AS
LEVEL

PHYSICS
FOR CCEA AS LEVEL

D1579096

COLOURPOINT
EDUCATIONAL

cea

Rewarding Learning

Pat Carson and Roy White

ISBN: 978 1 904242 43 7

First Edition
Third Impression 2012 (reprint with corrections)

Layout and design: Colourpoint Books
Printed by: W&G Baird Ltd, Antrim

COLOURPOINT EDUCATIONAL

Colourpoint Educational
An imprint of Colourpoint Creative Ltd
Colourpoint House
Jubilee Business Park
21 Jubilee Road
Newtownards
County Down
Northern Ireland
BT23 4YH

Tel: 028 9182 6339
Fax: 028 9182 1900
E-mail: info@colourpoint.co.uk
Web site: www.colourpoint.co.uk

The Authors

Roy White has been teaching Physics to A-level for over 30 years in Belfast. He is currently Head of Department and an enthusiastic classroom practitioner. He works for CCEA as Chair of Examiners for Double Award Science, Principal Examiner for GCSE Physics and as Chair of Examiners for Applied Science. In addition to this text, he has been the author or co-author of three successful books supporting the work of science teachers in Northern Ireland.

Pat Carson has been teaching Physics to A level for over 30 years in Belfast and Londonderry. He is currently Vice-Principal in a Londonderry Grammar school. He works for CCEA as Chief Examiner for GCSE Physics.

Picture credits

Apollo 17 crew, NASA	36
istockphoto:	84, 97, 154, 155, 156, 158, 159
Wesley Johnston	175
Authors	178, 182, 183, 184

Changes in this reprint
(CCEA endorsement does not apply to changes)

p138 Missing '=' inserted in second equation of 1st
   Overtone.

p145 Third column of table: $\frac{1}{T}$ to $\frac{1}{f}$

p150 X-rays in CT Scans added to Unit 2.7 Imaging
   Techniques *(pagination has changed)*

CONTENTS

Unit AS 1: Forces, Energy and Electricity

Unit AS 2: Waves, Photons and Medical Physics

Unit AS 3: Practical Techniques

Unit AS 1: Forces, Energy and Electricity

1.1 Physical Quantities

1.1.1   Describe all physical quantities as consisting of a numerical magnitude and unit.

1.1.2   State the base units of mass, length, time, current, temperature, amount of substance and be able to express other quantities in terms of these units.

Physical quantities

Physics is a science which relies heavily on measurement. To understand any physical phenomenon we have to be able to measure physical quantities. Examples of physical quantities are mass, length, time, force, and energy.

To describe a physical quantity we first define a characteristic unit. To state a measurement of some physical quantity e.g. force, we need to state two things:

1   **Magnitude (size) – a numerical value**

2   **Unit**

A force of 25 newtons would be written as **25 N**

International System of Units (SI units)

In 1971 it was agreed by the scientific community to use seven quantities as base quantities.

This formed the basis of the International System of Units, abbreviated SI from its French name.

In this system it was agreed that **only one unit** would be used to measure any physical quantity. However multiples and submultiples of these base units or quantities are commonly used. Length is measured in metres (m), but multiples such as kilometre (km) and submultiples such as centimetre (cm) and millimetre (mm) are in common use.

Base units

The SI system defines seven base units from which all other units are derived. The table below shows the six base units that you will come across in this A level course.

Quantity	Unit	Symbol
mass	kilogram	kg
time	second	s
length	metre	m
electric current	ampere	A
temperature	kelvin	K
amount of substance	mole	mol

Prefixes for units

Below is a list of the names of common multiples and submultiples of SI units.

Prefix	Multiplying factor	Symbol
pico	10^{-12}	p
nano	10^{-9}	n
micro	10^{-6}	μ
milli	10^{-3}	m
centi	10^{-2}	c
kilo	10^{3}	k
Mega	10^{6}	M
Giga	10^{9}	G
Tera	10^{12}	T

Derived units

Many SI units are derived i.e. they are defined in terms of two or more base units. For example, velocity is measured in metres per second, written as ms^{-1}. Some derived units have names, such as the newton (N) and the volt (V), but many do not.

The name of a unit when written in full is all in lower case, e.g. newton, joule, hertz.

The symbol has a capital letter, e.g. N, J, Hz

Do not add an 's' to indicate plural. For example, fifteen newtons is written 15 N. If you write this as 15 Ns then you are stating that the physical quantity is fifteen newton seconds and this is a measurement of impulse (momentum change) and not force.

Converting derived units to base units

It is sometimes useful to write a physical quantity in terms of its base units.
Energy is measured in joules (a derived unit). What are the base units of energy?
To calculate the base units for energy we can use any valid formula for energy such as that below for kinetic energy, E_k:

$E_k = \frac{1}{2}mv^2$ (the ½ being a number has no units)

In terms of physical quantities, we can write:

unit for energy = unit for mass × unit for velocity × unit for velocity
$$= kg \times ms^{-1} \times ms^{-1}$$
$$= kg \times m^2 \times s^{-2}$$

The base units of kinetic energy are therefore $kg\ m^2s^{-2}$. These are also the base units of **any form energy** and of **work**.

Homogeneous equations

For an equation to be valid it is necessary, but not sufficient, for the units on both sides of the equality sign to be the same. Such equations are called **homogeneous**.

Thus, **force = (momentum change) ÷ time taken**, is homogeneous because both sides have base units of kg ms⁻². On the other hand, **pressure = momentum × volume** is inhomogeneous because the left hand side has base units of kg m⁻¹s⁻², but the right hand side has base units of kg m⁴s⁻¹. Inhomogeneous equations are nonsensical.

Exercise 1

1 Express each of the following physical quantities in base units.

   If the derived unit of this physical quantity has a name then state it.

   Momentum   (Momentum = mass × velocity)

   Acceleration   (Acceleration = velocity change ÷ time taken)

   Force   (Force = mass × acceleration)

   Work   (Work = force × distance moved)

   Power   (Power = work done ÷ time taken)

   Frequency   (Frequency = speed ÷ wavelength)

2 On the planet Krypton the same laws of Physics apply as on the Earth. However the inhabitants of Krypton have decided to use force (F), acceleration (A) and time (T) as their base units.
   What are the base units of energy on the planet Krypton?

3 A simple pendulum consists of a mass on the end of a length of string. If the length of the string is L and g is the acceleration of free fall, then the time to complete one oscillation, called the period, is T, where:

$$T = 2\pi \sqrt{\frac{L}{g}}$$

   Show that the base units of both sides of the equation are identical.

4 A mass attached to a spring will oscillate up and down when disturbed. The period T of such oscillations is given by:

$$T = 2\pi \sqrt{\frac{m}{k}}$$

   The mass is m and k is the spring constant, i.e. the force needed to stretch the spring by 1 m. The units of k are Nm⁻¹.
   Show that the equation is homogeneous in terms of the base units on each side.

1.2 Scalars and Vectors

1.2.1   Distinguish between and give examples of scalar and vector quantities.

1.2.2   Calculate the resultant of two coplanar vectors by calculation or scale drawing, with calculations limited to two perpendicular vectors.

1.2.3   Resolve a vector into two perpendicular components.

A vector is a physical quantity that needs magnitude, a unit and a direction.

A scalar is a physical quantity that requires only magnitude and a unit.

For example speed is a scalar but velocity is a vector; mass is a scalar, but weight is a vector.

Here is a list of some of the vectors and scalars that you will encounter in the AS course.

Vector	Scalar
Displacement	Distance
Velocity	Speed
Acceleration	Rate of change of speed
Force	Time
Electric current	Electric charge
Momentum	Kinetic energy
	Temperature
	Area
	Volume
	Mass

Combining vectors

When we add vectors we have to take into account their direction as well as magnitude.

If the directions are in the same straight line then we can define any vector acting to the right as positive and any acting to the left as negative.

When we add two or more vectors then the final vector is called the **resultant**.

For two forces of 15 N and 10 N acting in the same direction, the resultant is 25 N.

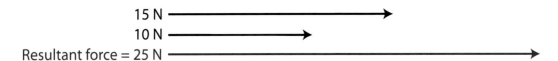

For two forces of 15 N and 10 N acting in opposite directions, the resultant is 5 N in the direction of the larger force.

15 N ——————————→
10 N ←——————————
Resultant force = 5 N ————→

Adding and Subtracting Vectors

If the vectors are not in a straight line then we use the **nose to tail method** to find the resultant.

Here are two vectors. The resultant of these two vectors is C. **C = A + B.**

The vector diagram on the right is obtained by placing the tail of vector B at the nose of vector A. The resultant C is the line joining the tail of A to the nose of B

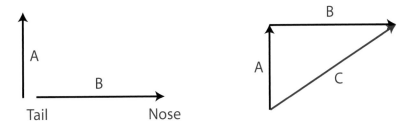

The resultant of subtracting the vector B from A is another vector D. **D = A – B.**

The vector **–B** is a vector of the **same magnitude as B** but in the **opposite direction.**

Effectively we add the negative vector so **D = A + (–B)**

To emphasise that certain quantities are vectors, we sometimes underline them (A) or draw an arrow above them ($\vec{A}$) to show direction. In books, vectors are often shown in bold type (**A**).

Exercise 2

Using the vectors A and B shown above, draw vector diagrams to show the resultant vector of each of the following:

(a) 2**A** + **B**

(b) **A** – 3**B**

(c) – **A** – **B**

Worked Examples

Example 1

Look at the diagram. Linda moved 3.0 m to the east (AB) and then 4.0 m to the north (BC).

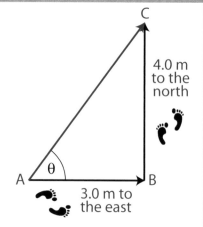

Although she has moved a total distance of 7.0 m, her displacement is 5.0 m (AC) from the start.

$$AC^2 = AB^2 + BC^2$$
$$= 3^2 + 4^2 = 25$$
$$AC = \sqrt{25} = 5.0$$

Since displacement is a vector, a magnitude and a direction are both needed.

$\tan \theta$ = opposite ÷ adjacent = 4 ÷ 3 = 1.333 giving θ = 53.13°

Linda's finishing point has a displacement, from her starting point, of 5.0 m at an angle of 53.13° to the north of east.

The above can also be done using a **scale drawing**. If we use a scale of 2 cm = 1 m, then **use a ruler** to draw a horizontal line, AB, 6 cm long to represent the 3.0 m travelled due east. Now, from B draw a vertical line 8 cm long to represent the 4.0 m travelled due north. Suppose this vertical line ends at point C. Then **join AC** to obtain the resultant displacement.

On the diagram AC will be 10 cm long, and with a scale of 2 cm = 1 m, it represents a real displacement of 5.0 m. Finally **use a protractor to measure the angle at C.** You should obtain an angle of 53° if sufficient care is taken.

Example 2

In this example we have a canoe that moves through the water at 1.5 ms⁻¹ and the water moves to the right at 1.2 ms⁻¹.

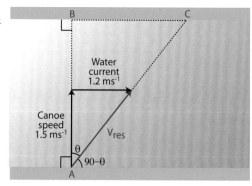

If the canoeist set off at A with the intention of rowing to B, he would not reach B, but would reach the opposite bank of the river at C.

The resultant velocity $\mathbf{v}_{res}$ is the vector sum of the speed of the canoe and the speed of the water current.

$$v_{res}^2 = 1.5^2 + 1.2^2$$

$$v_{res} = \sqrt{3.69} = 1.9 \text{ ms}^{-1}$$

The direction in which the canoe moves makes an angle θ with the perpendicular to the bank.

$\tan \theta$ = opp ÷ adj = 1.2 ÷ 1.5 = 0.8 θ = 38.7°

Example 3

If the canoeist in example 2 wants to cross from A to B, clearly he must paddle the canoe upstream. The direction in which he moves must combine with the speed of the river so that the resultant velocity is in the direction A to B.

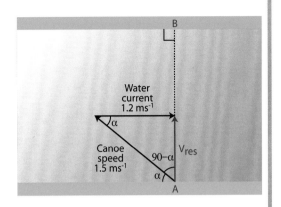

The angle to the bank that he must now direct the canoe is α.

$\cos \alpha = $ adj $\div$ hyp $= 1.2 \div 1.5 = 0.8$

Giving an angle $\alpha = 36.9°$.

The resultant velocity is then obtained:

$$\sin \alpha = \text{opp} \div \text{hyp} = v_{res} \div 1.5$$
$$0.6 = v_{res} \div 1.5$$
$$v_{res} = 0.9 \text{ ms}^{-1}$$

Exercise 3

1   A person starts from a point X and moves 20 m due east to a point Y. At Y the person turns, moves 15 m due north to a point Z, and then stops.

   (a) Calculate the distance the person moves from X.

   (b) Calculate the magnitude and direction of the displacement from X of the person at Z.

   [AS Physics Module 1 June 2002]

2   A light aircraft approaches a runway as shown in the diagram. A cross wind is blowing from the south causing the pilot to maintain a heading at an angle θ to the runway in order to approach it in the W–E direction. The speed of the aircraft in still air is 18 ms^{-1}.

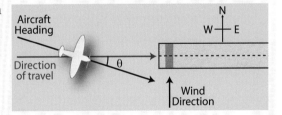

   The pilot can safely land the aircraft along the centre line provided the angle θ is no greater than 10°.

   (a) Calculate the maximum speed of the cross wind in which it is safe to land.

   (b) Draw a labelled vector diagram to show v_g, the velocity of the aircraft relative to the ground, when the cross wind has its maximum value.

   (c) Calculate the magnitude of v_g.

   [CCEA A Level Physics 1989]

Components of a vector

It is often useful to split or **resolve** a vector into two parts or components. Each component tells you the effect of the vector in that direction.

It is common to have these components act in directions that are perpendicular to each other, for example vertically and horizontally.

The diagram shows a vector F that has been resolved into two components that are at right angles to each other.

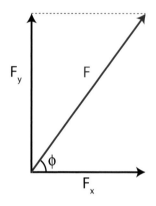

$$\sin \phi = \text{opp} \div \text{hyp} = F_y \div F$$
$$F_y = F \sin \phi$$

$$\cos \phi = \text{adj} \div \text{hyp} = F_x \div F$$
$$F_x = F \cos \phi$$

Exercise 4

1 A force has a vertical component of 23 N and a horizontal component of 14 N.

   Calculate the magnitude of this force and determine the angle it makes with the horizontal.

2 The displacement vector S_{BL} of London L from Belfast is 500 km in the direction 40° south of east as shown below. An aircraft flying from Belfast to London follows a two-leg flight path. The first leg is represented by the displacement vector S_{BW} of magnitude 160 km in the due east direction, to a point W directly above the town of Whitehaven. The second leg is represented by the displacement vector S_{WL} in the direction ϕ south of east

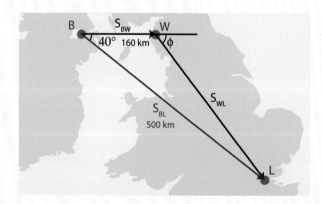

   (a) Show that the magnitudes of the components of S_{BL} are, to two significant figures, 380 km in the due east direction and 320 km in the due south direction.

   (b) Hence calculate S_{WL} and ϕ.

[AS Physics Module 1 January 2004]

Equilibrium of forces

If we consider the forces acting in two perpendicular directions such as up and down, left and right, then the object is in equilibrium if the up forces equal the down forces **and** the forces to the left equal those acting to the right. The object shown is acted upon by three forces that make angles with each other as shown.

Is the object in **translational equilibrium?** Is the resultant force equal to zero?

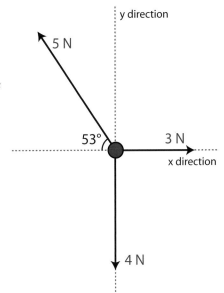

To answer the question let us resolve the forces in the x direction and the y direction.

On the right the 5 N force has been resolved into its components, one in the x direction the other in the y direction.

As you can see the forces in the x direction are equal and opposite **and** the forces in the y direction are also equal and opposite.

The resultant force is zero and the object is in translational equilibrium.

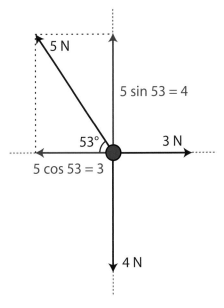

Triangle of forces

Force is a vector. Each of the three forces acting on the object can be represented by a line, the length of which indicates the size of the force and the direction of which represents the angle each force makes with the x and y directions.

When an object is in equilibrium the forces acting on it, taken in order, can be represented in size and direction by the sides of a closed triangle. 'Taken in order' means that the arrows showing the force directions follow each other in the **same direction** around the triangle.

The magnitude and direction of this additional force can be found either by calculation or by scale drawing.

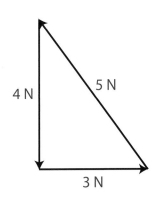

Worked Example

Consider how we might find the resultant of two forces which are not perpendicular to each other. We can either resolve and then add, or use a scale drawing. Suppose a force of 8 N acts due north and another force of 6 N acts at an angle of 45° to it as in the diagram.

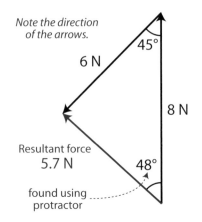

Note the direction of the arrows.

6 N

45°

8 N

Resultant force
5.7 N

48°

found using protractor

The resultant force (5.7 N) can be found by scale drawing and the angle measured (48°) using a protractor. Note that the resultant force is the line joining the tail of the 8 N force to the nose of the 6 N force.

The force required for equilibrium is one of the same size, but in the **opposite** direction.

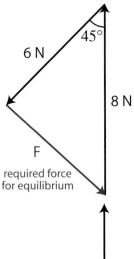

45°

6 N

8 N

F

required force for equilibrium

How is the resultant force found by calculation rather than by scale drawing? First resolve the 6 N force into a horizontal and vertical component as shown opposite. Then calculate the vertical component.

8 N and 6 cos 45° act in opposite directions.

This gives an upward force of 8 − 6 cos 45° = 3.76 N

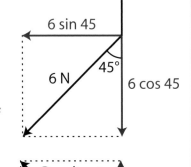

8 N

6 sin 45

6 N

45°

6 cos 45

To find the resultant we use the nose to tail method shown earlier. The Pythagoras theorem can be used to calculate the resultant since it forms the hypotenuse of a right angle triangle. The direction of the resultant force forms an angle ϕ to the vertical.

$\text{Tan } \phi$ = Opposite ÷ Adjacent
  = 4.24 ÷ 3.76
  = 1.127
 ϕ = 48.4°

So the resultant force is 5.7 N at an angle of 48.4° to the vertical.

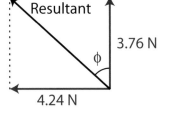

Resultant

3.76 N

ϕ

4.24 N

1.3 Linear Motion

Distance and displacement

Distance is a **scalar** quantity; it does not depend on direction.

Displacement is a **vector** quantity; it does depend on direction.

Displacement is the distance moved in a particular direction. An object that moves upwards has a positive displacement and one that moves down has a negative displacement.

To travel from Cookstown to Belfast by car, you can take the road shown on the map.

When you arrive the **distance you have travelled is 80 km**. When you reach Belfast, your **displacement**, shown by the dotted line, **is 50 km** in a direction east of your starting point of Cookstown.

(Distances and directions are approximate.)

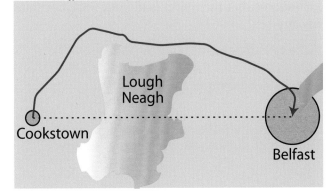

Speed and velocity

Speed is defined as the distance moved per second. Speed can also be defined as the rate of change of distance with time. Speed is a **scalar** quantity, it has magnitude (size) and a unit but not a direction.

$$\text{Average speed} = \frac{\text{Total distance travelled}}{\text{Total time taken}}$$

Velocity is a **vector** quantity, it has magnitude (size), a unit and a direction.

Velocity is defined as the displacement per second. It can also be defined as the rate of change of displacement with time.

$$\text{Average velocity} = \frac{\text{Total displacement}}{\text{Total time taken}}$$

Speed and velocity are measured in metres per second, written as ms^{-1}.

Acceleration

Acceleration is defined as the rate of change of velocity with time.

$$\text{Acceleration (ms}^{-2}) = \frac{\text{Change in velocity (ms}^{-1})}{\text{Time taken (s)}}$$

Acceleration is a **vector** quantity. Acceleration is measured in metres per second per second, written as ms^{-2}.

If an object is moving in a straight line and is slowing down, it has a negative acceleration.

If an object is speeding up, it has a positive acceleration.

Acceleration is described as **uniform** when it is constant i.e. equal changes of velocity take place every second. When the acceleration is **non–uniform** the velocity changes that take place every second are not equal.

Displacement–time graphs

In this graph the displacement increases by equal amounts in equal times.

This means that the object is moving with **constant velocity.**

Velocity = displacement ÷ time taken

Velocity = gradient of the line.

In this case velocity = 32 ÷ 8 or 16 ÷ 4 = 4 ms^{-1}.

The steeper the line, the greater the velocity.

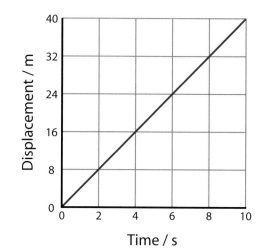

Velocity is a vector. A graph with positive gradient indicates a positive velocity. A graph with a negative gradient indicates a negative velocity. In this context, **positive and negative mean opposite directions.**

The displacement–time graph opposite shows an object moving with a constant velocity of 4 ms^{-1} in one direction for 10 seconds, remains stationary for 4 seconds and finally moves in the opposite direction with a constant velocity of 6.67 ms^{-1} for 6 seconds.

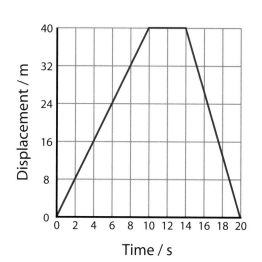

The object has finally arrived back its starting point; the overall displacement is zero.

The displacement–time graph opposite tells us that the velocity of the object is increasing; it is accelerating.

The gradient of the curve at time = 0 is zero, this tells us that the object accelerated from rest.

The **average velocity** for the object is found by dividing the total displacement by the time taken.

In this case, the average velocity **over 4 seconds** is $16 \div 4 = 4 \text{ ms}^{-1}$

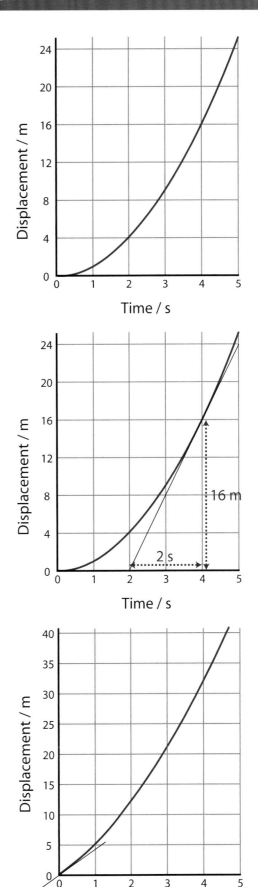

To find the **actual (instantaneous)** velocity at any time we need to **draw the tangent** carefully to the curve at that time and calculate its gradient. The tangent is a straight line that **touches** the curve but does not cut it.

For the graph shown the instantaneous velocity at 4 seconds is gradient of the tangent to the curve at 4 seconds.

$$\text{Gradient} = \frac{\text{rise}}{\text{run}} = 16 \div 2 = 8 \text{ ms}^{-1}.$$

It is worth noting that for an object undergoing uniform acceleration from rest, at any given time the instantaneous velocity at that time is aways **twice** the average velocity.

The displacement–time graph on the right shows an object moving with constant acceleration.

However in this example the object does not accelerate from rest: it already has an initial velocity.

It is possible to tell this because the graph has a positive gradient at time = 0, in other words the tangent to the graph at time = 0 has a positive slope.

The gradient of this tangent is the initial velocity. It is approximately 4.5 ms^{-1}.

If the acceleration of an object is not constant (non-uniform) the displacement–time graph is more complicated.

However the **average velocity** at a particular time can still be calculated as

Average velocity = s ÷ t

The instantaneous velocity is equal to the gradient of the displacement – time graph at that instant.

Instantaneous velocity = Δs ÷ Δt

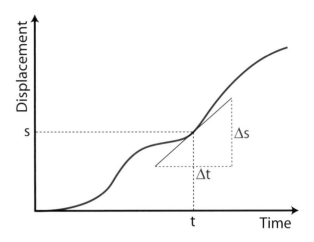

Note carefully that:

*   the gradient of a **distance–time** graph represents the **scalar quantity, speed.**
*   the gradient of a **displacement–time** graph represents the **vector quantity, velocity.**

Velocity–time graphs

This graph shows the motion of an object that is moving in a straight line and always in the same direction. It starts at rest, accelerates from 0 to 10 seconds, travels at constant velocity for 10 seconds, and then decelerates to a stop after a total time of 25 seconds.

The gradient of the line gives us the acceleration or deceleration.

Between 0 and 10 s the velocity change = 12 ms⁻¹.
Gradient = 12 ÷ 10 = 1.2 ms⁻²

Between 20 and 25 s the velocity change = –12 ms⁻¹.
Gradient = –12 ÷ 5 = –2.4 ms⁻².

This **negative acceleration could be described as a deceleration of 2.4 ms⁻² .**

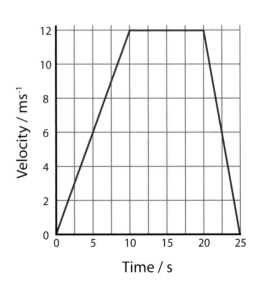

The steeper the line, the greater the acceleration. A positive gradient indicates acceleration. A negative gradient indicates a negative acceleration (deceleration). Straight lines indicate that the acceleration is constant or uniform.

Non-uniform acceleration

If the velocity–time graph is curved the acceleration is described as non-uniform.

The average acceleration at any time is the change of velocity up to that time divided by the time.

The instantaneous acceleration, i.e. the acceleration at any time, is found from the gradient of the tangent to the velocity–time graph at that time.

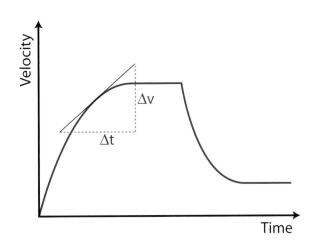

Instantaneous acceleration = Δv ÷ Δt

The velocity–time graph shown here is that of a parachutist. Just after she jumps from the aircraft her velocity increases rapidly; she has a large acceleration. However as the velocity increases so also does the upward frictional force and her acceleration gradually decreases until she is moving with a constant velocity, known as the **terminal velocity**. The parachutist then opens her parachute and the velocity decreases rapidly until once again she is moving with a new, lower **terminal** velocity. The area between a velocity–time graph and the time axis gives the displacement.

Calculate the displacement from the velocity–time graph shown.

From 0 to 10 s:

displacement = average velocity × time taken

$\qquad$ = (½ × 20 ms^{-1}) × 10 (area of triangle)

$\qquad$ = 100 m

From 10 s to 30 s:

displacement = constant velocity × time taken

$\qquad$ = 20 ms^{-1} × 20 s (area of rectangle)

$\qquad$ = 400 m

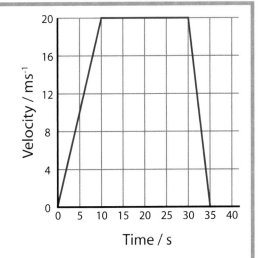

From 30 s to 35 s:

displacement = average velocity × time taken

$\qquad$ = (½ × 20 ms^{-1}) × 5 (area of triangle)

$\qquad$ = 50 m

So the total distance travelled in 35 s is 100 + 400 + 50 = **550 m, which is the area of the trapezium.**

Varying velocity

If the object is experiencing a non–uniform acceleration the velocity–time graph is a curve, as shown on the right.

As before, the area between the graph and the time axis will give the displacement.

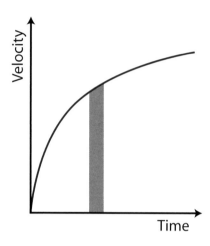

Exercise 5

1   A lift accelerates upwards at 0.5 ms^{-2} for 2 seconds then travels at constant velocity for another 8 seconds. It then decelerates uniformly to rest in another 2 seconds. It waits for 8 seconds to allow passengers to leave and enter before accelerating downwards at 0.5 ms^{-2} for 2 seconds. It then travels at a constant velocity for 3 seconds before coming to a rest in another 2 seconds. Draw the velocity–time for the motion of the lift.

2   A car accelerates from rest along a straight road. The graph is of the velocity v of the car against time t from the beginning of the journey.

   (a) State how the acceleration of the car at time t_1 could be obtained directly from the graph.

   (b) State how the distance travelled by the car from the start of the journey to time t_2 could be obtained from the graph.

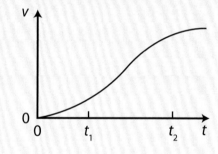

[CCEA Physics Module 1 January 2002]

3   Here is the velocity–time graph for an object undergoing acceleration.

   Use the graph to find:

   (a) the acceleration during the first 4 seconds.

   (b) the total distance travelled during the first 10 seconds.

   (c) the average speed for the first 10 seconds.

          [CCEA Physics Module 1 January 2001]

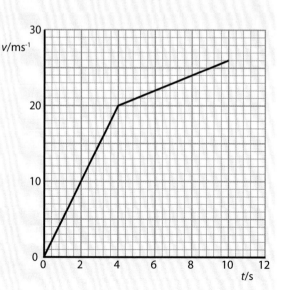

4   A body moves from rest in a straight line, starting at a point P. The initial motion of the body is from left to right.

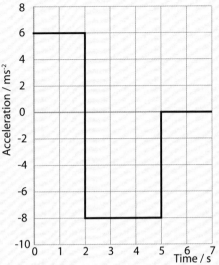

During a period of 7.0 seconds from the start, the body undergoes the series of accelerations shown on the right.

(a) Use the information on the graph to make appropriate calculations of velocity to enable you to plot a velocity–time graph for the motion of the body during these 7.0 seconds.

Sketch this velocity–time graph.

(b) Calculate the average speed of the body over the 7.0 second period.

(c) State the final position of the body, relative to P.

[CCEA Physics June 1999]

5   Opposite is a sketch of a velocity–time graph for a ball thrown up vertically from the surface of the Moon.

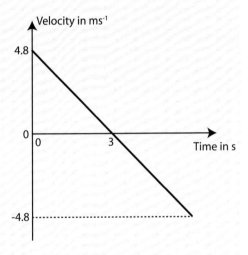

(a) Why does the velocity become negative after 3 seconds?

(b) Calculate the acceleration due to gravity close to the Moon's surface.

(c) Calculate the displacement after (i) 3 s and (ii) 6 s

(d) Calculate the distance travelled after (i) 3 s and (ii) 6 s

Equations of motion for uniform acceleration in a straight line

The following symbols are used in these equations:

u = initial velocity, v = final velocity, a = acceleration, t = time, s = displacement

Starting with the definition of acceleration, we can derive the relationship between initial velocity, final velocity, acceleration and time.

Acceleration = velocity change ÷ time taken, or a = (v − u) ÷ t

Re–arranging gives us $$v = u + at \tag{1}$$

Starting with the relationship between average velocity, displacement and time derive the relationship between initial velocity, final velocity, time and displacement.

Average velocity = displacement ÷ time = s ÷ t

Average velocity = (initial velocity + final velocity) ÷ 2 = ½ (u + v)

Equating and re–arranging gives us $$s = \tfrac{1}{2}(u + v)t \tag{2}$$

Equations (3) and (4) are algebraic combinations of equations (1) and (2).

Starting with the equation (2) we can eliminate final velocity using equation 1 so that we end up with the relationship between displacement, initial velocity, acceleration and time.

$s = \tfrac{1}{2} (u + v)t = \tfrac{1}{2} (u + u + at)t$

gives $2s = 2ut + at^2$

and re–arranging we get $$s = ut + \tfrac{1}{2}at^2 \tag{3}$$

We can use equation (1) to eliminate time from equation (3). This will give us relationship between displacement, initial velocity, final velocity and acceleration.

v = u + at and squaring both sides gives $\qquad v^2 = (u + at)^2 = u^2 + 2uat + a^2t^2$

Now take a factor of 2a out of the last two terms $\qquad v^2 = u^2 + 2a(ut + \tfrac{1}{2} at^2)$

But from equation (3),the term in brackets is s, so $\qquad v^2 = u^2 + 2as$

We have arrived at: $$v^2 = u^2 + 2as \tag{4}$$

You need not learn these derivations, but you need to remember the equations and know how to use them to solve problems.

Remember: these equations only apply when objects are moving with uniform acceleration.

Summary of equations of uniformly accelerated motion

Equation	Mainly used to find...
v = u + at	The velocity at a known time
s = ½ (u +v)t	The distance travelled after a known time
s = ut + ½at²	The distance travelled when the final velocity is unknown
v² = u² + 2as	The final velocity when the time taken is unknown

Exercise 6

1 Competitor A in a cycle race reaches a point 60.0 m from the finishing line. He then travels with uniform velocity of 18.0 ms^{-1} in a straight line towards the finish. Another competitor B reaches the same point 60.0 m from the finish 0.100 s after A, travelling with the same velocity (18.0 ms^{-1}) as A.

However, B then accelerates uniformly at 0.720 ms^{-2} until he reaches the finish.

(a) Calculate the velocity with which competitor B crosses the finishing line.

(b) Make appropriate calculations to determine which competitor wins the race.

[CCEA Physics Module 1 January 2003]

2 A skier accelerates from rest down a slope of constant gradient 20°. The constant acceleration down the slope is 2.5 ms^{-2}. How long does the skier take to travel through a vertical distance of 50 m?

[CCEA Physics Module 1 January 2002]

3 An object, initially at rest, can move along a straight line. From time $t = 0$ it accelerates uniformly until t= t_1, when its acceleration suddenly decreases to zero.

It continues until $t = t_2$ with zero acceleration. The graph shows how the acceleration a depends on time t.

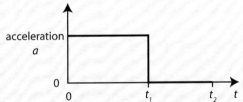

(a) (i) Sketch the velocity–time graph and the displacement–time graph for this object from time $t = 0$ until $t = t_2$.

(ii) State how the magnitude of the displacement at $t = t_2$ may be obtained from the graph of velocity against time.

(b) A vehicle is travelling at a speed of 120 km per hour along a straight road.

The driver brakes, causing a uniform retardation of 8.7 ms^{-2}.

(i) Show that a speed of 120 km per hour corresponds to a speed of 33 ms^{-1}.

(ii) Calculate the distance travelled from the moment of applying the brakes until the vehicle comes to rest.

(iii) Calculate the time taken for the vehicle to come to rest.

[CCEA January 2005]

Vertical Motion under gravity

An object dropped will accelerate due to the force of gravity. However gravity is not the only force acting on a falling object. Air resistance or drag acts upwards opposing the accelerating force of gravity. **We can describe an object as in 'free fall' if the** *only* **force acting on it is gravity.** All objects in **free fall** accelerate downwards at the same rate. **The acceleration does not depend upon the mass of the object.** The acceleration due to gravity, g, is approximately 9.81 ms^{-2}, but its value changes from one point to another over the Earth's surface.

Convention

It is convenient to adopt the convention that 'upwards is positive' when solving problems relating to motion under gravity. This means that an object moving vertically upwards has a positive velocity, while one moving vertically downwards will have a negative velocity. Objects above the surface have a positive displacement, while objects below the surface (such as those down a well) have a negative displacement.

Worked Example

A ball is dropped from a height of 10 m onto a hard surface and bounces a number of times. At the first bounce it rebounds to a height of 8.5 m. By making suitable calculations involving velocity and time, sketch a velocity–time graph for the motion of this bouncing ball to cover the time from release of the ball to just before it undergoes a second bounce.

Time to fall, from rest, from 10 m:

The ball moves 10 m towards the ground, so the displacement is –10 m.

Since the acceleration is also downwards, g = –9.81 ms^{-2}

$$s = ut + \tfrac{1}{2}\,at^2$$

$$-10 = 0 + \tfrac{1}{2} \times (-9.81) \times t^2 \qquad \text{giving } t = \textbf{1.43 s}$$

Velocity after falling 10 m

$$v = u + at$$

$$v = 0 + (-9.81) \times 1.43 \qquad \text{giving } v = \textbf{–14.0 ms}^{-1}$$

where the minus sign shows the ball is moving **towards the ground**. At this point, the ball undergoes its first bounce.

Initial velocity needed to reach a height of 8.5 m:

The ball is moving upwards, so the displacement and velocity are both positive. But the acceleration due to gravity, g, is towards the ground and is therefore negative.

$$v^2 = u^2 + 2as$$

$$0 = u^2 + 2 \times (-9.81) \times 8.5 \qquad \text{giving } u = \textbf{12.9 ms}^{-1}$$

Time to reach 8.5 m:

At this height the velocity = 0, but the acceleration is **still** –9.81 ms⁻² (even when the ball is stationary).

$$v = u + at$$

$$0 = 12.9 + (-9.81) \times t \qquad \text{giving } t = \textbf{1.32 s}$$

So the ball takes 1.43 s to fall 10 m from its original position and 1.32 s to reach a height of 8.5 m after its first bounce, a total of 2.75 s after it was first dropped

The ball then falls again, accelerating as it does. It will hit the ground, for the second time, after another 1.32 s (or 4.07 s after it was first released) with the same velocity as it left the ground after the first bounce.

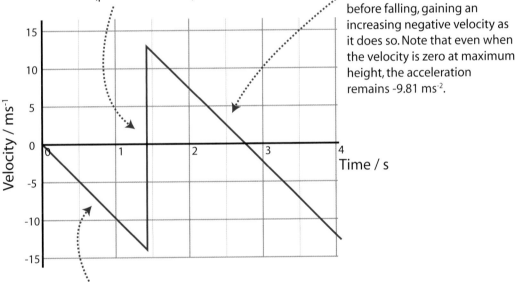

The first bounce is at 1.43 s. The direction of movement changes instantly from down (negative direction) to upward (positive direction).

The ball moves upwards, decelerating as it does. It reaches its maximum height at 2.75 s. It momentarily stops before falling, gaining an increasing negative velocity as it does so. Note that even when the velocity is zero at maximum height, the acceleration remains -9.81 ms⁻².

The ball accelerates uniformly at -9.81 ms⁻² as it falls. Note that the velocity and the gradient are negative, consistent with the convention. Velocity and acceleration are vectors, with downwards taken as the negative direction.

Exercise 7

Take g to be 9.81 ms^{-2}

1 A ball is thrown vertically upwards with an initial velocity of 39.24 ms^{-1}

   (a) Write down (no calculations required) its speed and its acceleration when it reaches maximum height.

   (b) Calculate the maximum height the ball reaches.

   (c) How long does it take the ball to reach maximum height?

2 A stone is dropped from rest down a well. Exactly 5.00 seconds after the stone is dropped, a splash is heard. Give all answers to three significant figures.

   (a) At what speed did the stone enter the water?

   (b) Calculate the average speed of the stone as it fell.

   (c) How far did the stone travel before it hit the water?

3 From the top of a tower 30.0 m high, a marble is thrown vertically upwards with an initial speed of 12.0 ms^{-1}. Calculate the following, giving all answers to three significant figures:

   (a) the maximum height reached above the **ground**.

   (b) the time taken for the stone to reach maximum height.

   (c) the time taken for the stone to fall from its maximum height to the **ground** below.

   (d) the speed of the stone when it strikes the **ground**.

4 A helicopter is at a height of 22.0 m and is rising vertically at 4.00 ms^{-1} when it drops a food parcel from a side door. Use the convention that 'upwards is positive'.

   (a) Write down the velocity and acceleration of the parcel at the instant it leaves the helicopter. Calculate the following to three significant figures.

   (b) The maximum height reached by the parcel before it starts to fall towards the ground.

   (c) Calculate the velocity of the parcel on impact with the ground.

   (d) Calculate the time between the parcel leaving the helicopter and it striking the ground.

5 A bouncing ball loses 10% of its incident kinetic energy every time it bounces off the floor. It falls from an initial height of 12.0 m.

   To what height will it rise after the third bounce? Give your answer to three significant figures. Does your answer depend on the value of g?

Experimentally measuring the acceleration of free fall using a timer

The acceleration of free fall can be measured using the apparatus shown. The metal contacts at the top of the apparatus are connected to the start terminals of an electronic timer. A short length of thread attached to the metal ball allows it to be held against the two contacts. When the metal ball is against them the circuit is complete and the clock remains stopped.

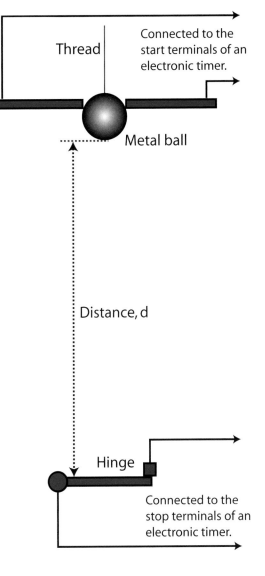

When the thread is released, the ball falls, the circuit is broken and the timer starts. When the ball reaches the bottom it strikes and opens a hinged contact, breaking another circuit which causes the timer to stop.

The distance, d, between the bottom of the metal ball and this hinged contact is measured. The distance d is increased from 0.2 m to 1.0 m in steps of 0.2 m and for each distance an average time of fall, t, is determined.

Since the ball starts from rest (u = 0) we can use the equation $d = \frac{1}{2}gt^2$ to find g (ie using $s = ut + \frac{1}{2}at^2$).

Re-arranging this gives $g = 2d \div t^2$.

One approach to finding g is to calculate a value of g for each value of s and t and find an average of g.

Alternatively, a graphical approach can be used. Plotting s on the y axis, and t^2 on the x axis will give a straight line that passes through the origin. The gradient is then $\frac{1}{2}g$.

This is because the equation of a straight line passing through the origin (0,0) is y = mx (where the gradient of the line is denoted by m).

$$d = \frac{1}{2} gt^2$$

$$y = mx$$

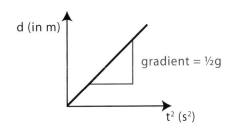

1.4 Dynamics

1.4.1   Describe projectile motion.

1.4.2   Explain motion due to a uniform velocity in one direction and a uniform acceleration in a perpendicular direction.

1.4.3   Apply the equations of motion to projectile motion, excluding air resistance.

A projectile is any object that is freely moving in the Earth's gravity, for example an object that is dropped from a height, an object that is fired vertically upwards. These two examples have been dealt with in a previous section.

Moving horizontally then falling over a cliff

We treat the horizontally motion as one of constant velocity **since we are ignoring friction.**

This means that whatever horizontal velocity the object might have had when it left the edge of the cliff, it does **not** change during its flight.

When it leaves the edge of the cliff it begins to fall vertically. Its downward acceleration is 9.81 ms^{-2}. You treat it as an object dropped vertically from rest.

Therefore, at any instant the velocity of the projectile is the resultant of:

(a)   the constant horizontal velocity

(b)   the vertical velocity gained as it falls

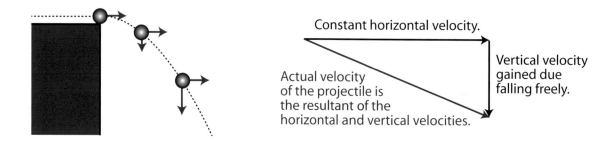

Exercise 8

A person stands 3.0 m from a dartboard. The dart is thrown horizontally towards the board and leaves the person's hand 1.70 m above the ground. The dart strikes the board 1.50 m above the ground.

(a) Calculate the time of flight, i.e. the time the dart takes to reach the dartboard.

(b) Calculate the initial speed of the dart.

(c) Find the magnitude and direction of the velocity of the dart as it enters the dartboard.

[CCEA A Level Physics 1999]

A projectile fired at an angle to the horizontal

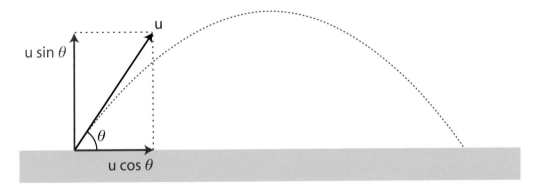

You treat this situation as follows:

1   Resolve the initial velocity into a horizontal component and a vertical component.

2   The horizontal component, **u cos** θ, does not change.

3   The vertical component **u sin** θ, decreases as the projectile moves upwards.

4   At the maximum height the **vertical** velocity is momentarily zero. The equation **v = u + at** can be used to find the time taken to reach the maximum height since v = 0 at this height and u = initial vertical = u sin θ

   Note that although the projectile does not have a vertical velocity (for an instant) at the maximum height, it **still** has a horizontal velocity.

5   The vertical component of the projectile's velocity increases again as the projectile falls. It takes the same time to fall from the maximum height as it did to reach it. The total time in the air is called the **time of flight** and equals twice the time to reach the maximum height.

6   The horizontal distance travelled is called the **range**.

   Assuming the projectile returns to the same vertical position:

   Horizontal range = constant horizontal velocity × time of flight.

7   At any instant the velocity of the projectile is the resultant of the constant horizontal velocity and the changing vertical velocity.

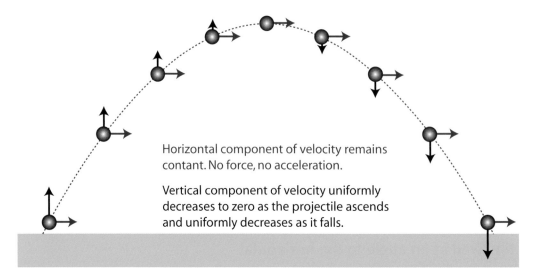

Horizontal component of velocity remains contant. No force, no acceleration.

Vertical component of velocity uniformly decreases to zero as the projectile ascends and uniformly decreases as it falls.

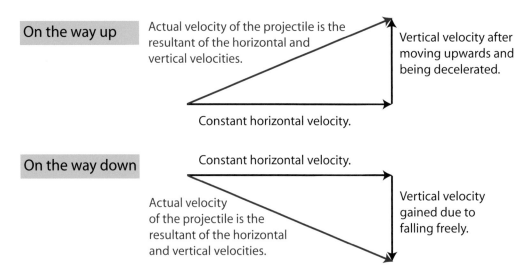

On the way up

Actual velocity of the projectile is the resultant of the horizontal and vertical velocities.

Vertical velocity after moving upwards and being decelerated.

Constant horizontal velocity.

On the way down

Constant horizontal velocity.

Actual velocity of the projectile is the resultant of the horizontal and vertical velocities.

Vertical velocity gained due to falling freely.

Worked Example

A stone is projected into the air from ground level with a velocity of 25 ms⁻¹ at an angle of 35° to the horizontal.

Calculate:

(a) the time to reach the maximum height
(b) the maximum height reached
(c) the magnitude and direction of the stone's velocity 2.0 s after it was released.

Solution

(a) At the maximum height the vertical component of the projectile's velocity is zero.
The initial vertical velocity = $25 \sin 35° = 25 \times 0.5736 = 14.34$ ms⁻¹.
Using $v = u + at$ we get $0 = 14.34 + (-9.81)\,t$
$t = 14.34 \div 9.81 = 1.46$ s

Time to reach the maximum height = 1.46 s

(b) The maximum height can be found in a number of ways.

Method 1	Method 2
$s = ut + \frac{1}{2}at^2$ $= 14.34 \times 1.46 + \frac{1}{2} \times (-9.81) \times 1.46^2$ $= 20.94 - 10.46 = 10.48$ m	$s = \frac{1}{2}(u + v)t$ $= \frac{1}{2}(14.34 + 0) \times 1.46$ $= 10.47$ m

The difference in the answers is due to rounding errors in the figures for u and t.

(c) After 2.0 s the horizontal component of the projectile's velocity is $25 \cos 35 = 20.48$ ms^{-1}. Remember **the horizontal component remains constant throughout the motion.**

After 2.0 s the vertical component can be calculated using $v = u + at$ where $v = 14.34$, $a = 9.81$ and $t = 2.0$. This gives -5.28. The **minus is important**, because it tells us that the projectile is now moving **down** with a velocity of 5.28 ms^{-1}

Draw the vector diagram showing both the horizontal and the vertical velocity at 2.0 s.

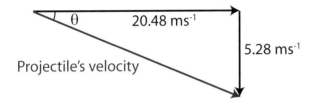

Projectile's velocity $= \sqrt{20.48^2 + 5.28^2}$
$= 21.15$ ms^{-1}

The direction of the velocity is θ. $\tan \theta = 5.28 \div 20.48 = 0.2578$
$\theta = 14.46$

Range

The **range** of the projectile is the horizontal distance it travels before returning to the ground.

Range (R) = Constant **horizontal** velocity × Time of flight (T).

The **time of flight** is the total time the projectile spends in the air. In this time the projectile travels upwards to its maximum height and down again, taking the same time for each half of this vertical journey. The time of flight (T) is therefore twice the time it takes the projectile to reach its maximum height.

At the maximum height the vertical component of the velocity is zero.

Using $v = u + at$ we find $0 = u \sin\theta - gt$ giving $t = u \sin\theta \div g$.

The time of flight $T = 2t = 2 u \sin\theta \div g$

Range $R = u \cos\theta \times T = u \cos\theta \times 2 u \sin\theta \div g = (u^2 \div g) 2 \sin\theta \cos\theta$ but $\sin 2\theta = 2 \sin\theta \cos\theta$, so

Range $R = (u^2 \div g) \sin 2\theta$

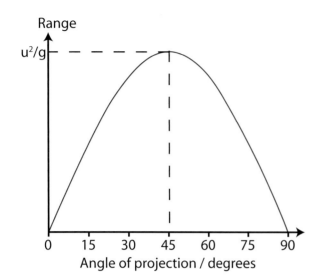

The range R depends on the angle of projection θ. sin 2θ has a maximum value of 1, i.e. when θ = 45°.

For a given initial velocity, the range R has a maximum value when the angle of projection is 45°.

Some angles of projection produce the **same range** but very different paths or trajectories. In general, the range when projected at an angle θ is the same as for a particle projected at an angle (90° − θ). So a particle projected at 30° has the same range as one projected with the same speed at 60°.

The diagram below shows the paths taken for some angles of projection.

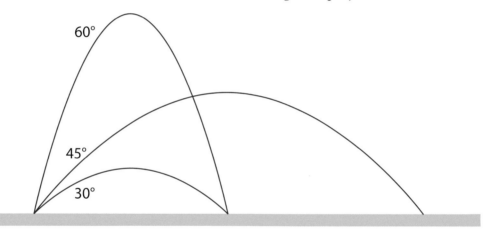

Exercise 9

1   One of the reasons for Wellington's victory at Waterloo was that the English field guns were much lighter, and hence more mobile, than the French. The muzzle speed of the shot from an English gun was about 150 ms⁻¹. At what **angles** with the ground could an English artilleryman have trained such a gun at a target 1200 m away? Assume the ground was level and neglect air resistance.

[CCEA AS Physics January 2004]

2   A stone is projected horizontally from the edge of a cliff. The initial velocity of the stone is v_o. The stone follows the curved path shown in the diagram. At the point A on its path, the stone has a velocity v. The direction of v makes an angle θ with the horizontal.

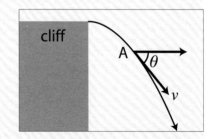

(a) Write down expressions, in terms of v and θ, for the horizontal and vertical components of the velocity of the stone at the point A.

(b) Sketch graphs to show how the horizontal and vertical components of the velocity of the stone vary with time from the moment the stone was thrown.

(c) At what point in its motion does the stone have the smallest speed?

[CCEA AS Physics January 2002]

1.5 Newton's Laws of Motion

Newton's laws of motion

Newton's 1st Law of Motion

If a body is at rest, it will remain at rest unless a resultant force acts on the object. If the body is moving in a straight line with a constant speed, it will continue to move in this way unless a resultant force acts on it.

The first law is another way of saying that all matter has a built-in opposition to being moved if it is at rest, or, if it is moving, to having its motion changed. This property of matter is called **inertia** (from the Latin word for laziness). The larger the mass of a body, the greater is its inertia, i.e. the more difficult it is to get it to move or to stop it moving or make it change direction.

Newton's 2nd Law of Motion

The acceleration of an object is inversely proportional to its mass, directly proportional to the resultant force on it and takes place in the same direction as the unbalanced force.

There are four ideas in this law:
* An unbalanced (resultant) force causes an object to accelerate.
* The direction of the unbalanced force is the same as that of the acceleration.
* The acceleration is inversely proportional to the object's mass.
* The acceleration is directly proportional to the size of the unbalanced force.

The car below has a mass m and is acted upon by a resultant force in the direction shown.

At time t = 0 the velocity = u   At time t the velocity = v
So the acceleration of the car, a, is (v − u) ÷ t.

Newton's 2nd law can be written: $F \propto ma$ (the sign $\propto$ means 'is proportional to')
                  or $F = kma$, where k is the constant of proportionality.

The unit of force, the newton, is defined as the force needed to cause a mass of 1 kg to have an acceleration of 1 ms^{-2}. This means that the constant of proportionality k equals 1.

The consequence of Newton's second law, and the definition of the newton, is that we can write:

$$\underline{F} = m\underline{a}$$

F = resultant force in N
m = mass in kg
a = acceleration in ms^{-2}

Some people like to underline 'F' and 'a' to emphasise that **force and acceleration are vectors in the same direction.**

Friction forces

Friction is a force that always opposes motion. Friction always acts in the **opposite** direction to the motion.

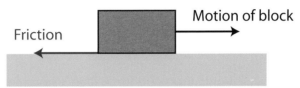

You need to be aware of the role of friction when determining a resultant force. The worked example below illustrates this.

Worked example

A person stands on a skateboard at the top of a rough sloping track. The total mass of the rider and skateboard is 73 kg. The track slopes at an angle of 9.5° to the horizontal. The rider and skateboard start from rest and move down the track with uniform acceleration of 0.46 ms^{-2}. During the motion the force of friction on the board is constant and air resistance is negligible.

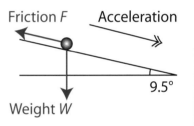

A simplified diagram of the situation, in which the rider and skateboard have been replaced by a point mass in contact with the track, is shown above.

[CCEA January 2005]

(i) Calculate the magnitude of the resultant force causing the skateboard and rider to accelerate down the slope.

(ii) Calculate the constant frictional force acting on the skateboard as it moves down the slope.

Solution

(i) The resultant force can be found using F = ma, where **F is the resultant force**.

F = 73 × 0.46 = **33.58 N**

(ii) If you look at the diagram you will see that friction is marked acting up the slope, opposing the motion of the rider and skateboard down the slope. What force acts downs the slope? The answer is a component of the combined weight of the rider and skateboard parallel to the slope.

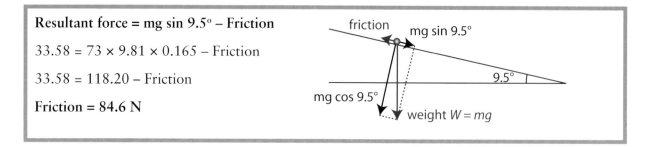

Resultant force = mg sin 9.5° – Friction

33.58 = 73 × 9.81 × 0.165 – Friction

33.58 = 118.20 – Friction

Friction = 84.6 N

friction   mg sin 9.5°

9.5°

mg cos 9.5°

weight *W = mg*

Newton's 3rd Law of Motion

If body A exerts a force on body B, then body B exerts a force of the same size on body A, but in the opposite direction.

Forces come in pairs. If a hammer exerts a force on a nail, the nail exerts a force of equal magnitude but opposite direction on the hammer. One of these forces is called the **action force** (it does not matter which). The other force is called the **reaction force**.

You might think that if every force has an associated force that is equal in magnitude but opposite in direction, why don't they cancel each other out? How can anything ever get moving?

The forces of an action – reaction pair **always** act on **different** bodies.

This means they do not combine to give a resultant force and cannot cancel each other.

Two forces that act on the **same** body are **not** an action – reaction pair, even though they may be equal in magnitude but opposite in direction.

How does Newton's 3rd Law apply to an apple resting on a table?

The Earth pulls the apple down with a force $\mathbf{F}_{EA}$ (EA means earth on apple) – this is the weight of the apple and we could call this the action force.

The apple attracts the Earth with a force of equal magnitude but opposite direction call this force $\mathbf{F}_{AE}$ (AE meaning apple on earth) – call this the reaction force.

The apple is in contact with the table. The apple exerts a downward force $\mathbf{F}_{AT}$ (AT meaning apple on table) – call this the action force. The table exerts an upward force on the apple, $\mathbf{F}_{TA}$ (TA meaning table on apple) – call this is the reaction force. **This is an example of the action – reaction pair of forces to which Newton's 3rd law refers.**

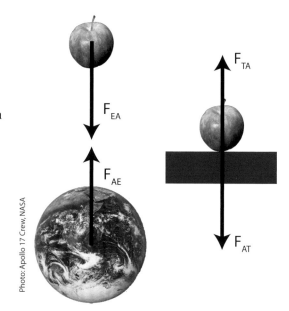

Photo: Apollo 17 Crew, NASA

F_{EA}

F_{AE}

F_{TA}

F_{AT}

If we look at the forces acting only on the apple, we have F_{EA} (weight of the apple) and F_{TA} the upward supporting force from the table.

The forces F_{EA} and F_{TA} are equal in magnitude and opposite in direction but they act on the **same** body, the apple. Remember, these do **not** constitute an action – reaction pair because they act on the same object, in this case the apple.

Worked Example

A golfer hits a golf ball of mass 80 g. If the golf club is in contact with the ball for a period of 50 ms and exerts a constant force of 200 N, calculate

(a) the acceleration of the golf ball and

(b) the speed of the golf ball at the moment it loses contact with the golf club.

Solution

(i) $a = F \div m = 200 \div 0.080 = \mathbf{2500 \ ms^{-2}}$

(ii) $v = u + at = 0 + 2500 \times 0.05 = \mathbf{125 \ ms^{-1}}$

Exercise 10

1 A parcel of mass 6 kg slides from rest down a slope inclined at 30° to the horizontal. The friction force acting on the parcel is 4.95 N. Calculate:

   (a) the resultant force on the parcel,

   (b) the acceleration of the parcel and

   (c) the distance travelled by the parcel in 2 s.

   Take the value of g to be 9.80 ms^{-2}.

2 A motorist has a reaction time* of 0.6 s. While travelling at 20 ms^{-1} she sees a child suddenly run into the road 40 m ahead of her. The motorist applies the brakes to make an emergency stop. If the mass of the car is 800 kg and the average braking force is 6400 N, calculate:

   (a) the distance travelled during the reaction time,

   (b) the deceleration of the car when the brakes are applied,

   (c) the total distance travelled by the motorist between the instant the child is seen and the time the car comes to rest, assuming the deceleration is constant.

   (d) Is the motorist likely to collide with the child?

   (e) Comment on the effects of (i) alcohol consumption and (ii) driving in wet conditions on the overall stopping distance.

   * Reaction time is time which elapses from the instant the brain receives a stimulus to the instant the brakes are applied.

3 A man of mass 60.0 kg stands on scales inside a lift. The scales measure the man's weight, not his mass. What readings would you expect to see on the scales when the lift is moving upwards with:

(a) a constant acceleration of 2.00 ms^{-2}

(b) a constant speed of 2.00 ms^{-1}

(c) a constant deceleration of 2.00 ms^{-2}. Take the value of g to be 9.81 ms^{-2}.

4 A car of mass 800 kg tows a trailer of mass 100 kg. The engine force is 3400 N, the friction forces opposing the motion of the car add up to 400 N and the friction forces opposing the motion of the trailer add up to 300 N.

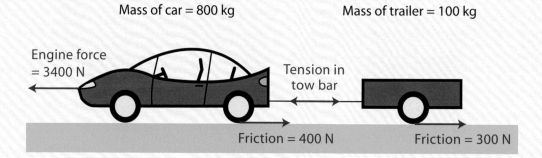

Mass of car = 800 kg   Mass of trailer = 100 kg

Engine force = 3400 N   Tension in tow bar

Friction = 400 N   Friction = 300 N

Calculate:

(a) the combined acceleration of car and trailer

(b) the tension in the tow bar.

5 Masses of 3 kg and 2 kg are joined by a light string over a pulley as shown in the diagram opposite.
When released, the 3 kg mass falls towards the ground and the 2 kg mass rises vertically. Ignoring all frictional forces and taking the acceleration of free–fall to be 9.81 ms^{-2}, calculate

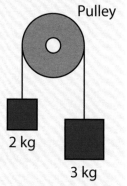

Pulley

2 kg

3 kg

(a) the common acceleration and

(b) the tension in the string.

Hint: Treat each mass separately. For each mass there are its weight and the tension to consider. Form an equation for each based on F = ma and solve simultaneously.

6 A large cardboard box has a mass of 0.80 kg. Its motion across a horizontal floor is opposed by a constant frictional force of 1.5 N and an air resistance force which increases with the speed of the box. The air resistance force, F_{air}, is given by the equation: $F_{air} = kv^2$, where the constant k = 0.16 kgm^{-1} and v is the speed of the box in ms^{-1}.

Patrick pushes the box across the floor with a force of 5.5 N.

(a) Sketch a large diagram to show all the forces acting on the moving box.

(b) Calculate the maximum acceleration of the box across the floor and state when it occurs.

(c) Calculate the maximum speed of the box when the forward force is 5.5 N

1.6 Principle of Moments

Moment of a force

The moment of a force about a point is defined as the product of the force and the perpendicular distance from the point to the line-of-action of the force.

Moment = Force × Perpendicular distance from the point to force

The force is measured in N and the distance in m.

Moments are measured in **newton–metres**, written as **Nm.** The direction of a moment can be clockwise or anti-clockwise.

Worked Example

A mechanic tries to remove a rusted nut from fixed bolt using the spanner shown opposite. The spanner is of length 0.18 m. However when he applies his maximum force of 300 N, the nut does not turn. By placing a steel tube over the handle of the spanner, the length is increased to 0.27 m. When the mechanic applies the same maximum force of 300 N at the end of the steel tube, the nut is just loosened.

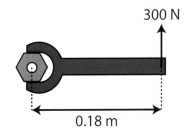

Calculate the minimum force that would have been necessary to loosen the nut if the length of the spanner had remained 0.18 m.

The moment required to loosen the nut is 300 × 0.27 = 81 Nm

If the force required to loosen the nut, when the length is 0.18 mm, is F.

$$F \times 0.18 = 81$$

$$F = \frac{81}{0.18} = 450 \text{ N}$$

Couples

A single force acting on an object will make the object rotate and move off in the direction of the force.

If only rotation of the object is required, a couple needs to be applied to the object.

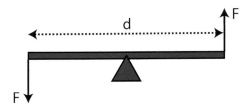

A **couple** is two forces that act in opposite directions, not along the same line, and which cause rotation. A couple produces **an unbalanced moment.**

The moment of each force about the pivot is F × ½ d

The sum of these two moments is therefore F × ½ d + F × ½ d = F × d

Moment of a couple = One force × Perpendicular separation of the forces

---

Worked Example

A driver applies parallel forces each of 15 N, in the plane of a steering wheel in the direction shown.

The radius of the steering wheel is 200 mm. The driver's hands are placed in the 'ten–to–two' position (the left hand is at the number 10 on an imaginary clock face and the right hand at the number 2).

The forces are applied to the dashed line in the diagram which joins the numbers 12 and 6 on the imaginary clock face.

Calculate the moment applied to the steering wheel.

[CCEA A Level Physics 2000]

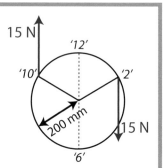

Solution

Angle between '10' and vertical = Angle between vertical and '2'
$$= 60°$$

Perpendicular separation of forces = d
$$= 2 × 200 × \sin 60° = 346.4 \text{ mm}$$
$$= 0.3464 \text{ m}$$

Moment about centre of wheel = 15 × 0.3464 = **5.20 Nm clockwise**

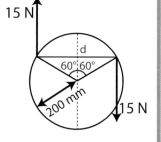

Note: that this is an unbalanced moment which will cause the wheel to turn. The Principle of Moments is not valid here.

Centre of gravity and centre of mass

This material is a recap of what you studied at GCSE. It is necessary to know this material in order to answer some questions on moments. At GCSE you may have learned:

The centre of gravity of an object is the point at which we can take its *weight* to act.

The centre of mass of an object is the point at which we take its *mass* to be concentrated.

This means that a resultant force acting through the centre of mass would cause the object to move in a straight line without causing it to rotate.

For most everyday situations the centre of gravity coincides with the centre of mass. For everyday objects the strength of the Earth's gravitational field is the same for all points on the object. An object on the Earth would have to be very large for the centre of mass and the centre of gravity to be in two different positions. A mountain would be an example of such an object. Alternatively you would need to be close to a black hole, where the gravitational force changes by large amounts in short distances, to detect any difference between the positions of the centre of gravity and the centre of mass of an object.

The centre of gravity of a uniform beam, a beam whose width, thickness and composition does not change along its length, is at the mid–point.

For a metre rule this would be at the 50 cm mark.

For a rectangular flat sheet (a lamina) it is at the centre, found by the intersection of the two diagonals.

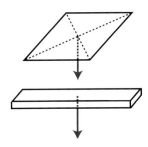

Principle of Moments

When an object is in *rotational equilibrium*, the sum of the clockwise moments about any point is equal to the sum of the anticlockwise moments about the same point.

Worked Example

A stage lighting batten consists of a uniform beam AB, 24 m long, which weighs 600 N.

The batten is suspended by two vertical cables C and D. The tensions in each cable are equal to 430 N. The batten supports two spotlights S_1 and S_2 each of weight 70 N and a floodlight F of weight 120 N. The arrangement and distances are shown in the diagram.

How far is cable C from end A?

[CCEA Module 1 January 2002]

Solution

Let the distance from A to the cable C be d and **take moments about end A.**

| Anti–clockwise moments due to the tensions in cables C and D | = | Clockwise moments due to the weights of F, S_2 and the weight of the beam |

The weight of S_1 does not have a moment about the point A.

$$430 \times d + 430 \times 22 = 120 \times 16 + 70 \times 24 + 600 \times 12$$

$$430 d + 9460 = 1920 + 1680 + 7200$$

$$430d = 1340$$

$$d = 3.12 \text{ m}$$

In this question the upward forces were the tensions in the cables. When objects rest on supports, the upward forces at the supports are called reactions.

Exercise 11

1 A uniform wooden rod AB weighs 1.2 N and is 120 cm long. It rests on two sharp supports at C and D placed 10 cm from each end of the rod. Weights of 0.2 N and 0.9 N hang from loops of thread 30 cm from A and 40 cm from B respectively.

   (a) Calculate the reactions at supports C and D.

   Hint: to find the reaction at C, take moments about point D.

   (b) Comment on the sum of the reactions at C and D.

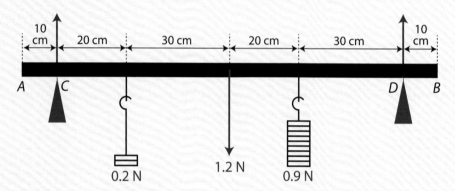

2 A uniform concrete paving slab has dimensions 750 mm × 600 mm × 75 mm and weighs 850 N.

   (a) Calculate the minimum force needed to raise one end of the slab when it lies flat.

   (b) Does it matter which side is used to lift the slab?

   Another uniform slab measuring 1500 mm × 900 mm × 25 mm also weighs 850 N.

   (c) Is the minimum force needed to lift this slab larger than, smaller than or equal to the force calculated in (a)?

3 A uniform beam, AB, of length 8 m and weight 480 N rests on two trestles C and D placed 2 m from one end and 3 m from the other. A painter of weight 600 N stands on the beam directly over trestle C.

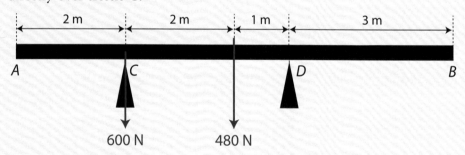

   (a) Calculate the upward reactions at trestles C and D.

   (b) The painter starts walking towards end B of the beam. At what distance is she from B when the beam tips at trestle C?

   Hint: What is the reaction at C when the beam starts to tip?

   (c) How far from A would the painter be standing when the beam begins to tip at trestle D?

Exercise 12

Examination Question

The diagram shows three identical uniform rectangular blocks stacked on a horizontal surface. The length of each block is 300 mm.

(a) Initially, the middle block overhangs the bottom one by 50 mm. The top block is placed as far to the right as possible before it tilts on the upper right–hand edge of the block below it. In this position, it overhangs the middle block by a distance x. Find x.

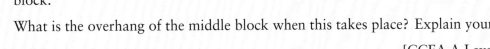

(b) With the upper block overhanging the middle block by the distance x, the upper and middle blocks are slowly moved together, maintaining the overhang x, so that the overhang of the **middle** block is increased beyond the initial 50 mm.

Eventually, both upper blocks topple by tilting on the upper right–hand edge of the bottom block.

What is the overhang of the middle block when this takes place? Explain your reasoning.

[CCEA A Level Physics 2000]

Worked Example

A wheel of radius 0.50 m rests on a level road at point C and makes contact with the edge E of a kerb of height 0.20 m, as shown in the diagram. A horizontal force of 240 N, applied through the axle of the wheel at X, is required just to move the wheel over the kerb.

Find the weight of the wheel.

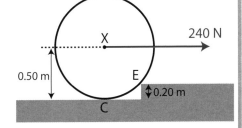

Solution

The first step is to mark the forces acting on the wheel not already shown on the diagram.

The weight of the wheel W, acts vertically downward from the centre of gravity of the wheel which is at the axle. The wheel is in contact with the kerb at E, so there is a normal reaction force R at this point.

The wheel is just on the point of moving over the kerb, so it is in equilibrium. This means that the three forces acting on the wheel, the weight, the pulling force of 240 N and the normal force (from E) must act through the same point. This point is the axle of the wheel.

Taking moments about the point E means that we can ignore the reaction force R as it does not have a moment about this point.

The perpendicular distance from E to the 240 N force is 0.3 m.

The perpendicular distance from E to the line of action of the weight W is 0.4 m (by Pythagoras)

Taking moments about E:

$$240 \times 0.3 = W \times 0.4$$

giving $W = 180$ N

Exercise 13

1 A car of mass 1200 kg has a wheelbase (the distance between the centres of the front and rear wheels) of 2.50 m. Its centre of gravity G is 1.05 m behind the centres of the front wheels. The car rests on a level road. Below is a simplified diagram of the situation.

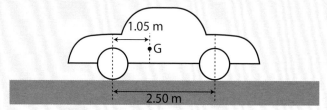

(a) Find the force exerted by the ground on each of the front wheels (assume this force to be the same on each wheel) and the force exerted by the ground on each of the rear wheels (also assumed to be the same on each wheel).

(b) Most of the mass of this car is concentrated in the engine unit. The distribution of mass throughout the body–shell, disregarding the engine unit, may be assumed to be approximately uniform. Deduce whether the car is front–engined or rear–engined, and explain your reasoning.

[CCEA February 2000]

2 The diagram below is a simplified side view of a car bonnet ABC raised at an angle of 30° to the horizontal. The bonnet of mass 1.4 kg is hinged at A. Its centre of gravity is at B, the mid–point of AC. The bonnet is held in the open position by a vertical support rod DC.

(a) Calculate the upwards force of the rod DC supporting the bonnet.

Hint: Let the distance AD = d and take moments about A.

(b) The bonnet is now held open at an angle of 60° to the horizontal by a new, longer, support rod, again placed vertically at C. What is the upward force of the new rod supporting the bonnet?

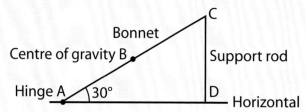

1.7 Work Done, Potential and Kinetic Energy

Work

When energy is transferred from one form to another it may be transferred by doing work. For example, when you lift an object you do work by transferring chemical energy to kinetic energy and gravitational potential energy. This concept of work gives us a way of defining energy.

Energy is defined as the stored ability to do work.

When we say that, for example, a battery stores 50 000 joules of energy, we simply mean that the battery has the capacity to do 50 000 joules of work. But what do we mean by 'work'?

We define the work done by a constant force as the product of the force and the distance moved in the direction of the force.

Work done = constant force × distance moved in the direction of the force

> **or W = F × s**
>
>> where W = work done in joules (or Nm)
>> F = constant force in N
>> s = distance moved in the direction of the force in m

At GCSE you did not pay much attention to the words 'in the direction of the force' used in the definition of work. At AS level it is important that you recognise and can apply this new definition when the force and the distance moved are not in the same direction. The following worked example shows why it is important to take into account the direction of the motion.

Worked Example

Consider an Arctic explorer dragging a sledge across a frozen lake. The explorer attaches the rope to his waist and the force of 200 N is applied at 30° to the horizontal. We can model this situation in the diagram below. How much work is done by the explorer in dragging the sledge 150 metres across the ice at a steady speed?

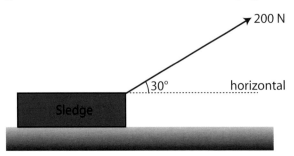

The difficulty here is that the force, F (200 N), and the displacement, s, are not in the same direction. The easiest solution is to resolve the 200 N force into its vertical and horizontal components as shown below.

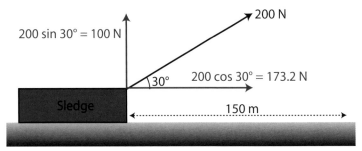

Provided the sledge does not rise above the ice, no work is done by the vertical force of 100 N. **Work is done only by the horizontal component of the applied force (173.2 N).**

Work done = constant force × distance moved in direction of the force = 173.2 N × 150 m
= **25 980 J**

Notice that since the sledge is moving at a steady speed there is no resultant force, so there is a frictional force of 173.2 N acting to the left. This is why we say 'the explorer is doing work against the frictional force'.

The situation described above occurs quite often and it is sometimes easier to use the general formula applicable when the force and distance moved are not in the same direction.

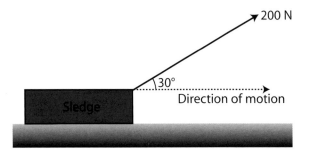

The general formula is:

$$W = Fs \cos \theta$$

where θ is the angle between the force and the direction of the motion.

To apply this formula to the sledge example above we would write:

$W = Fs \cos \theta = 200 \times 150 \cos 30° = 200 \times 129.9 = $ **25 980 J**

Potential energy

An object has gravitational potential energy when it is raised above the ground.

The gain in gravitational potential energy is equal to the work done in raising the object. If the object has zero potential energy when it is on the ground then the work done equals the amount of potential energy the object has when it is a height Δh above the ground.

If the object of mass m is raised a distance Δh then the amount of work done in raising the object is:

Work done = force needed × distance moved in direction of this force
        = weight × vertical distance moved
        = $mg\Delta h$ (where g is the acceleration of free fall)
        = gain in gravitational potential energy

$\Delta p.e. = mg\Delta h$

where $\Delta p.e.$ = change in potential energy in J
        m = mass in kg
        g = acceleration of free fall
        Δh = vertical distance moved in m

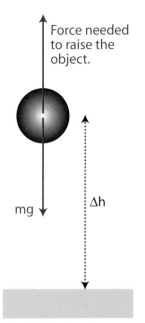

Force needed to raise the object.

mg

Δh

Kinetic energy

A moving object possesses kinetic energy.

An object of mass m is initially at rest. It is acted upon a resultant force F and the object accelerates. This force acts over a distance s. Having travelled this distance the object has a velocity v.

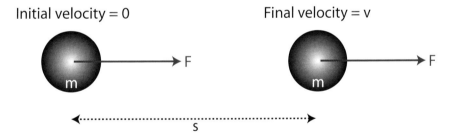

Initial velocity = 0

Final velocity = v

m

m

F

F

s

Work done in moving the object a distance s is W = F × s

Newton's 2nd law (F = ma) allows us to replace F in this expression, W = ma × s

The equation of motion $v^2 = u^2 + 2as$ allows us introduce velocity in our expression for W. The initial velocity of this object was 0 so **as = ½ v^2**

k.e. = ½ mv^2

where k.e. = kinetic energy in J
        m = mass in kg
        v = velocity in ms^{-1}

In general the work done on an object is equal to the **change** in the kinetic energy of the object. If the final speed v is greater than the initial speed u then W is the work done in accelerating the object over a distance s. If the final speed v is less than the initial speed u then W is the work done in slowing the object down over a distance s.

$$W = \tfrac{1}{2}\,mv^2 - \tfrac{1}{2}\,mu^2$$

$$\begin{aligned}
\text{where } W &= \text{work done in J} \\
m &= \text{mass in kg} \\
v &= \text{final velocity in ms}^{-1} \\
u &= \text{initial velocity in ms}^{-1}
\end{aligned}$$

Principle of Conservation of Energy

The Principle of Conservation of Energy states that energy cannot be created or destroyed but can be changed from one form to another.

Some forms of energy are more useful than others; they are more suitable for doing work and changing into other forms of energy. Electrical and chemical energy are in this category and are sometimes known as high-grade forms of energy.

On the other hand internal energy, i.e. the kinetic energy of gas molecules due to their random motion is a low-grade form of energy that is not easily converted to other forms.

The Principle of Conservation of Energy as it applies to a falling object

An object held above the ground and then released will gradually convert potential energy to kinetic energy. At any time its total energy (E_T) i.e. the sum of its kinetic (E_k) and potential (E_p) energies, is constant. At any point along its path, as it falls, the total energy E_T is also constant.

How does the kinetic energy and the potential energy vary with the vertical distance it falls?

As the object accelerates from rest (u=0) its velocity at any instant is v = at.

$$E_k = \tfrac{1}{2}\,mv^2 = \tfrac{1}{2}\,ma^2t^2$$

E_k is proportional to t^2.

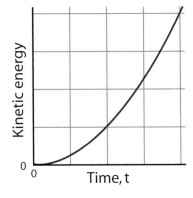

As the object falls its E_p decreases. At any instant the E_p equals the initial potential energy (E_T) less the kinetic energy (E_k)

$$E_p = E_T - E_k$$

$$E_p = E_T - \tfrac{1}{2}\,ma^2t^2$$

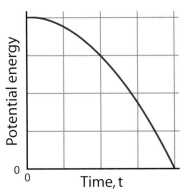

If the object falls a distance y then its potential energy at this point is

$$E_p = E_T - mgy$$

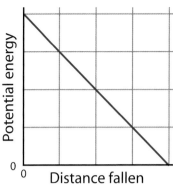

As the object falls a distance y we can use the equation of motion $v^2 = u^2 + 2as$ to find its velocity at this point. This gives $v^2 = 2gy$

$$E_k = \tfrac{1}{2}mv^2 \quad , \text{but we can substitute, giving}$$

$$E_k = mgy$$

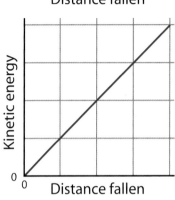

The following shows the strength of using energy interchange to solve problems in mechanics.

Worked Examples

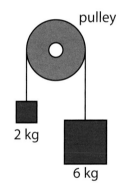

1 Masses of 6.0 kg and 2.0 kg are connected by a light inextensible string passing over a smooth pulley. The string is taut when the masses are released. The smaller mass accelerates upwards and the bigger mass accelerates downwards. Using the Principle of Conservation of Energy, calculate the speed of the masses when the larger one has descended 2.0 m.

Solution

The 2.0 kg mass is accelerating upwards and is gaining both kinetic and potential energy. The 6.0 kg mass is accelerating downwards and is gaining kinetic energy and losing potential energy.

Let the speed of each mass be v (in ms⁻¹) when the larger one has descended 2.0 m.

Net loss in energy of 6.0 kg mass = p.e. − k.e. = $mgh - \tfrac{1}{2}mv^2 = 6 \times g \times 2 - \tfrac{1}{2} \times 6 \times v^2$
$$= 12g - 3v^2$$

Net gain in energy of 2.0 kg mass = p.e. + k.e. = $mgh + \tfrac{1}{2}mv^2 = 2 \times g \times 2 + \tfrac{1}{2} \times 2 \times v^2$
$$= 4g + v^2$$

By the Principle of Conservation of Energy:
the net loss in energy of the 6.0 kg mass = net gain in energy of the 2.0 kg mass

$$12g - 3v^2 = 4g + v^2 \text{, which rearranges to give}$$

$$8g = 4v^2 \text{, which simplifies to}$$

$$v = \sqrt{(2g)} = \sqrt{(2 \times 9.81)} = \textbf{4.4 ms}^{-1}$$

An equally valid approach is to use the idea that the total loss in p.e. is equal to the total gain in k.e.

This leads to:

Loss in p.e. = (mgh) $_{for\ 6\ kg\ mass}$ − (mgh) $_{for\ 2\ kg\ mass}$ = 6 × g × 2 − 2 × g × 2 = 8g

Gain in k.e. = (½ mv²) $_{for\ 6\ kg\ mass}$ + (½ mv²) $_{for\ 2\ kg\ mass}$ = ½ × 6 × v² + ½ × 2 × v² = 4v²

Hence, 8g = 4v² , which simplifies as above to give v = **4.4 ms⁻¹**

Note: This problem can also be solved by first finding the common acceleration of the masses and then applying Newton's equations of uniform acceleration.

2 A small block of wood passes through point P at a speed of 2.00 ms⁻¹ and slides down a smooth curved track.

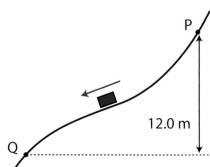

   (a) Calculate the speed of the block as it passes point Q, 12.0 m vertically below P.

   (b) Explain why it would be inappropriate to use Newton's equations of uniform acceleration in this situation.

   (c) Does the time taken to travel from P to Q depend on the equation of the curved slope? Explain your answer.

Solution

   (a) Let the speed of the block as it passes Q be v.
By Principle of Conservation of Energy,
Loss in gravitational p.e. = gain in k.e.

mgΔh = ½ mv² − ½ mu²

Substituting,	m × 9.81 × 12 = ½ mv² − ½ mu²
cancelling m,	117.72 = ½(v² − 2²)
and solving.	v = 15.5 ms⁻¹

   (b) The acceleration is not uniform (and not in a straight line).

   (c) Yes. The steeper the slope the greater the average acceleration and the smaller the time taken.

Exercise 14

Examination Question

   (a) Distinguish between kinetic energy and gravitational potential energy.

   (b) A particle possesses energy in two forms only: kinetic energy and gravitational energy. It has a total energy of 3.0 J and is initially at rest. Its potential energy E_p changes causing a corresponding change in its kinetic energy E_k. No external work is done on or by the system. Copy the grid on the next page and draw a graph of kinetic energy E_k against potential energy E_p.

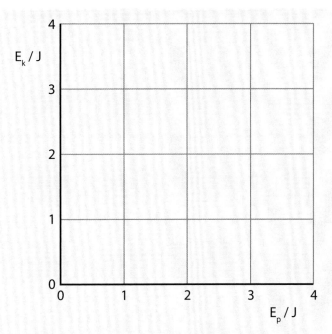

Explain how your graph illustrates the principle of conservation of energy.

(c) An AS Physics student plans to enter for the high jump event at the School Sports.

She estimates that, if she is to have a chance of winning, she will have to raise her centre of mass by 1.6 m to clear the bar. She will also have to move her centre of mass horizontally at a speed of 0.80 ms^{-1} at the top of her jump in order to roll over the bar.

(i) The student's mass is 75 kg. Estimate the total energy required to raise her centre of mass and roll over the bar.

(ii) The student assumes that this energy can be supplied entirely from the kinetic energy she will have at the end of her run-up. Estimate the minimum speed she will require at the end of the run-up.

[CCEA AS Physics 2006]

Power

Power is defined as the rate of doing work.

The definition can be expressed as an equation:

$$\text{Power} = \frac{\text{Work done}}{\text{Time taken}}$$

or

$$P = \frac{W}{t}$$

where P = power in watts (W) or joules per second (Js^{-1})
W = work done in joules (J)
t = time taken in seconds (s)

If the work is being done by a **constant** force, F, then we know that the work done, W, can be written as W = Fs. Making this substitution for W in the power equation gives P = Fs ÷ t. If the **displacement occurs at a steady rate**, then speed, v = s ÷ t and we arrive at:

P = Fv

where P = power in watts (W) or joules per second (Js^{-1})
F = force being applied in newtons (N)
v = constant speed at which force is moving in ms^{-1}

Worked Examples

1 An electric motor has an output power of 2400 W and is used to raise a ship's anchor. If the tension in the cable is 8 kN, at what constant speed is the anchor being raised?

Solution

P = Fv, so v = P ÷ F = 2400 ÷ 8000 = **0.3 ms^{-1}**

2 A car of mass 1200 kg has an output power of 60 kW when travelling at a speed of 30 ms^{-1} along a flat road. What power output is required if the same car is to travel at the same speed up a hill of gradient 10%? (Such a hill has an angle of slope of $\tan^{-1}(0.1)$ or 5.7°.)

Students are advised to re-visit the material on resolution of forces on the inclined plane (page 35) before attempting this question.

Take g as 9.81 ms^{-2}.

Solution

Additional force to be overcome due to hill = mg.sin θ = 1200 × g × sin 5.7° = 1169.19 N
Additional power required = Fv = 1169.19 × 30 = 35 076 W ≈ 35 kW

Total power required = 60 + 35 = **95 kW**

3 The engine of a motor boat delivers 36 kW to the propeller while the boat is moving at 9 ms^{-1}. Calculate the tension in the tow rope if the boat were being towed at the same speed.

Solution

Force (tension) = P ÷ v = 36000 ÷ 9 = 4000 N = **4 kN**

4 The dam at a certain hydroelectric power station is 170 m deep. The electrical power output from the generators at the base of the dam is 2000 MW. Given that 1 m^3 water has a mass of 1000 kg, calculate the minimum rate at which water leaves the dam in m^3s^{-1} when electrical generation takes place at this rate.

Why is this figure the **minimum** rate of flow? Take g as 9.81 ms^{-2}.

Solution

In 1 s, the potential energy converted to electrical energy is 2×10^3 MJ = 2×10^9 J
Gravitational p.e. = mgh = m × 9.81 × 170 = 1667.7 × m
So mass removed from dam **every second** = $(2 \times 10^9) ÷ 1667.7 \approx 1.20 \times 10^6$ kg
So rate of flow = $(1.2 \times 10^6) ÷ 1000$ = **1200 m^3s^{-1}**

Calculated flow rate is a **minimum** because it has been assumed that all the gravitational potential energy has been converted into electrical energy and no allowance has been made for the wasted heat and sound energy.

Efficiency

Efficiency is a way of describing how good a device is at transferring energy from one form to another in an intended way.

If a light bulb is rated 100 W, this means that it normally uses 100 J of electrical energy every second. But it might only produce 5 J of light energy every second. The other 95 J are wasted as heat. This means that only 5% of the energy is transferred from electrical energy into light energy. This light bulb therefore has an efficiency of 0.05 or 5%. If the same light bulb were used as a heater, its efficiency would be 95% or 0.95, because the intended output energy form would be heat, not light.

Opposite are two equivalent equations which can be used to define efficiency. Since efficiency is a ratio of two quantities each with the same unit, efficiency itself is dimensionless, that is, **efficiency has no unit.**

$$\text{efficiency} = \frac{\text{useful power output}}{\text{total power input}}$$

or

$$\text{efficiency} = \frac{\text{useful energy output in a given time}}{\text{total energy input in the same time}}$$

Worked Examples

1   A filament lamp rated 60 W has an efficiency of 0.04 (4%). A modern long-life lamp is rated 12 W and produces the same useful output power as the filament lamp. Calculate (a) the useful output power of the filament lamp and (b) the efficiency of the long-life lamp.

   Solution

   (a) useful output power = efficiency × total input power = 0.04 × 60 = 2.4 W

   (b) $\text{efficiency} = \dfrac{\text{useful power output}}{\text{total power input}} = \dfrac{2.4}{12} = 0.2 = 20\%$

2   A wheel-and-axle is a simple machine in which a small effort force can be used to raise a heavy load. In the wheel-and-axle shown in the diagram, a rope under 200 N tension (the effort) is wrapped around a 'wheel' of radius 20 cm to raise a load of weight 600 N.

   Calculate the machine's efficiency.

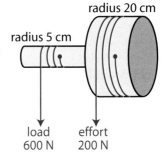

radius 20 cm
radius 5 cm
load 600 N
effort 200 N

   Solution

   When the wheel rotates once, the effort falls a distance of (2 × π × 0.2) metres and at the same time the load rises through a distance of (2 × π × 0.05) metres.

   For every revolution, the work done by the effort = Fs = 200 × (2 × π × 0.2) = 80π joules and the work done on the load = Fs = 600 × (2 × π × 0.05) = 60π joules

   $$\text{efficiency} = \frac{\text{useful energy output in a given time}}{\text{total energy input in the same time}} = \frac{60\pi}{80\pi} = 0.75 = 75\%$$

Exercise 15

Where relevant take g as 9.81 ms^{-2} and give your answer to an appropriate number of significant figures.

1 To enable a train to travel at a steady speed of 30 ms^{-1} along a level track, the engine must supply a pulling force of 50 kN.

   (a) How much work is the engine doing every second?

   (b) If the power is proportional to the cube of the velocity, how much power is needed to drive the train at a speed of 40 ms^{-1}?

2 A car of mass 600 kg moves at a constant speed of 20.0 ms^{-1} up an inclined road which rises 1 m for every 40.0 m travelled along the road. Calculate

   (a) the constant kinetic energy of the car and

   (b) the rate at which the gravitational potential energy of the car is increasing.

3 A lorry of mass 35 000 kg moves at a constant maximum speed, v, up an inclined road which rises 1.00 m for every 10.0 m travelled along the road. The output power of the engine is 175 kW. Calculate (a) the value of v, if friction forces can be ignored and
(b) the value of v, if the friction force is 4665 N.

4 A simple pendulum has a length of 1.00 m. The bob is pulled to one side so that the angle between the taut string and the vertical is 60.0°. The pendulum is then released.

   (a) Why can Newton's equations of motion not be applied in this situation?

   (b) Show that the maximum speed of the pendulum in its motion is 3.13 ms^{-1}.

5 Several stones are projected upwards with the same initial speed, u, but at different angles α (α >0) to the horizontal. A student claims that at any common height reached by all of the stones, the *speed* of each stone is the same. Is the student right?

   A stone projected at 15.0 ms^{-1} at an unknown angle α (α >0) to the horizontal.

   Show that when it is 2.00 m above the ground the stone's speed is 13.6 ms^{-1}

Exercise 16

1 You lift your schoolbag from the floor to your desk, and leave it resting there. Describe the energy changes that take place. Explain also how the principle of conservation of energy applies to this operation.

[CCEA AS Physics January 2002]

2 A model helicopter of mass 0.60 kg, initially at rest on the ground, rises vertically into the air with uniform acceleration. At a height of 35 m above the ground its speed is 5.9 ms^{-1}.

   (a) calculate the change in kinetic energy of the helicopter as it rises from the ground to a height of 35 m.

(b) calculate the change in gravitational potential energy of the helicopter as it rises to this height.

[CCEA AS Physics June 2003]

3 (a) (i) State the principle of conservation of energy.

   (ii) A rugby ball is kicked from the ground towards the goalposts directly against the wind. The ball rises from ground level to a maximum height, and then falls. Explain how the principle of conservation of energy applies to this situation from the instant that the ball leaves the ground until it reaches its maximum height. Air resistance cannot be neglected.

(b) In this part of the question, neglect air resistance. An object falls from rest from a certain height H to the ground. As it falls, its potential energy E_p and its kinetic energy E_k both change.

   (i) Sketch a graph to show the potential energy E_p varies with time from the moment of release until it reaches the ground.

   (ii) Sketch a graph to show the kinetic energy E_k varies with time from the moment of release until it reaches the ground.

   (iii) Sketch a graph to show the kinetic energy E_k depends on the height h of the object above the ground until it reaches the ground.

[CCEA June 2002]

1.8 Deformation of Solids

Hooke's Law

You will be familiar with Hooke's Law from your studies at GCSE. **At GCSE the 'elastic limit' and the 'limit of proportionality' were treated as meaning the same thing. In fact, this is not so and at AS level we must make the distinction clear.** Hooke's Law, for any elastic material, states that:

Up to a maximum load, known as the limit of proportionality, the extension of an elastic material is proportional to the applied load.

For many materials, the limit of proportionality and the elastic limit are the same. This is why the form of Hooke's Law you may have learned for GCSE was accepted even if was in terms of elastic limit (which is wrong) rather than the limit of proportionality (which is correct).

Hooke's Law may be written as an equation:

$$F = kx$$

where F = applied load in N

k = the Hooke's Law constant in Nm^{-1} (or Ncm^{-1} or Nmm^{-1})

x = the extension of the specimen under test in m (or cm or mm)

The graph opposite illustrates how the load and extension are related for a typical metal wire. From (0,0) up to the limit of proportionality the line is straight. This is the region where the wire obeys Hooke's Law. Beyond **the limit of proportionality,** the line curves: there is no longer direct proportion between load and extension. A point is then reached where any further load will cause the wire to become **permanently** stretched. This is the **elastic limit.**

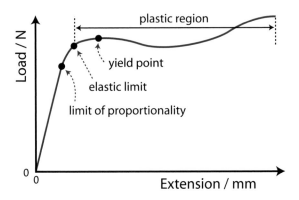

The elastic limit is therefore the maximum load a specimen can experience and still return to its original length when the deforming force is removed. Beyond the elastic limit the wire reaches a 'yield point'. The internal molecular structure is being permanently changed as crystal planes slide across each other. **A wire stretched beyond its elastic limit is said to be 'plastic'** and may stretch enormously before it finally breaks.

Exercise 17

1 Two identical springs are joined in series. One has a spring constant of 12 Ncm⁻¹ and the other has a spring constant of 18 Ncm⁻¹. One free end is connected to a fixed point and from the other a weight of 36 N is applied. Calculate

(i) the extension in the combination caused by the 36 N load and

(ii) the spring (Hooke's Law) constant of the combination.

(iii) State the tension in each spring.

(iv) Show that if two springs having Hooke's Law constants, k_1 and k_2 are joined end-to-end, then their combined spring constant is $\dfrac{k_1.k_2}{(k_1 + k_2)}$

2 Two springs are joined together in parallel with each other as shown in the diagram opposite. One spring has a stiffness constant of 15 Ncm⁻¹ and the other 25 Ncm⁻¹. The lengths of the springs are such that a metal bar weighing 100 N suspended as shown rests horizontally. Calculate the tension and extension of each spring.

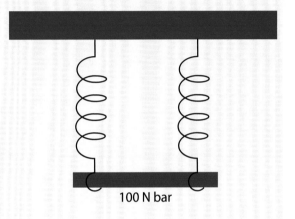

100 N bar

Show that if two springs having spring constants k_1 and k_2 are joined in parallel, then their combined spring constant is:

$k_1 + k_2$.

3 A nylon guitar string is in tune when it is under 32.0 N tension. The length of the string from the fixed point to the tension key is 850 mm. On average, each turn of the tension key increases the length of the string by 40.0 mm and the key must be turned exactly ten times to bring the string into tune. Assuming the string obeys Hooke's Law when in tune, calculate (a) the stiffness constant and (b) the total length of the stretched string.

4 A metal cube of side 200 mm is held in a vice. Each turn of the handle of the vice moves the jaws 0.500 mm closer together. The vice is tightened up by a quarter turn. A strain gauge attached to the metal shows the compressive force to be 600 kN. Assuming the metal obeys Hooke's Law at this compression, calculate the reduction in the length of the metal and its stiffness constant.

5 When carrying out an experiment to see if a steel wire obeyed Hooke's Law, a teacher insisted on (a) all students wearing safety spectacles and (b) measurements of length being taken both when the wire was being loaded and unloaded. Why were these requirements of the teacher good experimental practice?

Stress, Strain and Young Modulus

The definitions of these quantities need to be learned in preparation for the AS examination. All of them can be expressed as equations.

Stress (σ) is defined as the applied force per unit area of cross section.

$$\sigma = \frac{F}{A}$$

where:

F is the applied force in N
A is the cross section area in m^2
σ is the stress in Nm^{-2} or Pa

Strain (ε) is defined as the ratio of the change in the length of a specimen to its original length.

$$\varepsilon = \frac{\Delta L}{L_0}$$

where:

ΔL is the change in the length
L_0 is the original length
ε is the strain (no units)

Generally the application of a tensile stress to a material produces a corresponding strain. Provided the stress is not too large, the strain is directly proportional to the stress. Within the limit of proportionality, the ratio of stress to strain is defined as the Young Modulus (E).

$$E = \frac{\sigma}{\varepsilon}$$

where:

σ is the stress in Nm^{-2} or Pa
ε is the strain (no units)
E is the Young Modulus in Nm^{-2}
or Pa

During your AS course you should get the experience of determining the Young Modulus of the material of a metal wire. This is a prescribed experiment which you may be required to describe in the examination.

Measuring the Young Modulus of a metal

The method below uses two long wires suspended from a common support in the ceiling. One wire is called the reference wire because the extension of the wire under test is measured with respect to it.

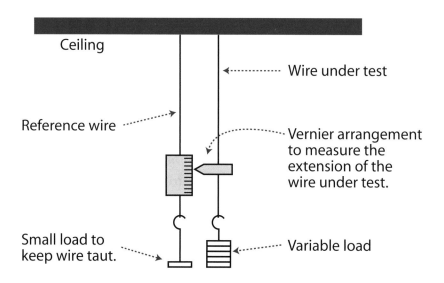

Both the reference wire and the wire under test should be made of the same material, have the same cross-section area and be approximately the same length. This ensures that errors arising from thermal expansion as a result of temperature changes in the wires are minimised. The wires should be as long as possible (at least 2 m) so as to obtain the greatest possible extension of the test wire. Even so, a Vernier gauge is necessary to measure the small extension with respect to the reference wire.

At the outset the **length, L, of the test wire is measured** in mm using a metre stick. The measurement should be taken from the point of suspension to the Vernier scale. For information about how to use a Vernier scale see the section in Module 3.

Using a micrometer screw gauge, the diameter, d, of the test wire is measured at about six places spread out along its length. It is necessary to measure the diameter in this way to avoid the possibility of small kinks in the wire giving rise to erroneous results. The cross section area, A, can then be found from the equation $A = \pi <d>^2 \div 4$ where $<d>$ is the average diameter of the wire from the measurements made.

The reference wire is loaded with about 5 N to keep it taught. The test wire is loaded in steps of 10 N from 10 N to about 100 N. For each load on the extension wire, the extension is found from the Vernier and the stress, σ, ($\sigma = F \div A$) and strain, ε, ($\varepsilon = \Delta L \div L_o$) calculated and recorded in a suitable table. Typical results are shown below.

Typical Results for Young Modulus Experiment on a metal			
Length of test wire in metres:	2.055		
Diameter of test wire in mm:	1.38, 1.38, 1.37, 1.39, 1.38, 1.38		
Average diameter of test wire in mm:	1.38		
Area of cross section in m²:	1.496×10^{-6}		

Force (in N)	Extension (in mm)	Stress (in MPa)	Strain (x 10^{-4} no units)
10	0.07	6.68	0.334
20	0.14	13.37	0.668
30	0.21	20.05	1.003
40	0.27	26.74	1.337
50	0.34	33.42	1.671
60	0.41	40.11	2.005
70	0.48	46.79	2.340
80	0.55	53.48	2.674
90	0.62	60.16	3.008
100	0.69	66.84	3.342

It is left as an exercise for the reader to plot a graph of stress (y-axis) against strain and draw the straight line of best fit. The gradient of this **straight line** is the Young Modulus.

If we continue to measure stress and strain for increasing loads on a wire, we would be able to plot a graph like the one shown opposite.

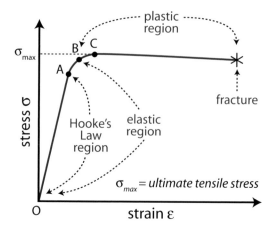

The gradient of the straight line region (OA) is the Young Modulus. Point A represents the limit of proportionality – beyond A the wire will not obey Hooke's Law. Point B represents the elastic limit – beyond B the wire is plastic and will not return to its original length when the stretching force is removed. Point C marks the position of **ultimate tensile stress** (UTS).

The UTS is defined as the maximum stress which can be applied to a wire without it breaking.

Exercise 18

1 A lift and its occupants have a combined mass of 2500 kg. The lift is supported by a steel safety cable which the manufacturers say is safe up to a maximum stress of 100 MPa. The lift manufacturers require the lift to be able to accelerate up and down the lift shaft at a maximum rate of 0.500 ms⁻². Calculate:

(a) the minimum cross section area and

(b) the diameter of the safety cable.

2 In the showroom of an Irish crystal manufacturer, a chandelier of mass 11.0 kg hangs from the ceiling, supported only by a solid aluminium rod of diameter 2 mm and length 2 m.

What is the (a) stress (b) strain and (c) extension of the aluminium rod if the Young Modulus for aluminium is 70 GPa?

3 A copper wire of length 900 mm and cross section area 0.9 mm² is welded to an iron wire of length 1400 mm and cross section area 1.3 mm². The compound wire is stretched so that its length increases by 10.0 mm. The Young Modulus for copper is 130 GPa and that for iron is 210 GPa.

(a) Write down the length and cross section area of each wire in m and m² respectively.

(b) Show that the extension of each wire is given by the formula: $\Delta L = (FL_o) \div (AE)$ where the symbols have their usual meanings.

(c) Given that the force in each wire is the same, calculate (i) the ratio of the extensions of the wires, using the formula given in part (b), (ii) the extension of each wire and (iii) the tension in each wire.

4 A nylon rope of length 10.0 m and diameter 10.0 mm is used by a tow truck to tow a car which has broken down. The rope obeys Hooke's Law while being used for this purpose. The Young Modulus for nylon is 3.00 GPa.

While towing at a constant speed on level ground the extension of the tow rope is 25.0 mm Calculate:

(a) the strain in the tow rope

(b) the stress in the tow rope

(c) the tension in the tow rope

(d) the sum of the forces which oppose the motion of the car.

(e) In what way, if at all, would the tension and the extension of the tow rope change if it has a larger cross section area? Assume the other factors remain as before.

The ultimate tensile stress of the rope is 21.8 MPa and the combined mass of the car and its driver is 750 kg.

(f) Calculate the acceleration of the car which is just enough to break the rope, assuming that the friction forces are unchanged.

1.9 Electric Current and Charge

Conduction in solids

Materials exhibit a very wide range of electrical conductivities. The best conductors, such as silver and copper, are over 10^{23} times better than the worst conductors such as polythene. Between these extreme cases are materials known as semiconductors of which the most important are germanium and silicon.

The first requirement for conduction is a supply of charge carriers that can wander freely through the material. In solid, metallic conductors, the carriers are loosely held outer electrons. With copper, for example, every atom contributes, on average, one 'free' electron which is not attached to any particular atom and so can participate in conduction. On the other hand, if all electrons are required to form the bonds (covalent or ionic) that bind the atoms of the material together, then the material will be an insulator. In semiconductors only a small proportion of the charge carriers are 'free' to move throughout the lattice.

The 'free' electrons in a solid conductor are in a state of rapid motion, moving within the crystal lattice at speeds which depend on the lattice temperature. At room temperature, typical thermal speeds are around 1×10^6 ms^{-1}. This motion is normally completely random, like that of gas molecules in the air. This means that as many electrons with a given speed move in one direction as in the opposite direction. Since the free electron motion is entirely random, we do not observe an electric current.

metallic conductor, eg copper

metallic conductor with a p.d. applied across it

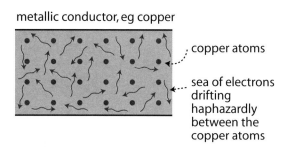

copper atoms

sea of electrons drifting haphazardly between the copper atoms

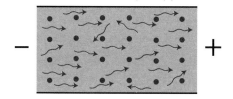

With no applied p.d., there is no net flow of charge and so no current flows.

When a p.d. is applied, there is a net drift of electrons towards the region of higher potential.

However, when a battery is applied across the ends of a conductor, an electric field is created causing the electrons to accelerate towards the region of positive potential and to gain kinetic energy. Collisions between these accelerating electrons and the vibrating atoms in the crystal lattice cause the electrons to slow down and give up some of their kinetic energy to the atoms themselves. The effect is to transfer some of the chemical energy from the battery to the internal energy of the vibrating atoms in the lattice. This causes the atoms to vibrate more rapidly about their mean positions. Externally, we observe this increased internal energy as a temperature rise in the conductor. Electrical resistance is explained by collisions between the 'free electrons' and the vibrating atoms in the crystal lattice of the metal.

Following any collision, the electrons accelerate once again and the process continues. The overall acceleration of the electrons is zero on account of these frequent collisions. However, there is a **drift of negative charge** towards the region of positive potential. **It is this drift of electrical charge which constitutes an electric current in a metal.** A typical drift velocity, for currents you might experience in an AS course, is less than 1 mms^{-1}.

Current and charge

You will be aware from GCSE of the convention that current flows from the region of positive potential to that of negative or zero potential. However, in normal circumstances, the current, I, in metals is entirely due to the motion of electrons in the opposite direction to that of the conventional current. The quantity of electric charge flowing past a fixed point is defined in terms of the current. Thus, for a constant current I flowing for a time Δt we can write:

$$\Delta Q = I \times \Delta t$$

or

$$I = \Delta Q \div \Delta t$$

ΔQ = charge flowing past a fixed point, in coulombs

I = constant current in Amperes

Δt = time taken for charge to flow past fixed point in seconds

This tells us that a current of 1A flowing in a circuit is equal to a charge of 1C passing a fixed point in the circuit every second.

Exercise 19

What steady current flows when a charge of 300 mC flows past a fixed point in 5 s?

Worked example

If the charge on a single electron is -1.6×10^{-19} C, how many electrons flow past a fixed point every minute when a current of 2 A is flowing?

$$\Delta Q = I \times \Delta t = 2 \times 60 = 120 \text{ C}$$

Number of electrons = (Total Charge) ÷ (Charge on a single electron)

$$= 120 \div 1.6 \times 10^{-19}$$
$$= 7.5 \times 10^{20} \text{ electrons}$$

The fact that electrons have a negative charge has no bearing on this calculation.

Exercise 20

Examination Questions

1 A metal rod of circular cross section is narrower in one part, as shown to the right. The diameter of the narrower part is D, and that of the wider part is 2D.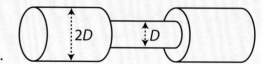

   When there is a certain current in the rod, 7.84×10^{18} electrons pass through a cross-section of the narrower part in one second.

   (a) Calculate the current corresponding to this rate of flow of electrons.

   (b) What is the current in the wider part of the rod at this time?

   [CCEA January 2005]

2 Electric current in a metal wire can be described as the flow of charged particles.

   (a) Name the particles involved.

   (b) A wire carries a current of 1.5 mA. How many charge carriers pass a point in the wire in one second?

   [CCEA January 2004]

3 A certain wire carries a current of 25.0 μA when a potential difference is applied between its ends. Calculate the time taken for 1.10 coulomb of charge to pass a given cross-section of the wire.

   [CCEA January 2003]

1.10 Potential Difference and Electromotive Force

You should be able to:

1.10.1 Recall and use the equations $V = \dfrac{W}{q}$, $V = \dfrac{P}{I}$

1.10.2 Define the volt

1.10.3 Define electromotive force

1.10.4 Distinguish between electromotive force and potential difference

Electromotive force

Batteries and generators are able to maintain one terminal positive (i.e. deficient in electrons) and the other negative (i.e. with an excess of electrons). We can picture a battery as a pump which moves electrons from the negative terminal to the positive terminal around a circuit. **A battery therefore does work on charges and so energy must be changed within it.**

The work done is a measure of this energy transfer. When current flows in the filament of a torch bulb, for example, this stored chemical energy in the battery is first converted into electrical energy in the circuit, which in turn is changed to heat and light energy in the bulb.

A battery or generator is said to produce an electromotive force (e.m.f.), defined in terms of energy change.

The electromotive force (e.m.f.) of a battery is defined as the energy converted into electrical energy when unit charge (1 C) passes through it.

> e.m.f. = electrical energy converted ÷ electric charge moved

$E = W \div Q$

> where E = e.m.f. in volts
> W = electric energy converted in J
> Q = charge in coulombs

The unit of e.m.f., like the unit of potential difference, is the volt.

The volt can be thought of as a joule per coulomb (or, as we shall see later, a watt per ampere.)

You should remember that:

The potential difference between two points is the energy generated for every coulomb passing between them.

The potential difference between two points is 1 volt if, when 1 coulomb passes between them, 1 joule of energy is generated.

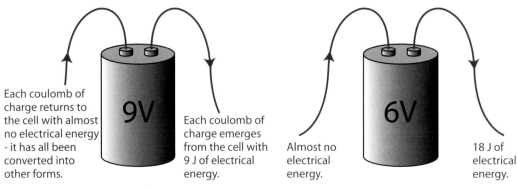

Each coulomb of charge returns to the cell with almost no electrical energy - it has all been converted into other forms.

Each coulomb of charge emerges from the cell with 9 J of electrical energy.

1 C of charge carries 9 J of energy away from a 9 V battery.

Almost no electrical energy.

18 J of electrical energy.

3 C of charge carries 18 J of energy away from a 6 V battery.

A car battery with an emf of 12 volts supplies 12 joules for every coulomb that passes through it; a power station generator with an e.m.f. of 25 000 volts is a much greater source of energy and supplies 25 000 joules per coulomb, 2 coulombs would receive 50 000 joules and so on.

In general, if a charge Q (in coulombs) passes through a source of e.m.f. E (in volts), the electrical energy supplied by the source W (in joules) is given by:

$$W = QE$$

Potential difference (p.d.)

It should be noted that although e.m.f. and potential difference have the same unit, they deal with different aspects of an electric circuit. **Emf applies to a source supplying electrical energy.** Potential difference refers to the conversion of electrical energy by a device **in a circuit.**

The term 'e.m.f.' is misleading to some extent, since it measures **energy per unit charge** and not force. It is true, however, that the source of e.m.f. is responsible for moving charges round the circuit. A voltmeter measures p.d. and one connected across the terminals of an electrical supply, such as a battery, records what is called the **terminal p.d.** of the battery.

If the battery is not connected to an external circuit and the voltmeter has a very high resistance, then the current through the battery will be negligible. We can regard the voltmeter as measuring the number of joules of electrical energy the battery supplies per coulomb, i.e. its e.m.f. Some people will therefore prefer to think of e.m.f. of a battery as **the p.d. across its terminals** *on open circuit*, **that is, when no current is drawn from it.**

Our definition of the volt allows us to write:

$$W = QV$$

where W = work done or energy transformed in joules
Q = charge moved in coulombs
V = potential difference in volts

All sources of e.m.f. have an **internal resistance** from which the source cannot be separated. When the source provides an electrical current to some external load resistor, a voltage is also developed across this internal resistance. The difference between the e.m.f., E, and the voltage across the external load resistor, V, is equal to the voltage lost in the internal resistor. We have more to say about the internal resistance of a source of e.m.f. in section 1.12.

Electrical power

Electrical power is defined as the rate at which electrical energy is converted into other forms of energy by a circuit or a component, such as a resistor, in a circuit.

Electrical power, like mechanical power, is measured in watts (W).

If we divide both sides of the equation W = QV by time, t, we arrive at:

$$\frac{W}{t} = \frac{QV}{t} = \frac{Q}{t}.V = I.V$$

And since work ÷ time is equal to power, we can write:

P = IV

$$\begin{aligned} \text{where } P &= \text{power in watts} \\ I &= \text{current in amperes} \\ V &= \text{potential difference in volts} \end{aligned}$$

Re-arranging this gives $V = \frac{P}{I}$, so the volt can also be thought of as **watt per ampere.**

Worked Examples

1   A battery of negligible internal resistance and emf 12 V is connected to a lamp marked 12 V, 24 W.

   (a) What current flows through the lamp in normal use?

   (b) How much electrical energy is used when this lamp is left on for 1 hour?

Solution

   (a) Current = power ÷ current = 24 ÷ 12 = 2 A

   (b) Power = 24 W = 24 Js^{-1}
       Energy (in J) = power (in W) × time (in s) = 24 × 360 = 86 400 J

2   An electron in a cathode ray tube is accelerated from rest through a potential difference of 150 kV.

   (a) Calculate the kinetic energy of the electrons when they collide with the screen.

   (b) If the current in the tube is 32 mA, how many electrons strike the screen per second?

   (c) At what rate must heat be dissipated from the screen when it reaches its working temperature?

Solution

   (a) W = QV = $1.6 \times 10^{-19} \times 150 \times 10^3$ = **2.4 × 10^{-14} J**

   (b) From the definition of charge, the total charge arriving per second = 3.2 mC
       Since the charge on each electron is (−) 1.6×10^{-19} C, the number of electrons arriving per second = $(3.2 \times 10^{-3}) \div (1.6 \times 10^{-19})$ = 2×10^{16}.

   (c) P = IV = $3.2 \times 10^{-3} \times 150 \times 10^3$ = **480 W**

3 A fully charged 12 V battery can deliver 1 A for 20 hours before it becomes flat. Calculate for the fully charged battery the total charge stored and the total energy stored.

Solution

Charge $Q = It = 1 \times 20 \times 3600 = 72\ 000\ C = $ **72 kC**

Energy $= QV = 72\ 000 \times 12 = 864\ 000\ J = $ **864 kJ**

Exercise 21

1 Define the electromotive force (e.m.f.) of a battery.

2 The e.m.f. of a rechargeable battery is 15 V. Its internal resistance is negligible. During charging, a charge of 2.5 C passed through the battery in a time of 5.0 s.

(a) In this time, how much work is done by the charger against the e.m.f. of the battery?

(b) Calculate the power of the charger.

[CCEA June 2002]

1.11 Resistance, Resistivity

Current-Voltage Relationship

The ammeter-voltmeter circuit (two meter method) shown below allows us to vary and measure the p.d. V across a bulb and measure the corresponding current I. By removing the bulb and replacing it with another component such as length of wire or a thermistor the circuit can be used to obtain voltage and current measurements for that component.

A graph of I against V showing the relationship between these two quantities is called the **characteristic** of the component. It summarises pictorially how the component behaves.

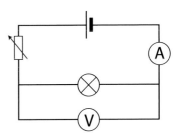

At GCSE level you may have come across graphs with voltage V on the y-axis and current I on the x-axis. For A level and beyond the practice is to show the relationship as a graph of **voltage on the x-axis** and **current on the y-axis**.

Metals and their alloys give I-V graphs which are straight lines through the origin, provided the temperature remains constant.

Ohm's Law

This states that the current through a metallic conductor is directly proportional to the applied p.d., *provided the temperature is constant.*

These materials are called **ohmic** conductors. This is because they follow Ohm's Law. Observe that the **graph passes through 2 quadrants**. When a voltage of opposite polarity is applied, the current flow is in the reverse direction.

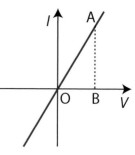

I-V graph for a metal at constant temperature

Since **I is directly proportional to V** it follows that $\dfrac{V}{I}$ = a constant

(equal to the reciprocal of the slope of the graph, i.e. by OB ÷ AB).

This ratio $\dfrac{V}{I}$ is called the resistance, R of a conductor and is measured in ohms (Ω).

Resistance is calculated using the formula

$$R = \frac{V}{I}$$

where R = resistance in ohms Ω
V = potential difference in volts
I = current in amperes

You will recall from the definition of potential difference, V, in section 1.10, that we were able to write the familiar equation for electrical power, P = IV. We can combine this equation with that for Ohm's Law above.

Since P = IV and V = IR, then

substituting for V gives $P = I^2R$ and

substituting for I gives $P = \dfrac{V^2}{R}$

We arrive therefore at the set of equations listed below. These should be memorised.

$$P = IV = I^2R = \frac{V^2}{R}$$

Collectively, these equations are referred to as **Joule's Law** of electrical heating.

Worked Examples

1 A train of mass 100 000 kg operates from a 25 kV supply and can accelerate to a speed of 20 ms^{-1} in 50 seconds along a level stretch of track. Calculate the average current it uses, assuming no energy losses.

Solution

Average mechanical power = k.e. ÷ time = ½ × 100 000 × 20² ÷ 50 = 400 000 W

$I = \dfrac{P}{V}$ = 400 000 ÷ 25 000 = 16 A

2 A consumer requires to use 5 kW at a pd of 240 V which is connected to a distant generator by leads which have a total resistance of 2.0 Ω. Calculate the current flowing in the leads and the p.d. across the leads at the generator.

Solution

Current $I = \dfrac{P}{V}$ = 5000 ÷ 240 = 250 ÷ 12 = 20.83 A

Voltage lost in resistance of leads = IR = 20.83 × 2 = 41.66 V

Voltage at generator = 41.66 + 240 = 281.66 V

3 An electric boiler is rated 2645 W and has a heating element of resistance 20 Ω. Calculate the resistance of its heating element.

Solution

$P = I^2R$, so 2645 = I^2 × 20   thus $I = \sqrt{(2645 ÷ 20)} = \sqrt{(132.25)} = 11.5$ A

Current, voltage and resistance in series and parallel circuits

Resistors in series

The current in a series circuit is the same everywhere. The supply voltage is equal to the sum of the voltages across each of the series components. We can demonstrate mathematically how this leads to the **series** resistance formula.

What single resistor R_T could replace these three resistors yet allow the same current I to pass for the same total p.d.?

Total Resistance, R_T = (Total PD) ÷ (Current)

$\qquad\qquad = (V_1 + V_2 + V_3) ÷ I$

$\qquad R_T = V_1 ÷ I + V_2 ÷ I + V_3 ÷ I$

$\qquad R_T = R_1 + R_2 + R_3$

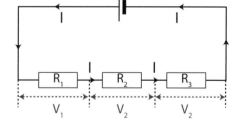

You will be familiar with this idea from GCSE and will gain further practice in its application in section 1.12.

Resistors in parallel

When resistors are in parallel the p.d. across each resistor is the same. The sum of the currents through each resistor is equal to the total current taken from the supply. Opposite is a demonstration which leads to the **parallel** resistance formula.

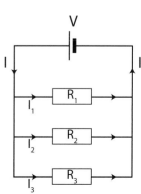

Total Resistance, $R_T = V \div I$ and since $R_1 = V \div I_1$,

$R_2 = V \div R_2$ and $R_3 = V \div I_3$ and $I = I1 + I_2 + I_3$

Then, $I = V \div R_1 + V \div R_2 + V \div R_3$ so,

$$I = \frac{V}{R_T} = \frac{V}{R_1} + \frac{V}{R_2} + \frac{V}{R_3}$$

Dividing by V gives:

$$\frac{1}{R_T} = \frac{1}{R_1} + \frac{1}{R_2} + \frac{1}{R_3}$$

When there are **just two resistors** the equation $\frac{1}{R_T} = \frac{1}{R_1} + \frac{1}{R_2}$ reduces to

$$R_T = \frac{R_1 \times R_2}{R_1 + R_2}$$

This is often easier to use, but it must be applied repeatedly when there are three or more resistors.

It is important to remember that:

- the **total resistance** of any **series** arrangement is always **greater than the largest resistance** in that network

- the **total resistance** of any **parallel** arrangement is always **less than the smallest resistance** in the parallel network

- the **total resistance of N equal resistors R** arranged in parallel is simply **R ÷ N**

You may recall using the last point at GCSE to calculate the resistance of two, equal parallel resistors as the half of one of them.

Hybrid circuits

Hybrid circuits consist of a mixture of parallel and series elements, such as the one shown on the right. Here a heating element of resistance 3 Ω is placed in parallel with a series arrangement of two other heaters of resistance 2 Ω and 4 Ω. How could we find the total resistance of the combination?

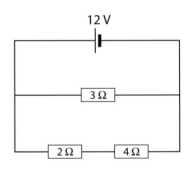

Applying the series equation first gives the resistance of the 2 Ω and 4 Ω combination as 6 Ω.

Now applying the equation for parallel networks,

$$\frac{1}{R_T} = \frac{1}{R_1} + \frac{1}{R_2} = \frac{1}{6} + \frac{1}{3} = \frac{1}{2}$$

Hence, **$R_T = 2\ \Omega$.**

The voltage across the 3 Ω resistor = the voltage across the 2 Ω + 4 Ω combination = 12 V

The current in each of the series elements is given by $I = V \div R = 12 \div 6 = $ **2 A.**

The current in the 3 Ω resistor is similarly $12 \div 3 = $ **4 A.**

The current drawn from the battery, $I_b = V_b \div R_T = 12 \div 2 = 6$ A, which is the sum (2 A + 4 A) of the currents in the parallel branches of the circuit.

Ohmic & Non-Ohmic behaviour

As we have seen, when the current flowing through a material is directly proportional to the p.d. across it, that material is said to be ohmic. Copper wire at constant temperature is an example of an ohmic material.

If the temperature is allowed to rise with increasing current, as occurs in the filament of a lamp, then the I-V characteristic curve is as shown opposite. This means that with increasing current (and hence increasing temperature) the resistance of a metal wire increases. However, as the temperature is increasing, the conditions pertaining to Ohm's Law are not constant, so we call this non-Ohmic behaviour. We will return later to explain the reasons for this increasing resistance.

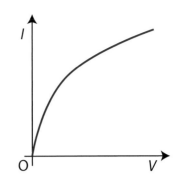

I-V characteristic curve for a filament lamp

Thermistors

These are made of semiconductor materials such as silicon or germanium. The I-V characteristic curve for a thermistor is shown opposite. The resistance of this thermistor decreases as it heats up. An explanation for this behaviour will be given later.

The symbol for a thermistor is shown below.

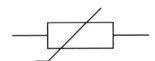

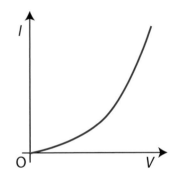

I-V Characteristic curve for a thermistor

Variation of resistance with temperature

You should be aware of how the resistance of **a metal** and **an NTC thermistor** change with increasing temperature. The variation is illustrated graphically opposite.

The resistance of the metal rises linearly with temperature. Although there is linear relationship, **the resistance is not directly proportional to the temperature,** because the graph does not pass through the origin. At 0°C the metal still has resistance.

The resistance of an NTC thermistor falls exponentially with temperature as shown in the graph.

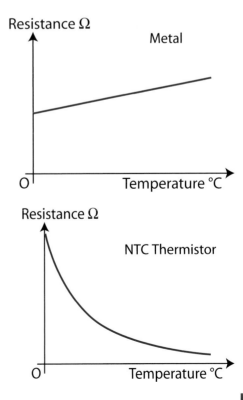

73

Why do metals and thermistors behave so differently?

When the temperature of a metal increases, **the atoms vibrate with greater amplitude and much more violently than before**. This **causes the free electrons to collide more frequently** and with greater force **with the atoms in the lattice**. These more frequent collisions **reduce the average drift speed of the electrons** and hence increase the time they take to move between two fixed points in the circuit. This in turn means that, for a given p.d., the current is reduced. Hence the **resistance of the metal increases**.

With thermistors **two effects are taking place simultaneously**. The increase in temperature would tend to increase the free electron-atom collision frequency and hence increase the resistance, as occurs with metals. However, only **a small amount of energy binds the electrons to the thermistor's atoms within the lattice**. With rising temperature, the lattice atoms vibrate with increasing amplitude. If the vibration is sufficiently violent, many, many electrons break free. There is such **an enormous increase in the number of free electron charge carriers** that there is a **huge increase in the current for a given voltage**. Since R = V ÷ I, this results in a reduction in the thermistor's resistance. Of the two effects, the increase in the number of free charge carriers (which would tend to decrease resistance) and the decrease in the electrons' average drift speed (which would tend to increase resistance), the former **is by far the greater**. The consequence is a net reduction in the resistance of the thermistor.

As the temperature rises, the resistance of a thermistor generally falls, giving rise to the name **NTC thermistor** ('negative temperature coefficient').

Thermistors can be used as thermometers, and as part of electronic circuits which are switched on and off automatically by a change in temperature.

Resistivity

The resistance of a metal conductor at a constant temperature depends on its length, l, its area of cross section, A, and the material from which it is made.

Experiment shows that the resistance of a metal wire is **directly proportional** to its length. So, if the length of wire is doubled, the resistance also doubles.

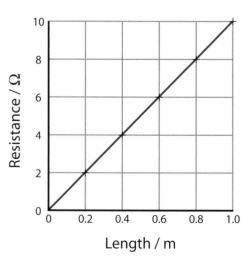

As the area of cross section increases, the resistance of the wire decreases. This is shown by the graph on the right. In fact the resistance of the wire is **inversely proportional** to the area of cross section. This means as the area of cross section is doubled then the resistance is halved. Mathematically, the curve opposite is called a hyperbola and it follows the equation:

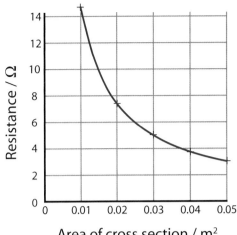

R = k, a constant,

where R = resistance and

A = cross-section area.

In this case, RA is approximately equal to 0.15 Ωm^2.

How else might we show this graphically? Can we obtain a straight line graph? From the equation above, we see have that:

$R = k(\dfrac{1}{A})$ where k is a constant

So we need to plot a graph of resistance against 1 / area of cross section, as shown on the right.

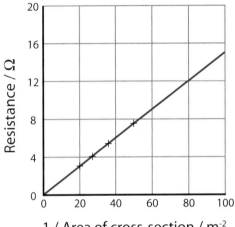

The resistance also depends on the material of the conductor. A piece of copper with the identical dimensions to a piece of steel will have a very different resistance.

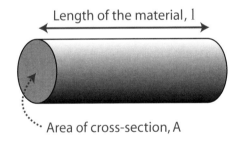

Each material has a constant known as its **resistivity** and is given the symbol ρ (pronounced 'rho'). If we combine all these ideas, we have:

$$R = \frac{\rho l}{A}$$

where R = Resistance in Ω

A = area of cross section in m^2

l = length in metres

ρ = resistivity in Ω m

Re-arranging this to give $\rho = \dfrac{RA}{l}$ provides us with a definition of resistivity.

The resistivity of a material is defined as numerically equal to the resistance of a sample of the material 1 m long and of cross sectional area 1 m^2.

The resistivities of materials vary widely as shown in the table below.

Type of Substance	Material	Resistivity in Ω m	Use
METALS	Silver	1.8×10^{-8}	Switch contacts
	Copper	1.7×10^{-8}	Connecting cables
	Aluminium	2.9×10^{-8}	Power cables
	Tungsten	5.5×10^{-8}	Lamp filaments
ALLOYS	Manganin	44×10^{-8}	Standard resistors
	Eureka	49×10^{-8}	Variable resistors
	Nichrome	110×10^{-8}	Heating elements
NON-METAL	Carbon (graphite)	185×10^{-8}	Radio resistors
SEMICONDUCTORS	Germanium	0.6	Transistors
	Silicon	2300	Transistors
INSULATORS	Glass	$10^{10} - 10^{14}$	
	Polystyrene	10^{15}	

While there is absolutely no requirement to know any of the details in the above table, you should be able to recall that metals have resistivity of around 1×10^{-8} Ω m, while good insulators have resistivity of around 1×10^{15} Ω m.

Measuring resistivity experimentally

This is an experiment which is prescribed within the specification. It is important that you do the experiment as part of your training in practical classes and that you can give a detailed description of the procedure for the theory examination.

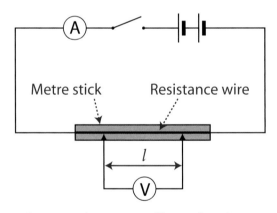

The resistance wire under investigation, which has been previously freed from bends and kinks, is laid along a metre stick and secured in position at each end by means of insulating tape. The electrical circuit is then set up as shown in the diagram. Connections to the resistance wire are usually made using crocodile clips.

The experiment involves measuring the voltage across different lengths of resistance wire and the current passing through for lengths l ranging from about 20 cm to about 90 cm. From the voltage, V, and current, I, the resistance, R, can be found using R = V ÷ I. This is done at least twice per length of resistance wire to reduce the possibility of random error. At this stage we should plot a graph of R against l. The graph will be a straight line through the origin. Now we find the gradient of this line to determine the resistance per metre length of wire (R ÷ l).

Using a micrometer screw gauge we now measure the diameter of the wire at about six points along its length. From this data we can determine the average diameter <d> and using A = π<d>^{2} ÷ 4 we can find the wire's average cross section area, A.

The last stage is to calculate the resistivity of the material of the wire, ρ. Since the resistivity is defined by the equation:

$$\rho = \frac{RA}{l} = \frac{R.\pi<d>^2}{4l} = \text{gradient of R-}l\text{ graph} \times \frac{\pi<d>^2}{4}$$

Below is a typical table of results for nichrome wire.

Resistivity Experiment Data

Diameter, d, in mm: 0.32, 0.31, 0.32, 0.32, 0.32, 0.33

Length (m)	Voltage (V)	Current (A)	Resistance (Ω)	Average resistance (Ω)
0.10	0.50	0.36	1.37	1.37
0.10	0.50	0.36	1.37	
0.20	0.90	0.33	2.73	2.74
0.20	0.90	0.33	2.75	
0.30	1.00	0.24	4.11	4.11
0.30	1.00	0.24	4.11	
0.40	1.20	0.22	5.48	5.48
0.40	1.20	0.22	5.48	
0.50	1.50	0.22	6.86	6.85
0.50	1.50	0.22	6.84	
0.60	1.70	0.21	8.22	8.22
0.60	1.70	0.21	8.22	
0.70	1.90	0.20	9.59	9.59
0.70	1.90	0.20	9.59	
0.80	2.00	0.18	10.96	10.96
0.80	2.00	0.18	10.96	

It is left as an exercise to the reader to draw the appropriate graph and to use the data provided to calculate the resistivity of the material.

Worked Examples

1 What length of resistance wire must be cut from a reel if the material has resistivity 1.57×10^{-8} Ωm, diameter 0.18 mm and is required to have a resistance as close as possible to 2.50 Ω?

Solution

Rearranging $\rho = (R \div l)A$ gives $l = RA \div \rho = R\pi d^2 \div 4\rho$

Hence $l = 2.50 \times \{\pi \times (0.18 \times 10^{-3})^2\} \div (4 \times 1.57 \times 10^{-8})$

$l = 4.05$ m

2 An electric hot plate consists of a 20 m length of manganin wire of resistivity of 4.4×10^{-7} Ωm and cross section area 0.23 mm². Calculate the power of the plate when connected to a 200 V electrical supply.

Solution

$$P = IV = V^2 \div R = V^2 A \div \rho l$$
$$= (200^2 \times 0.23 \times 10^{-6}) \div (4.4 \times 10^{-7} \times 20)$$
$$= 1045 \text{ W}$$

3 A 960 Ω filament for an electric light bulb is made of 60 cm of tungsten wire of resistivity 5.5×10^{-8} Ωm. Calculate the diameter of the wire.

Solution

$$A = l\rho \div R = (0.6 \times 5.5 \times 10^{-8}) \div 960$$
$$= 3.4375 \times 10^{-11} \text{ m}^2$$

$$D = \sqrt{(4A \div \pi)}$$
$$= \sqrt{\{(4 \times 3.4375 \times 10^{-11}) \div \pi\}}$$
$$= 6.62 \times 10^{-6} \text{ m}$$

Exercise 22

1 (a) Define electrical resistivity.

(b) A student plans to conduct an experiment to measure resistivity. The plan is to take a reel of constantan wire and cut a number of pieces from it. First, the resistance of each piece will be measured.

(i) Draw a labelled diagram of a circuit using the ammeter-voltmeter method which could be used to measure the resistance of one such piece of wire.

(ii) Assume that the resistances of the pieces of wire have been determined. Describe how the quantities which are required to calculate the resistivity would be measured. Include experimental detail.

(iii) Having completed the experiment, the student writes a report. He states: "The resistivity of the wire is 4.9×10^{-7} Ω m⁻¹". The student's numerical values are correct, but two errors have been made in the statement. Identify the errors and show how they should be corrected.

(c) The resistivity of iron is 6.7 times the resistivity of silver. An iron wire of length L and diameter d has resistance R. Obtain an expression for the diameter of a silver wire which is also of length L and resistance R. Give your answer in terms of the diameter d of the iron wire.

[CCEA June 2005]

2 To show whether a material exhibits ohmic or non-ohmic behaviour, a graph of current I through a sample of the material against potential difference V across it (a current-voltage or I-V characteristic) is often drawn.

(a) Sketch the current–voltage characteristic for an ohmic conductor. Remember an I–V characteristic has V on the x-axis and I on the y-axis.

(b) The current-voltage characteristic for the tungsten filament in a small lamp is shown on the right. Tungsten is a metal, and metals are ohmic conductors. Comparing your graph in part (a) with that shown here, give reasons for any difference in their shape.

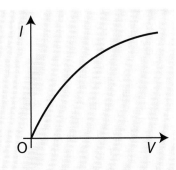

(c) Using information from the graph in part (b), sketch a graph to show how the resistance R of the filament of the lamp depends on the potential difference V across it.
Use the x-axis for V and the y-axis for R.

(d) Using a particle model of conduction, suggest an explanation for the shape of your graph in part (c).

[CCEA January 2004]

3 (a) Electrical conductors may be classified as ohmic or non-ohmic.
(i) State Ohm's Law.

(ii) Name one example of an ohmic conductor. Sketch the I–V characteristic of the conductor you have named. Use the x-axis for V and the y-axis for I.

(iii) The current-voltage graph for a certain device is shown on the right. Is this device an ohmic conductor? Explain your answer.

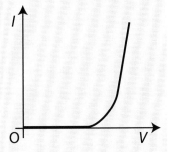

(b) The table below gives information about the resistivities of some metals.

Metal	Resistivity ρ/Ωm
Aluminium	2.90×10^{-8}
Copper	1.72×10^{-8}
Iron	9.71×10^{-8}
Silver	1.80×10^{-8}

Reels of wire of the metals in the table are available. Each of the wires has a uniform circular cross-section of diameter 0.500 mm. A resistor of resistance 6.80 Ω is to be made from a length of one of these wires. The wire selected is to be made of the **shortest** length possible to make the resistor.

State the metal to be used for this resistor and calculate the length of wire required.

[CCEA January 2003]

Internal resistance

Sources of e.m.f. (electromotive force), such as batteries and power packs, have themselves some resistance to the electric current that passes through them. This is called their **internal** resistance.

The internal resistance of a source of e.m.f. has two effects:

1 As more current is drawn from the battery or power pack, the voltage across the terminals of the supply falls.

2 The source of e.m.f. is less than 100% efficient as energy is dissipated as heat within it.

The voltage stated on the label of a source of e.m.f. such as a battery is the voltage measured across its terminal when **no current** is being drawn from it. This is called the **open-circuit voltage**. The internal resistance of a source of e.m.f. may be thought of as a **resistance r in series with the supply**.

In the circuit shown opposite and in the discussion below:

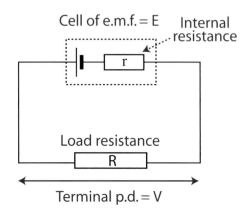

Cell of e.m.f. = E   Internal resistance

Load resistance
R

Terminal p.d. = V

E = e.m.f. of the cell
V = voltage across the terminals
r = internal resistance
R = load resistance
v = voltage lost in internal resistance

Total resistance = R + r

Current $I = \dfrac{E}{(R + r)}$

The potential difference across the load resistance is known as the terminal potential difference V:

V = IR

The potential difference lost in the internal resistance is v = Ir, so:

E = V + v

  = IR + Ir

The maximum current that can be taken from a power supply occurs when the cell is short-circuited (so there is no load resistance, R = 0):

$I_{max} = \dfrac{E}{R}$

Internal resistance and maximum power transfer

Internal resistance limits the current and power that can be supplied to a load by a power supply. Remember that because of this resistance, some of the energy is dissipated as heat within the power supply.

It is often desirable to transfer as much electrical energy as possible to a load. An example is starting a motor car engine. As much electrical energy as possible needs to be delivered to the electric motor that turns the engine over. The graph shows how the power delivered varies with the load resistance.

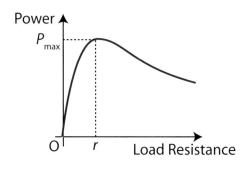

Notice that it peaks when load resistance = *r*, the internal resistance of the cell.

Internal resistance and the law of conservation of energy

Analysis of the circuit above shows that

    E = V + Ir

If both sides of the equation are multiplied by I, the result is:

$$\underset{\substack{\text{Power released by} \\ \text{chemical energy in the} \\ \text{battery}}}{\text{EI}} \quad = \quad \underset{\substack{\text{Power delivered to} \\ \text{the external} \\ \text{circuit}}}{\text{VI}} \quad + \quad \underset{\substack{\text{Power dissipated in the} \\ \text{internal resistance of the} \\ \text{battery}}}{\text{I}^2\text{r}}$$

This is simply an application of the law of conservation of energy to a battery with an internal resistance.

Worked examples

1   When the current drawn from a dry cell is 1 A, the voltage across the cell's terminals is 0.5 V. When the current drawn is 0.5 A, the terminal p.d. is 1 V. Calculate the e.m.f. of the cell and its internal resistance.

Solution

Using E = I(R + r) and R = V ÷ I,

Terminal p.d. = 0.5 V, I = 1 A, so R = 0.5 ÷ 1 = 0.5 Ω and E = 1(0.5 + r) = 0.5 + r [1]

Terminal p.d. = 1.0 V, I = 0.5 A, so R = 1 ÷ 0.5 = 2 Ω and E = 0.5(2 + r) = 1 + 0.5r [2]

Subtracting [2] from [1] gives 0 = −0.5 + 0.5r

Hence, **r = 1 Ω and E = 1.5 V**

2   When a 12 V battery is short-circuited, the current drawn is 6 A. What current would you expect to flow when the load resistor is 4 Ω?

Solution

Internal resistance = V ÷ I = 12 ÷ 6 = 2 Ω.

When the load is 4 Ω, the total resistance is 2 + 4 = 6 Ω, and I = 12 ÷ 6 = 2 A.

3   Three identical cells each have an internal resistance of 0.5 Ω. They are connected in series with each other across a load resistor of 1.5 Ω. If the e.m.f. of each cell is 2.0 V, calculate the current drawn from the battery and the power dissipated in the load resistor.

Solution

$$\begin{aligned} \text{I} = \text{battery voltage} \div \text{circuit resistance} &= (3 \times 2.0) \div (3 \times 0.5 + 1.5) \\ &= 6.0 \div 3.0 \\ &= \textbf{2.0 A} \end{aligned}$$

Power in external resistor = I^{2}R = 2.0^2 × 1.5 = **6.0 W**

4   When a 2.5 Ω resistor is connected across a battery of e.m.f. 6.0 V, the terminal p.d. is 5.0 V.

(a) What resistor could be **added** to the circuit to reduce the total load resistance to 0.5 Ω and how should it be connected?

(b) What power does the battery deliver to the load when this resistance is added?

Solution

(a) Current = V ÷ I = 5.0 ÷ 2.5 = 2.0 A.

Total resistance = 6.0 ÷ 2.0 = 3.0 Ω, so internal resistance = 3.0 – 2.5 = 0.5 Ω.

To obtain a total load resistance (0.5 Ω) **less** than the present external resistance (2.5 Ω), the extra resistor must be placed **in parallel with the 2.5 Ω**.

$$\frac{1}{R_{total}} = \frac{1}{R_1} + \frac{1}{R_2}$$

So, if R_{total} = 0.5 Ω, R_1 = 2.5 Ω and the required resistance is R_2, then

$$\frac{1}{0.5} = \frac{1}{2.5} + \frac{1}{R_2}$$

$$\frac{1}{R_2} = \frac{1}{0.5} - \frac{1}{2.5} = 1.6$$

So, additional resistance R_2 = 1 ÷ 1.6 = **0.625 Ω**

(b) Total resistance = R_{load} + $R_{internal}$ = 0.5 + 0.5 = 1.0 Ω

Current from battery = V ÷ I = 6.0 ÷ 1.0 = 6.0 A = current through load combination (0.5 Ω)

Power in load = I^2R = 6.0^2 × 0.5 = **18 W**

Experiment to find the internal resistance of a cell

Determination of the internal resistance of a cell is an experiment prescribed by the specification. You should therefore have carried out the experiment in practical classes and be able to describe the procedure in detail.

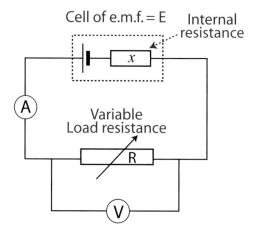

Cell of e.m.f. = E   Internal resistance

Variable Load resistance

Procedure

The experiment involves recording values of terminal voltage, V, and current drawn from the cell, I, for different load resistances, R. A 'D' cell (commonly called a torch battery) is suitable for the purpose. It is not necessary to know the values of the load resistance, but typically it should range from zero to about 5 Ω.

Theory

Since

E = I(r + R) = Ir + IR,
E = Ir + V

Rearranging,

V = E – Ir

So a graph of V against I gives a straight line of slope –r and y-axis intercept of E.

Typical results for this experiment are shown on the next page.

Terminal Voltage in Volts	0.50	0.64	0.75	0.83	0.90	0.95	1.00	1.04	1.07	1.10	1.13	1.15	1.17
Current in Amperes	1.00	0.86	0.75	0.67	0.60	0.55	0.50	0.46	0.43	0.40	0.38	0.35	0.33

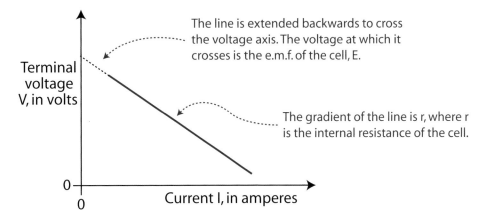

It is left as an exercise to the reader to plot the graph using the data above and to find the internal resistance of the cell and its e.m.f.

An interesting side aspect of this experiment is that the data collected can also be used to plot a graph of power, P, developed in the load resistor (P = IV) against the load resistance, R (R=V ÷ I). The graph follows the same shape as that shown on page 80. The reader can check that the power developed is a maximum when the load resistance, R, is equal to the internal resistance of the cell, r.

Superconductivity

As we have seen, even metals, regarded as good conductors, have a measurable electrical resistance and that this resistance decreases as the temperature falls. In 1908, a physicist called Kammerlingh Onnes succeeded in cooling helium to a temperature around –269°C, which corresponds to a temperature of around 4 Kelvin. This allowed the investigation of the electrical properties of metals at really low temperatures.

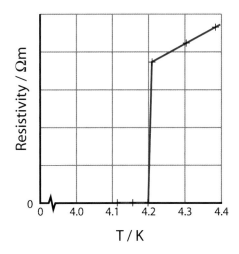

One of the first metals studied was mercury. Below –40°C mercury is a solid. What astonished Onnes was that at around 4 Kelvin the resistance of mercury fell to zero as shown in the graph opposite. This was the first **superconductor**.

We can define a material as a superconductor if it loses all its electrical resistivity to become a perfect conductor when it is below its critical (or Curie) temperature.

Since the effect was discovered, many metallic alloys have been found which exhibit superconductivity and the search has been on for superconductors at room temperature (around 20°C or 293 Kelvin). At the moment the most promising materials are ceramic alloys, of which one is a superconductor at around –148°C (125 Kelvin), so there is still a long way to go.

Superconductors are likely to be found in **very many applications** later this century. They are already used to produce the extremely strong magnetic fields needed for **Magnetic Resonance Imaging (MRI) scanners** used in hospitals for diagnostic purposes. Here the major expense is the liquefied gases needed to keep the superconductor sufficiently cold.

A MagLev train

Another application is **Maglev (magnetic levitation) Transport.** Here superconducting magnets are used to get vehicles (notably modern railway carriages) to float on strong superconducting magnets. This almost completely eliminates friction between the train and the track. In both applications a superconductor at room temperature would be a major technological breakthrough.

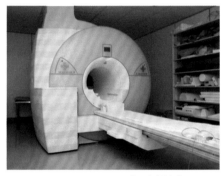

A third application is **the transmission of electrical power** – the need for huge transmission voltages would be all but eliminated if superconductors could be developed at 'ordinary' temperatures.

An MRI Scanner

Exercise 23

Examination Questions

1 Electromotive force (e.m.f.) and terminal potential difference (terminal p.d.) are terms applied to the voltage which can be obtained from a battery.

 (a) Define **electromotive force**.

 (b) Under a certain condition, the e.m.f. and the terminal p.d. of a battery may be identical. What is this condition?

 (c) In normal operation, the terminal p.d. of a battery is **less than** its e.m.f. Explain why.

 (d) Suggest a situation when the terminal p.d. of a battery is **greater than** its e.m.f.

[CCEA January 2002]

2 (a) The diagram on the right shows an electrical circuit. A student states that the electromotive force (e.m.f.) of the battery in this circuit is the same as the potential difference between the points X and Y.

 Discuss briefly whether this statement is correct or incorrect.

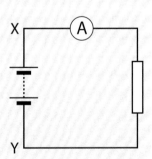

 (b) A source of electrical power with an internal resistance of 0.6 Ω supplies a current of 0.25 A to a resistor of resistance 5.0 Ω as shown overleaf.

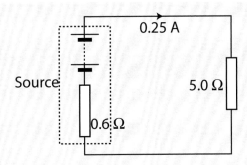

(i) Calculate the e.m.f. of the source.

(ii) Calculate the power dissipated internally in the source.

[CCEA January 2003]

3 (a) State what is meant by the internal resistance of a battery.

(b) The circuit diagram below shows a resistor of resistance R connected to a battery of e.m.f. E and internal resistance r. The current in the circuit is I.

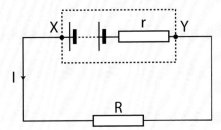

(i) Write down an equation connecting the e.m.f. E of the battery to the potential difference V between its terminals X and Y. Use the symbols E, I, r and V.

(ii) The e.m.f. of the battery is 1.50 V, the circuit current is 0.50 A and the external resistor has a resistance of 2.94 Ω. Calculate the internal resistance of the battery.

(iii) Calculate the power dissipated in the internal resistance of the battery.

(iv) Suggest a reason why the power dissipated in the internal resistance of the battery is sometimes described as "the rate of energy loss".

[CCEA January 2005]

1.12 Direct Current Circuits

1.12.1 Use conservation of charge and energy in simple d.c. circuits

1.12.2 Recall and use the equations for resistors in series and in parallel

1.12.3 Understand the use of a potential divider as a source of variable p.d.

1.12.4 Use $V_{out} = R_1 V_{in} \div (R_1 + R_2)$

Conservation of charge

One of the fundamental laws of physics is that **electrical charge** is conserved. Electrons cannot be created or destroyed inside a material. As the electrons move around the circuit their total number must remain the same. When a neutral plastic rod is charged by friction by rubbing it with a neutral duster, the rod and the duster obtain equal amounts of charge, but of the opposite sign. Their total charge is therefore zero, as it was at the beginning.

The sum of the charges entering a junction must therefore be equal to the sum of the charges leaving it, to be in agreement with the law of conservation of electric charge.

Sum of charges entering junction, Q_{in} = Sum of charges leaving junction Q_{out} **in the same time**.

Therefore, $Q_{in} \div t = Q_{out} \div t$ where t represents the time taken

But $I = Q \div t$, so

Sum of currents entering junction = Sum of currents leaving junction

$$\Sigma I_{in} = \Sigma I_{out}$$

The mathematical symbol Σ (sigma) simply means 'the sum of'.

The statement above is called **Kirchhoff's First Law** or Kirchhoff's law of electric charge and is a direct consequence of the law of conservation of charge. Some students prefer to express the law: **'The algebraic sum of the currents at a junction is zero.'** The word **algebraic** means we must take direction into account. In this formulation of the law, currents flowing **into** the junction are positive, while currents **leaving** it are negative. This is illustrated in this worked example:

Worked Example

Suppose a current of 8 A flows into a junction and currents of 2 A and 1 A flow out of it as illustrated in the diagram opposite. How much current, I, flows in the remaining fourth arm and in what direction does it flow?

Applying Kirchhoff's Law gives us: $8 + (-2) + (-1) + I = 0$

So, $I = -5$ A.

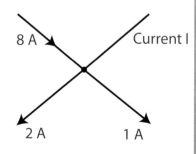

This is interpreted as meaning the current I has a magnitude of 5 A and its direction is out of the junction.

Exercise 24

Use the data in the diagram to calculate the size and direction of the current in AB and BC.

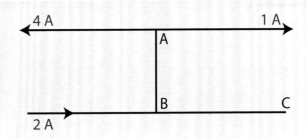

Conservation of energy

A simple d.c. circuit contains a cell and a resistor. In the cell, electrical energy is being produced from the chemical energy (reactions) within the cell. In the resistor, electrical energy is being converted into heat.

In a period of time the quantity of electrical energy generated within the cell is equal to the heat energy dissipated by the resistor.

We can develop this idea further using the notion that the sum of the power generated by the cells in a circuit must equal the sum of the power dissipated in the resistors. Hence:

Sum of power produced by cells = Sum of power developed in resistors

$I \times$ algebraic sum of e.m.f.s of cells = algebraic sum of ($I \times$ (IR products))

where I = the current in the circuit
R = the resistance of one of the resistors

Dividing both sides by I gives:

Algebraic sum of e.m.f.s of cells = Algebraic sum of (IR products)

or

$$\Sigma E = \Sigma IR$$

A few examples will show just how powerful this equation can be.

Worked Examples

Example 1

A battery charger has an internal resistance of 0.4 Ω and variable output voltage E. It is used to charge a car battery of e.m.f. 12.0 V and internal resistance 0.2 Ω. The cables supplying the current have a combined resistance of 1.0 Ω and this can be thought of as a load resistance as shown in the diagram. Calculate:

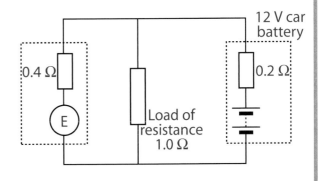

(i) the minimum output voltage from the battery charger, E, above which the car battery begins to charge

(ii) the charging current in the car battery when E = 20 V.

Solution

(i) Suppose the current from the charger and the battery are I_1 and I_2 respectively, so that the current in the load is $I_1 + I_2$ as shown opposite. Consider the circuit containing the charger, battery and their internal resistances. Then

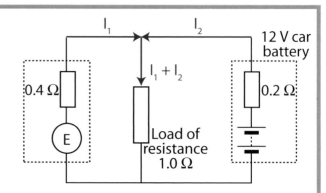

$$E - 12 = 0.4\,I_1 - 0.2\,I_2 \;\ldots\ldots\text{ this is equation 1}$$

Now consider the circuit containing the battery, its internal resistance and the load.

Then $12 = 0.2\,I_2 + 1.0 \times (I_1 + I_2) \;\ldots\ldots\text{ this is equation 2}$

The battery just begins to charge when **E** is just big enough to cause I_2 to fall to zero (and then to start flowing in the opposite direction). Solving equations 1 and 2 simultaneously, with I_2 set as zero gives: $E - 12 = 0.4\,I_1$ and $12 = I_1$, so the minimum charging voltage is:
$12 + 0.4 \times 12 = 16.8$ V

(ii) With a charger voltage of 20 V, equations 1 and 2 become:

$8 = 0.4\,I_1 - 0.2\,I_2$ and $12 = 0.2\,I_2 + 1.0 \times (I_1 + I_2)$ which solve to give $I_2 = -4.7$A

The charging current is 4.7 A flowing towards the positive terminal of the 12 V car battery.

Example 2

In the diagrams opposite the batteries have negligible internal resistance. Calculate the current in each of the resistors.

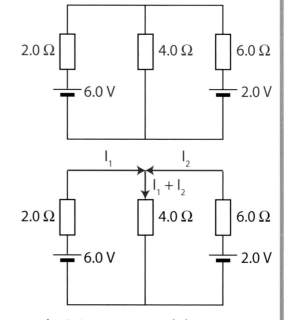

Solution

Suppose the current from the 6.0 V battery and the current from the 2.0 V battery are I_1 and I_2 respectively, so that the current in the 4.0 Ω resistor is $I_1 + I_2$ as shown opposite.

Consider the circuit containing the 6.0 V battery, the 2.0 Ω resistor, the 6.0 Ω resistor and the 2.0 V battery only. Then

$$6 - 2 = 2I_1 - 6I_2 \;\ldots\ldots\text{ this is equation 1}$$

Now consider the circuit containing the 6.0 V battery, the 2.0 Ω resistor and the 4.0 Ω resistor only. Then

$$6 = 2I_1 + 4 \times (I_1 + I_2) \;\ldots\ldots\text{ this is equation 2}$$

Solving these equations simultaneously gives

$$I_1 = 1\frac{2}{11}\,A \quad I_2 = \frac{-3}{11}\,A \quad I_1 + I_2 = \frac{10}{11}\,A$$

Note: The minus sign with I_2 means that the current ($\frac{3}{11}$ A) flows towards the positive terminal of the 2.0 V battery.

Resistors in series and in parallel

Recall that in the previous chapter we established the rules for resistors in series and in parallel. These were:

The total resistance of resistors R_T in a **series** network is given by:

$$R_T = R_1 + R_2 + R_3 + \ldots$$

The total resistance of resistors R_T in a **parallel** network is given by:

$$\frac{1}{R_T} = \frac{1}{R_1} + \frac{1}{R_2} + \frac{1}{R_3} + \ldots$$

Below we give some worked examples to illustrate the use of these equations.

Worked Examples

Example 1

In the network opposite all the resistors have a resistance of 4 Ω. Find the total resistance between points:

(i) A and B
(ii) B and C
(iii) A and C
(iv) B and D
(v) A and D

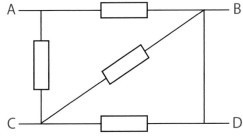

Solution

(i) The 4 Ω in CD is in parallel with the diagonal 4 Ω resistor between B and C and together these give 2 Ω. This 2 Ω combination is in series with the 4 Ω resistor in AC to give 6 Ω.

This 6 Ω is in parallel with the 4 Ω resistor in AB to give a total resistance of **2.4 Ω.**

(ii) In BAC there is a total resistance of 8 Ω. BC therefore is a combination of 8 Ω, 4 Ω and 4 Ω, all in parallel with each other. This gives a total resistance of **1.6 Ω.**

(iii) The 4 Ω in CD is in parallel with the diagonal 4 Ω resistor between B and C and together these give 2 Ω. This 2 Ω combination is in series with the 4 Ω resistor in BA to give 6 Ω.

This 6 Ω is in parallel with the 4 Ω resistor in AC to give a total resistance of **2.4 Ω.**

(iv) 0 Ω (short circuits the other parts of the network)

(v) Points B and D are electrically identical. So the total resistance between AD is exactly the same as the total resistance between AB, which is **2.4 Ω.**

Example 2

A resistor is marked 4 Ω, 0.25 W. This means the manufacturer claims the nominal resistance is 4 Ω, but only when the power dissipated is 0.25 W or less. An unlimited supply of such resistors is available. How could such resistors be combined to give a total resistance of 4 Ω, but with a combined power rating of 4 W?

Solution

If we need to dissipate 4 W in total and each resistor can dissipate only 0.25 W, then a minimum of **16 resistors** is required. If four resistors, each marked 4 Ω, 0.25 W are combined in a series chain, their total power rating is 1 W and their combined resistance is 16 Ω. If four such chains are combined in parallel with each other, their combined resistance is 4 Ω, and their total power rating is 4 W.

Example 3

The diagram shows a series circuit containing three batteries B_1, B_2 and B_3 and two resistors of resistance 6.0 Ω and 3.0 Ω respectively. All the batteries have negligible internal resistance. The e.m.f. of battery B_2 is 8.0 V, and that of B_3 is 7.0 V. The current in the circuit is 3.0 A. What would a high resistance voltmeter read when connected

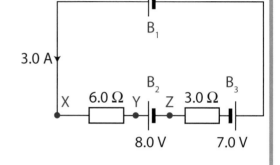

(a) between X and Y,

(b) between X and Z,

(c) across battery B_1?

[CCEA June 2001]

Solution

(a) Voltage drop across XY = IR = 3 × 6 = **18 V**

(b) Since the polarity of B_2 opposes the 3.0 A current,

Voltage across XZ = Voltage across XY – e.m.f. of B_2

So, voltage across XZ = 18 – 8 = **10 V**

(c) Total voltage supplied = current flowing × total resistance

$$= 3.0 \times (6.0 + 3.0) = 27 \text{ V}$$

Adding the battery e.m.f.s and taking battery polarity into account,

E.m.f. of B_1 + (–8.0) + 7.0 = 27

E.m.f. of B_1 = 27 + 1 = **28 V**

Hence a high resistance voltmeter across B_1 would read **28 V**

Exercise 25

1 The circuit diagram shows four resistors, each of resistance 12 Ω, connected to a battery of e.m.f. 8.0 V and negligible internal resistance.

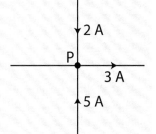

   (a) Calculate the current in the circuit.

   (b) One of the three resistors connected in parallel develops a fault which gives it infinite resistance. Calculate the potential difference across the parallel combination of two resistors each of resistance 12 Ω and one of infinite resistance.

   (c) The faulty resistor is replaced by another, which soon develops a fault giving it zero resistance. Calculate the current now drawn from the battery.

[CCEA January 2005]

2 (a) State how the principle of conservation of charge applies to currents at a junction in a circuit.

   (b) The diagram shows a junction P in a circuit. The magnitude and direction of the currents in three of the wires are shown on the diagram. What is the magnitude and direction of the current in the 4th wire?

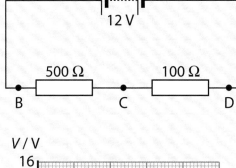

   (c) The circuit diagram shows resistors of resistance 500 Ω and 100 Ω connected in series with a battery of e.m.f. 12 V. The battery has negligible internal resistance. The connecting wires have negligible resistance also.

   (i) Calculate the current in the circuit.

   (ii) On the right is an incomplete graph to show voltage V at various positions in the circuit. The voltage between the points A and B has already been shown on the graph. Copy and complete the graph.

[CCEA June 2005]

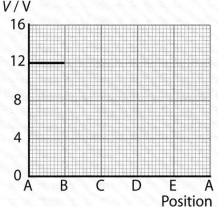

Potential divider

A potential divider is an arrangement of resistors which allows a fraction of the p.d. supplied to it to be passed on to an external circuit.

In the circuit below the current, I in resistor R_1 is given by:

$$I = \frac{V_{IN}}{R_1 + R_2}$$

The output voltage is the potential difference across R_1:

$$V_{OUT} = IR_1$$

Appling Ohm's Law to R_1:

$$V_{OUT} = \frac{R_1 V_{IN}}{R_1 + R_2}$$

The output voltage is generally applied across some external device known as the load. This type of potential divider is particularly useful where the power supply provides a greater voltage than that required by the load. However, **it does not permit the user to vary the voltage across the load.** To do that **the fixed resistors are replaced by a continuously variable resistor called a rheostat.** The output voltage is then continuously variable.

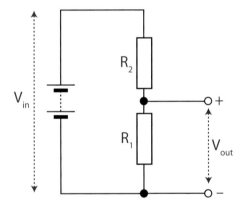

Potential divider with fixed resistors

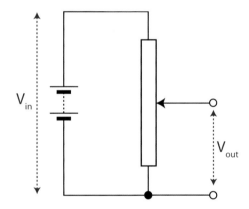

Potential divider with a rheostat

Worked example

The circuit shows a potential divider. The battery has an e.m.f. of 6.0 V and has negligible internal resistance.

(a) What is the magnitude of the potential difference between the terminals P and Q?

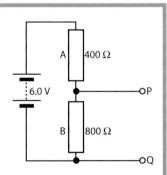

(b) A resistor of resistance 400 Ω is now connected in parallel with the 800 Ω as shown. Calculate the new potential difference between the terminals P and Q.

[CCEA January 2002]

Solution

(a) The p.d. between P and Q is the output voltage V_{OUT}.

Substituting the values into the formula $V_{out} = R_1 V_{in} \div (R_1 + R_2)$ gives

$$V_{OUT} = \frac{800 \times 6}{800 + 400} = 4.0 \text{ V}$$

(b) The resistance between P and Q is no longer 800 Ω, it is the effective resistance of 800 Ω and 400 Ω connected in parallel.

$$\frac{1}{R_T} = \frac{1}{800} + \frac{1}{400} = \frac{3}{800}$$

$$R_T = 266.7 \Omega$$

The resistances that make up the potential divider now have the effective values shown in the circuit diagram opposite.

When these are used in the potential divider equation we obtain a value for the output voltage much smaller than the original value of 4.0 V.

$$V_{OUT} = \frac{266.7 \times 6}{266.7 + 400} = 2.40 \text{ V}$$

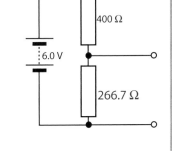

Effect of loading on V_{OUT}

In the example above, the addition of the 400 Ω across the terminals P and Q has reduced the maximum output voltage of the potential divider from 4.0 V to 2.4 V. In general, the voltage across the load decreases as the resistance of the load decreases.

In the extreme case, where there is infinite load resistance V_{OUT} is a maximum.

If there is zero load resistance, the potential divider is short-circuited and V_{OUT} is zero.

In general engineers and circuit designers use a rule-of-thumb which states that the load resistance must always be greater than ten times the potential divider's resistance to ensure that that there is no appreciable voltage drop caused by adding the external resistance (the load).

Exercise 26

1   A potential divider circuit is shown opposite. Calculate the potential difference between the terminals P and Q.

[CCEA June 2003]

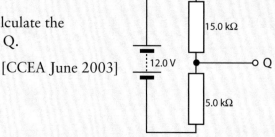

2   The circuit shown below provides a voltage V which depends on the brightness of the lighting in a room. The battery has an e.m.f. of 12 V and negligible internal resistance. The light sensor is a light dependent resistor (LDR). The resistance of the LDR is 5.0 kΩ in the dark and 0.20 kΩ when the illumination in the room is a maximum.

(a) The variable resistor R is initially set to its maximum resistance of 5.0 kΩ. Show that the value of the voltage V when the illumination of the room is a maximum is about 0.4 V.

(Remember that under these conditions the resistance of the LDR is 0.20 kΩ)

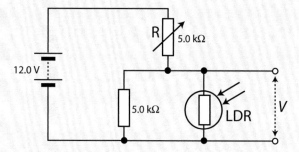

(b) The variable resistor R acts as a sensitivity control for the circuit. By changing this resistance, the voltages V obtained for illuminated and dark conditions can be altered. Explain why reducing R to its minimum value of zero resistance would not be a good idea.

[CCEA January 2003]

3   It is required to provide a voltage supply, continuously variable from 0 to 6 V. A fixed 9 V supply, a rheostat (which may be used as a potential divider) of total resistance 10 kΩ and a selection of resistors are available.

(i) Draw a suitable circuit to provide this variable supply. Calculate the resistance of the additional resistor required. Label the components of your circuit with their values, and mark the polarities of the 9 V supply and the output terminals.

(ii) A voltmeter of resistance 20 kΩ is connected across the output terminals and the rheostat is set at its mid-point value. Calculate the reading on the voltmeter.

4   A technician is asked to construct a potential divider circuit to deliver an output voltage of 1.2 V, using a battery of e.m.f. 3.0 V and negligible internal resistance. To conserve the life of the battery, it is desirable that the current drawn from it should be about 10 µA.

(a) Draw a diagram of a suitable circuit in which the current drawn from the battery is 10 µA. Calculate the values of any resistors used. Show where connections would be made to obtain the 1.2 V output. Label the terminals T+ and T– to indicate their polarity.

(b) A resistor of resistance 1.0 kΩ is now connected across the output terminals. Explain why the output voltage and the current drawn from the battery are affected by making this connection. Determine the new values of output voltage and current drawn.

Unit AS 2:
Waves, Photons and Medical Physics

2.1 Waves

Waves are everywhere. We encounter sound waves when we listen to a radio, which itself detects radio waves. We see the world around us because our eyes are sensitive to visible light waves. You might even have used a microwave oven to cook your breakfast.

Waves are created by a disturbance which results in a vibration. For example, when a stone is dropped into water it creates ripples (water waves). The water vibrates up and down as the energy from the stone is distributed outwards in all directions.

Any object floating on the water will move up and down as the water waves reach it.

This means that waves transport energy. The energy is transported to the floating object not by the water but by the wave that is propagated through the water.

A wave that transports energy by causing vibrations in the material or medium through which it moves is called a progressive wave.

Mechanical waves, such as sound and water waves, require a substance (medium) through which to travel. Electromagnetic waves do not require a medium through which to travel.

Progressive waves can be categorized as either transverse or longitudinal.

Transverse and longitudinal waves

In transverse waves the vibration of the medium is perpendicular to the direction in which the wave travels (i.e. carries energy or propagates). The diagram overleaf shows how transverse waves can be sent along a string. The hand is moved up and down as shown. As the transverse wave passes through the medium the particles vibrate at right angles to the direction of propagation of the wave. Electromagnetic waves are transverse waves.

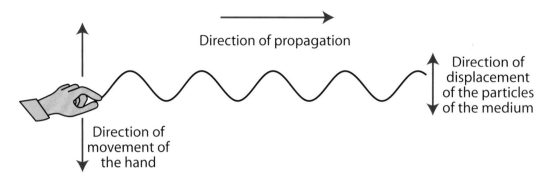

In a longitudinal wave the vibrations of the medium are parallel to the direction of propagation. The diagram below shows a how a longitudinal wave can be sent along a slinky coil. The hand is moved back and forth as shown. As the longitudinal wave passes through the medium these particles vibrate parallel to the direction of propagation of the wave.

A **compression** is where the coils of the slinky are close together. A **rarefaction** is where the coils are further apart. Sound and ultrasound are longitudinal waves.

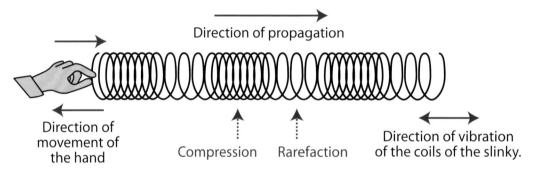

Polarisation

A light wave is an electromagnetic wave. Light waves are produced by vibrating electric charges. For the moment, it is sufficient to say that an electromagnetic wave is a transverse wave which has both an electric and a magnetic oscillating component. These two components oscillate in planes that are perpendicular to each other. In the diagram below, the electric component is oscillating in the plane of the page and the magnetic component is oscillating in and out of the page.

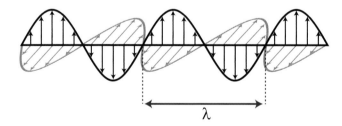

If you could view an electromagnetic wave travelling towards you, then you would observe both the electric component and the magnetic component of the wave occurring in more than one plane of vibration. In this section we will concentrate on the electric component of the electromagnetic wave since it is the component that our eyes are sensitive to.

A light wave which is vibrating in more than one plane is referred to as **unpolarised** light. Sunlight and light from a filament lamp are unpolarised. Unpolarised light waves are created by an electric charge which vibrates in a variety of directions, thus creating an electromagnetic wave which oscillates in a variety of directions.

It is possible to change unpolarised light into **polarised** light. Polarised light waves are light waves in which the vibrations occur in a single plane. The process of transforming unpolarised light into polarised light is known as polarisation.

The most common method of polarisation involves the use of a Polaroid filter. A Polaroid filter is able to polarise light because of the chemical composition of the filter material.

You can observe the polarisation of light by carrying out the following experiment.

Place a Polaroid filter in front of a filament bulb as shown on the right. The light from the bulb is unpolarised but is plane polarised after passing through the filter. This first filter is called the polariser.

Now view the plane polarised light using a second Polaroid filter. This second filter is known as the analyser. At a certain angle, the light intensity viewed through the second filter will be a maximum.

As you rotate the second filter, the intensity of the light will change. You will see that the intensity of the light transmitted by the second filter falls to minimum after it has been rotated 90° from the position at which the intensity was a maximum.

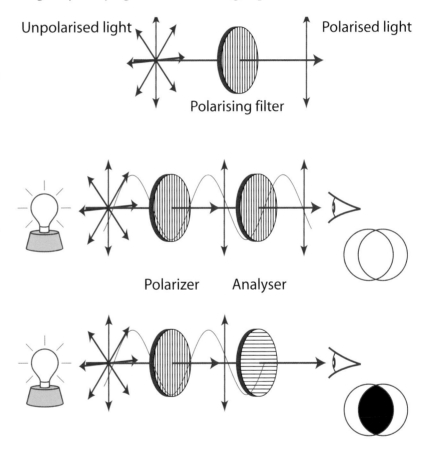

The graph on the right shows how the intensity of the light transmitted by the second polaroid filter changes as this filter is rotated.

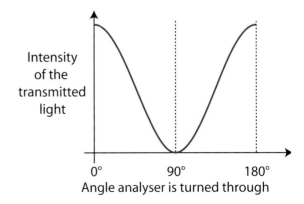

99

Velocity of the wave

The velocity of the wave can be calculated from its wavelength and frequency using the following equation:

Velocity = Frequency × Wavelength

$$v = f\lambda$$

The velocity is measured in ms^{-1}.
The frequency is measured in Hz
The wavelength is measured in m

Spectrum of electromagnetic waves

Electromagnetic waves exist with a very large range of wavelengths. This continuous range of wavelengths is known as the **electromagnetic spectrum**. The entire range of the spectrum is usually broken into specific regions. The subdividing is done mostly on how each region of electromagnetic waves interacts with matter.

The table below shows the electromagnetic spectrum and its various regions. You should note that the boundaries between the different regions of the electromagnetic spectrum are not well defined. However you should have some idea of a typical wavelength for the waves found in each region.

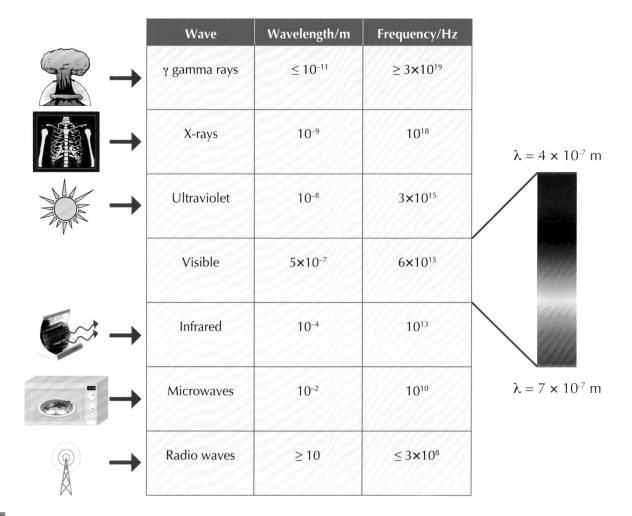

Wave	Wavelength/m	Frequency/Hz
γ gamma rays	$\leq 10^{-11}$	$\geq 3\times10^{19}$
X-rays	10^{-9}	10^{18}
Ultraviolet	10^{-8}	3×10^{15}
Visible	5×10^{-7}	6×10^{15}
Infrared	10^{-4}	10^{13}
Microwaves	10^{-2}	10^{10}
Radio waves	≥ 10	$\leq 3\times10^{8}$

$\lambda = 4 \times 10^{-7}$ m

$\lambda = 7 \times 10^{-7}$ m

How electromagnetic waves are generated and their uses

Region of the EM Spectrum	How they are generated	Uses
Radio	Electronic circuits in which the electrons are made to vibrate.	Communications, from radio to television.
Microwaves	Electronic circuits in which the electrons are made to vibrate.	Communications Satellite television Cooking food
Infra-red	All warm objects emit this type of electromagnetic wave.	Remote controls for TVs etc Detecting intruders Cooking and heating
Visible	Hot objects such as filament lamps, flames, the Sun.	Seeing Photography
Ultra-violet	Very hot objects such as the Sun. Gas discharge lamps. Both of these involve exciting the electrons within atoms.	Making vitamin D Sun tan lamps Detecting forged bank notes
X-rays	These are produced when electrons are accelerated to high energy and allowed to strike a metal target. This is the process used in X–ray tubes found in hospitals.	Detecting broken bones. Detecting hidden objects, e.g. in luggage. Treatment of some cancers
γ (Gamma) rays	Radioactive materials emit gamma rays	Killing cancerous cells Sterilisation of medical supplies

Exercise 27

1 (a) Name seven regions of the complete electromagnetic spectrum.
     List them in order of increasing wavelength.

   (b) State typical wavelengths for the first and last regions in your list.

   (c) Electromagnetic waves are transverse. Name one other type of transverse wave and describe briefly how it may be generated.

   (d) Sound waves are longitudinal waves. Explain what is meant by a longitudinal wave.

   (e) Can sound waves be polarised? Explain your answer.

                                                                [CCEA June 2002]

2 (a) For visible light and microwaves, give a typical wavelength, state whether it is transverse or longitudinal and whether it can be polarised.

   (b) State one property, apart from anything you stated in part (a), that these waves have in common.

                                                                [CCEA January 2004]

Graphical representation of a wave

Both transverse and longitudinal waves can be represented graphically in two ways.

Displacement of a particle of the medium against time.

This graph shows how the displacement, from its equilibrium position, of a particle of the medium through which the wave is moving, varies with time.

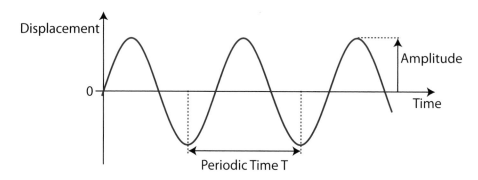

Periodic Time

Period refers to the time which it takes to do something. When an event occurs repeatedly, then we say that the event is periodic and refer to the time for the event to repeat itself as the period. The period of a wave is the time for a particle on a medium to make one complete vibrational cycle.

Frequency

The frequency of a wave refers to how often the particles of the medium vibrate when a wave passes through the medium. The frequency is the number of complete waves that pass a point in one second. Frequency is measured in hertz, (Hz). A frequency of 100 Hz means 100 waves per second pass a point, or the particle of the medium completes 100 oscillations in one second.

$$\text{Frequency} = \frac{1}{\text{Periodic Time}}$$

Displacement of the particles of the medium against distance along the wave.

This graph shows how the displacement, from their equilibrium position, of particles of the medium through which the wave is moving, varies with distance along the direction in which the wave is travelling.

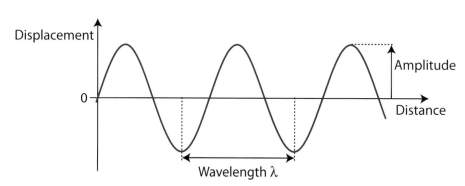

Amplitude

The amplitude of a wave refers to the maximum displacement of a particle of the medium from its rest position. You can think of the amplitude as the distance from rest to crest. Similarly, the amplitude can be measured from the rest position to the trough position.

The amount of energy carried by a wave is related to the amplitude of the wave. A high energy wave is characterised by a high amplitude; a low energy wave is characterized by a low amplitude.

Wavelength

The wavelength is defined as the distance the wave form progresses in the periodic time, T.

The wavelength can be measured as the distance from crest to next crest or from trough to next trough. In fact, the wavelength of a wave can be measured as the distance from a point on a wave to the corresponding point on the next cycle of the wave. Wavelength is measured in metres.

Phase

The particles of the medium through which a wave passes vibrate. If two particles are vibrating so that at the same instant they are at the same distance and same direction (same displacement) from their equilibrium positions they are said to be in phase.

Phase is also used to describe the relative positions of crests and troughs on two waves of the same frequency. If the crests of one wave coincides with the crests of the other we say the waves are in phase. If the crests of one wave coincide with the troughs of the other then we describe then as being out of phase by ½ λ.

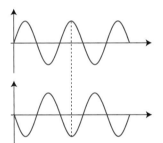 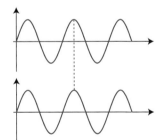 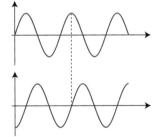

These two waves are out of phase. The crests of one exactly coincide with the troughs of the other. Their phase difference is ½ λ.

These two waves are in phase. The crests of one exactly coincide with the crests of the other.

These two waves are out of phase. The crests of one exactly coincide with the point where the displacement of the other wave is zero. Their phase difference is ¼ λ.

Exercise 28

1 Two transverse waves A and B travel in a medium. Here is a graph of displacement y against time t for a particle in the medium, due to each wave separately.

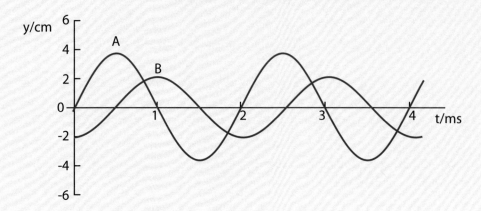

Use the information from the graph to find the values and units of the following quantities.

(a) The amplitude of wave A.

(b) The frequency of wave B.

(c) The phase difference between the two waves.

[CCEA January 2003]

2 A student defines the amplitude of a wave as follows:

"*The amplitude of a wave is the displacement of a particle in the wave from its equilibrium position.*"

He defines the frequency of the wave as:

"*The number of cycles of oscillation of a particle in the wave per unit time.*"

He defines the wavelength as:

"*The time taken by a particle in the wave to complete one cycle.*"

He gives the following relationship between velocity, wavelength and period:

"*The velocity of the wave is the wavelength divided by the period.*"

What, if anything, is wrong with each of these statements?

[CCEA January 2005]

2.2 Refraction

You should be able to:

2.2.1 Describe an experiment to verify Snell's law

2.2.2 Recall and use the formula $\dfrac{\sin i}{\sin r} = n$

2.2.3 Perform and describe an experiment to measure refractive index

2.2.4 Demonstrate knowledge and understanding of total internal reflection

2.2.5 Recall and use the formula $C = \dfrac{1}{n}$

Refraction occurs when a wave, for example light, travels from one medium to another, for example from air into glass. Its direction of travel is changed. The angle between the incident ray and the normal is called the angle of incidence i. The angle between the normal and the refracted ray is called the angle of refraction r. Note that the angles are measured from the normal.

Notice that there is also a weak reflected ray. Transparent materials do not allow all the light that is incident to pass through. Glass typically reflects about 4% of the incident light. This weak reflected ray obeys the laws of reflection.

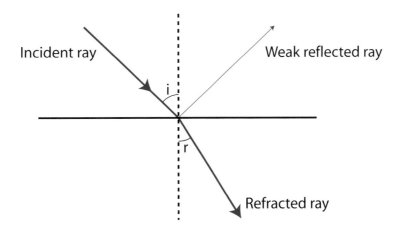

Snell's Law states:

For light travelling from one material to another, the ratio $\dfrac{\sin i}{\sin r}$ is a constant.

Experimental verification of Snell's Law and measurement of the refractive index

This can be done by **ray tracing** through a glass block.

1 Place the glass block on a sheet of paper and carefully trace around it.

2 Remove the glass block and mark the normal at one edge and extend this line into the position of the glass block.

3 Replace the glass block.

4 A ray box is used to produce a narrow ray.

5 Shine the ray into the block so that it meets the block at the point where the normal meets the block.

6 Mark this path carefully with crosses.

7 Mark the emergent ray in a similar fashion.

8 Remove the glass block, join up the crosses to show the incident, refracted and emergent rays.

9 Using a protractor measure the angles of incidence and refraction.

10 Carefully replace the glass block and repeat this procedure for a number of incident rays with differing angles of incidence.

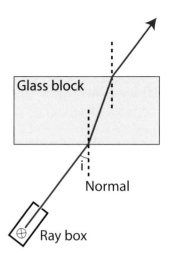

Results

The table below shows a set of results from such an experiment.

The graph of sin i (y-axis) and sin r (x-axis) is drawn.

The straight line through the origin is verification of Snell's Law.

The refractive index is the gradient of the line.

Angle of incidence i	Angle of refraction r	sin i	sin r
10°	7°	0.174	0.122
20°	13.5°	0.342	0.233
30°	20°	0.500	0.342
40°	26°	0.643	0.438
50°	31.5°	0.766	0.522
60°	36°	0.866	0.588

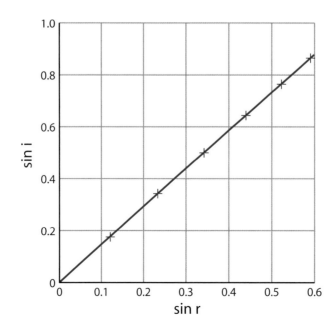

Since the graph is a straight line that passes through the origin, sin i and sin r are proportional or we can state that $\frac{\sin i}{\sin r}$ is a constant. This constant is known as the refractive index, n.

$$n = \frac{\sin i}{\sin r}$$

The gradient of this line is 1.47 so the refractive index of the material of the block used in the experiment is 1.47.

The refractive index of a material is a constant. It is the ratio of the speed of light in a vacuum to the speed of the speed of light in the material.

$$\text{Refractive index of a material} = \frac{\text{Speed of light in vacuum}}{\text{Speed of light in material}}$$

The speed of light in a vacuum is almost equal to the speed of light in air. This means that the refractive index for light traveling from vacuum to glass is for most practical purposes the same as that for light traveling from air to glass.

Say the refractive index for light travelling from air into glass is 1.5.

$$1.5 = \frac{\text{velocity of light in vacuum}}{\text{velocity of light in glass}}$$

This tells us that the velocity of light in this glass is 2×10^8 ms^{-1}.

When a ray of light enters or leaves a transparent material along the normal, the angle of incidence i = 0 and the angle of refraction r = 0. However the light's velocity **does** change. For example, travelling from air into glass the velocity decreases. Travelling from glass into air, the velocity increases. Note that the frequency of the light **does not** change.

Relationship between refractive indices

The diagram show a ray of light passing from air into glass. The refractive index can be written as

$$_{air}n_{glass} = \frac{\sin i}{\sin r}$$

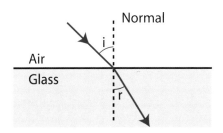

If the path of the ray were reversed, i.e. glass to air, the refractive index for glass to air can be written as

$$_{glass}n_{air} = \frac{\sin r}{\sin i}$$

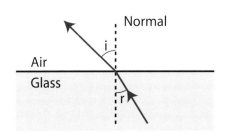

Examination of the two relationships shows that

$$_{air}n_{glass} = \frac{1}{_{glass}n_{air}}$$

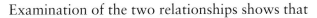

Exercise 29

1 The diagram shows a ray of light in a vacuum, striking the plane surface of a block of glass. The ray contains blue light and red light.

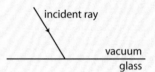

The refractive index for blue light in the glass is 1.64 and the refractive index for the red light in the glass is 1.61.

(a) Copy the diagram and draw the paths of the blue light and the red light after refraction. Label the blue ray B and the red ray R.

(b) For the case where the incident ray meets the block at an angle of 55° to the glass surface, calculate the angle between the blue and red rays in the glass.

[CCEA Feb 2001]

2 The diagram shows the path of a ray of monochromatic light through a prism made of glass of refractive index 1.52.

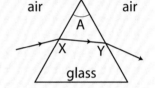

(a) Copy the diagram and mark clearly the angles of incidence and refraction for the ray entering at X.

(b) If the angle of incidence at X is 55° calculate the angle of refraction.

(c) The angle marked A is 60°. Using your calculated value of the angle of refraction at X, obtain the angle of incidence in the glass at Y, where the ray leaves the prism.

(d) Calculate the angle of refraction at Y.

(e) Calculate the speed of light in the prism.

[CCEA 1997]

3 A thick glass container holds some oil as shown in the diagram. The refractive index of the glass is 1.54. A ray of monochromatic light is incident on the air-glass boundary at A.

The angle of incidence is 44°.

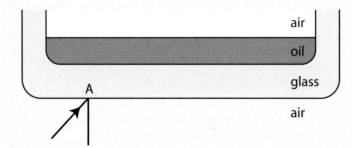

(a) Copy the diagram and sketch the refracted ray in the glass. Mark the angle of incidence **i** and the angle of refraction **r** at the air-glass boundary.

(b) Calculate the angle of refraction r in the glass.

(c) Calculate the speed of light in the glass.

[CCEA June 2002]

Critical angle

Consider what happens when light travels from a material of high refractive index to one of lower refractive index, for example from glass into air. As the angle of incidence in the glass increases so does the angle of refraction in the air.

The largest angle of refraction is 90°. The angle of incidence in the glass that produces this angle of refraction of 90° is called the critical angle C. Note that there is still a weak reflected ray.

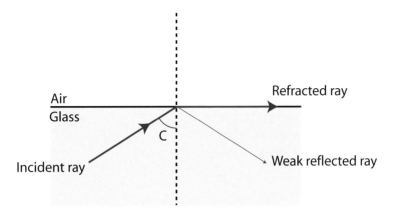

The value of the critical angle depends on the refractive index of the material.

The relationship between the critical angle and the refractive index of the material can be derived by applying Snell's law.

$$_{glass}n_{air} = \frac{\sin C}{\sin 90} = \sin C$$

$$_{glass}n_{air} = \frac{1}{_{air}n_{glass}}$$

$$\sin C = \frac{1}{_{air}n_{glass}}$$

Total internal reflection

When the angle of incidence in the material with the higher refractive index is greater than the critical angle, a phenomenon known as total internal reflection occurs. Total internal reflection (TIR) involves the reflection of all the incident light at the boundary between two materials.

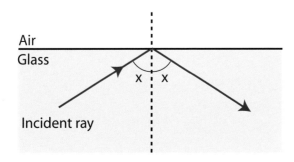

Remember, total internal reflection takes place only when both of the following two conditions are met:

(a) the direction of the light is from one material to one of **lower** refractive index;

(b) the angle of incidence in the material of higher refractive index is greater than the critical angle.

Total internal reflection is possible for light travelling from water towards air, but it will not happen for light traveling from air towards water. Total internal reflection is possible for light travelling from glass to water but not from water to glass.

A right angled prism can be used to deviate a ray of light by 90° using total internal reflection. The ray meets the side AB along the normal so no refraction takes place and the ray continues into the glass. When it reaches the side AC the angle of incidence from glass to air is 45°, the critical angle for the glass is 42° so total internal reflection takes place. Finally the ray travels to side BC and since it meets it along the normal no refraction takes place and the ray emerges into the air.

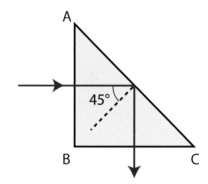

Optical fibres

The use of a long strand of glass to send light from one end of the medium to the other is the basis for modern day use of **optical fibres**. Optical fibres are used in communication systems and micro-surgery. On each occasion when the ray of light meets the glass/air boundary the angle of incidence exceeds the critical, and total internal reflection takes place. None of the incident energy is ever lost due to the transmission of light across the boundary. The intensity of the signal remains constant.

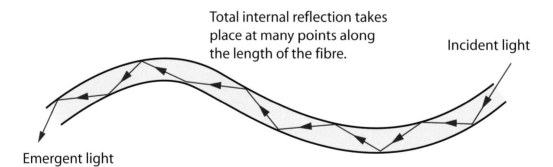

Total internal reflection takes place at many points along the length of the fibre.

Incident light

Emergent light

Measuring the refractive index using total internal reflection

Total internal reflection can be demonstrated using a semi-circular glass block as shown below. This method also provides us with a way to measure the refractive index, although it must be stated that it is not a very accurate one.

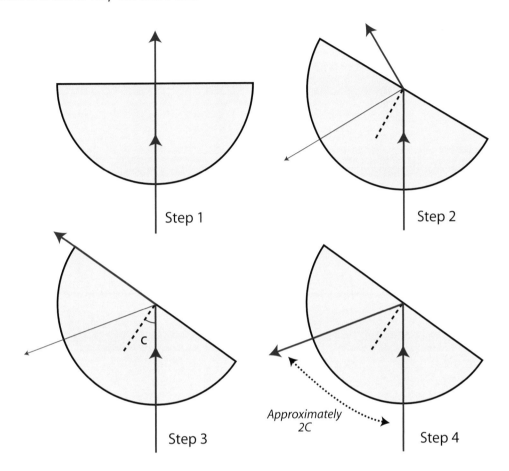

1   A ray is directed towards the centre of a semi-circular glass block. This ensures no refraction at the curved edge. The ray of light meets the curve at right angles.

2   The block is slowly rotated. The emergent ray is now bent away from the normal as shown. Note the weak reflected ray.

3   At a particular angle, the critical angle, the emergent ray is refracted at an angle of 90° to the normal. It travels along the straight edge of the glass block. This can be difficult to see.

4   However, if the angle the incident ray makes with the straight edge of the glass is increased by a very small amount, total internal reflection takes place. This is very noticeable since the weak reflected ray suddenly becomes bright.

The angle between the two rays is now just slightly greater than 2C. Measure this angle and use the value to calculate an approximate value for the refractive index using the equation below.

$$\sin C = \frac{1}{_{air}n_{glass}}$$

Exercise 30

1   A ray of light is incident on a plane glass-air boundary, making an angle of 25° with the normal as shown. The refractive index of the glass is 1.50.

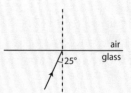

(a) Determine the angle of incidence at the glass-air boundary which would result in the angle of refraction becoming 90°.

(b) Describe, with the aid of a diagram, the path taken by the light when the angle of incidence is increased beyond the value you have calculated.

[CCEA 1999]

2   The diagram shows a ray of monochromatic light incident at an angle of 75° at the mid-point of one side AB of a rectangular glass block ABCD.

The ray enters the glass and meets the side BC. The critical angle for the glass of the block is 41°.

(a) Calculate the refractive index of the glass.

(b) Show by appropriate calculation that the ray of light will not emerge from the block through the side BC.

3   Describe, in detail, an experiment to demonstrate total internal reflection of light in a semicircular glass or perspex block, and how to use the arrangement to determine the critical angle. Your answer should include:

(a) a labelled diagram of the apparatus;

(b) a description of the procedure;

(c) a statement of the measurements to be taken to determine the critical angle;

(d) details of how to ensure as accurate a result as possible;

(e) a statement of how to calculate the refractive index of the material of the block from the measured value of the critical angle.

[CCEA June 2001]

2.3 Lenses

You should be able to:

2.3.1 Draw ray diagrams for converging and diverging lenses

2.3.2 Use the equation $\dfrac{1}{u} + \dfrac{1}{v} = \dfrac{1}{f}$ for converging lenses

2.3.3 Perform and describe an experiment to measure the focal length of a converging lens

2.3.4 Recall and use the equation $m = \dfrac{v}{u}$

2.3.5 Describe the use of lenses to correct myopia and hypermetropia

2.3.6 Perform calculations on the correction of long sight

2.3.7 Perform calculations involving the lens power of converging lenses

A lens consists of a piece of glass or other transparent material with one or two curved surfaces. Lenses can be classified into converging (convex) and diverging (concave). The effect of these two types of lens on a parallel beam of light is shown below.

When parallel rays of light pass through a converging lens they are refracted so that they pass through the focal point or principal focus of the lens. This type of principal focus is described as **real.**

In the case of a diverging lens the parallel rays are refracted so that they to spread out (diverge) from the focal point or principal focus of the concave lens. This type of principal focus is described as **virtual.**

The distance from the centre of a lens to the focal point is the **focal length f.**

Converging or convex lens

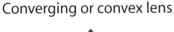

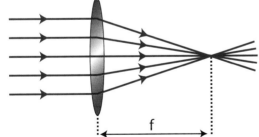

Diverging or concave lens

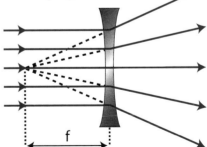

Images formed by converging lenses

The apparatus shown below can be used to investigate how the image formed on the screen by the converging lens changes as the distance between the lens and the illuminated wire mesh on the lamphouse is changed.

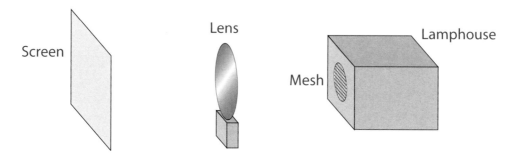

You should initially place the lamphouse at a distance from the lens of approximately three times the focal length of the lens. An approximate method for the focal length can be found using the method described on page 118.

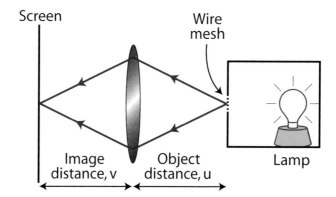

The screen is then moved until a sharp image is obtained. The lamphouse is then gradually moved closer to the lens and for a number of positions the screen is re-positioned until the image is again sharp.

Converging lens: ray diagrams

To find the position, size and nature of the image formed by a convex lens we need to find where at least two rays of light meet having passed through the lens from the object. The diagrams on the following pages show what happens to three particular rays when they pass through a convex lens. In the diagram the thickness of the lens is ignored: the lens is represented by a straight line (dashed). All refraction happens at this line, the 'curved lens' shape simply acts as label for the type of lens.

The horizontal line that passes through the optical centre of the lens is called the principal axis. On each side of the lens the focus F is marked and a point at twice this distance from the lens, 2F, is also marked. The object is small and upright and sits on the principal axis at various distances from the lens.

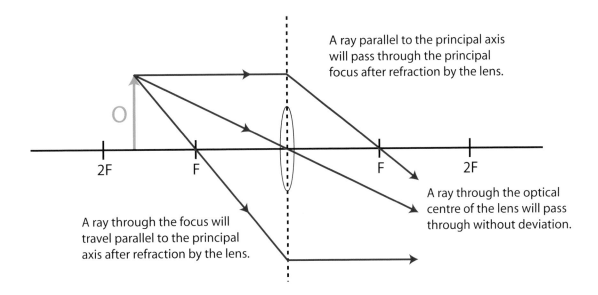

A ray parallel to the principal axis will pass through the principal focus after refraction by the lens.

A ray through the optical centre of the lens will pass through without deviation.

A ray through the focus will travel parallel to the principal axis after refraction by the lens.

The following diagram shows how a convex lens can produce an image for different positions of the object.

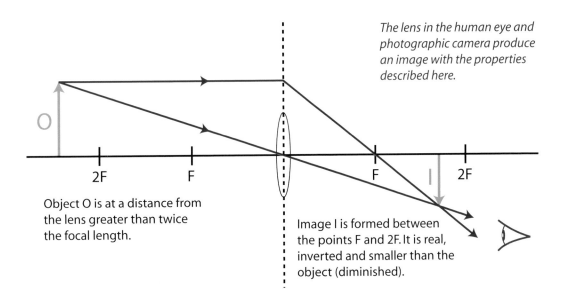

The lens in the human eye and photographic camera produce an image with the properties described here.

Object O is at a distance from the lens greater than twice the focal length.

Image I is formed between the points F and 2F. It is real, inverted and smaller than the object (diminished).

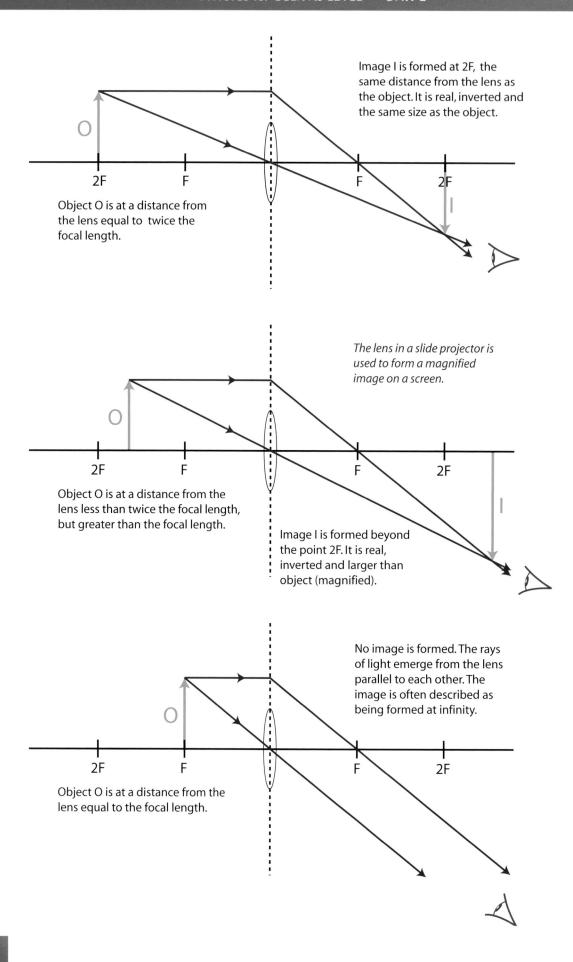

Image I is formed at 2F, the same distance from the lens as the object. It is real, inverted and the same size as the object.

Object O is at a distance from the lens equal to twice the focal length.

The lens in a slide projector is used to form a magnified image on a screen.

Object O is at a distance from the lens less than twice the focal length, but greater than the focal length.

Image I is formed beyond the point 2F. It is real, inverted and larger than object (magnified).

No image is formed. The rays of light emerge from the lens parallel to each other. The image is often described as being formed at infinity.

Object O is at a distance from the lens equal to the focal length.

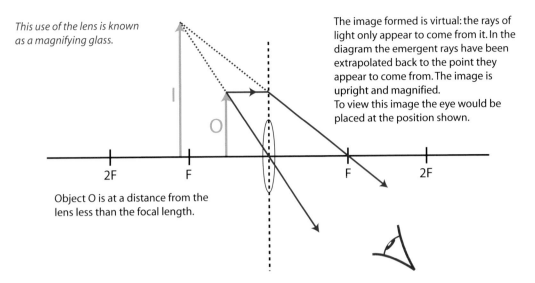

This use of the lens is known as a magnifying glass.

The image formed is virtual: the rays of light only appear to come from it. In the diagram the emergent rays have been extrapolated back to the point they appear to come from. The image is upright and magnified.
To view this image the eye would be placed at the position shown.

Object O is at a distance from the lens less than the focal length.

Diverging lens: ray diagrams

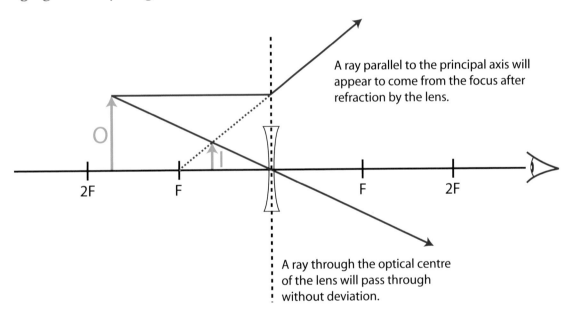

A ray parallel to the principal axis will appear to come from the focus after refraction by the lens.

A ray through the optical centre of the lens will pass through without deviation.

The image formed is virtual. With the exception of the ray through the optical centre of the lens, all other rays only appear to come from the image. The image is upright and diminished. These are properties of the image formed by a concave lens regardless of the position of the object. The two rays shown in the diagram above can be used to locate the image for all positions of the object.

Measurement of the focal length of a converging lens

1 **Approximate method – using a distant object**

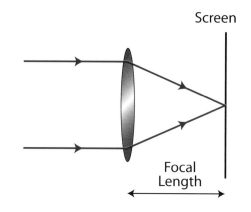

Light from a distant object, more than 10 m away, is approximately parallel. A convex lens will form an image of this object at approximately the focus.

Arrange the lens so that the image of a such an object is formed on a screen. Adjust the distance from the lens to the screen so that image is as sharp as possible.

Measure this distance; it is approximately the focal length. This should be repeated a number of times and the average taken.

2 **Using a plane mirror**

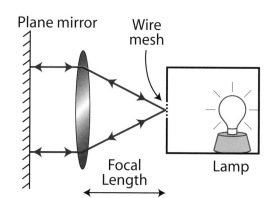

If an illuminated object is placed at the focus of a convex lens the light emerging from the lens is parallel. If these parallel rays are reflected back upon themselves, by a plane mirror, an image is formed beside the object.

The object is an illuminated wire mesh.

Place the plane mirror as close as possible to the lens. Move the lens and plane mirror together until a sharp image of the wire mesh appears on the front of the lamp house. Measure the distance from the lens to the lamp house; this is the focal length of the lens. Repetition and the taking of an average improves the reliability of the result.

3 **Measuring object and image distance**

This method also allows you to verify an important relationship between the object distance, the image distance and the focal length, called the **lens formula**. The object is the illuminated wire mesh.

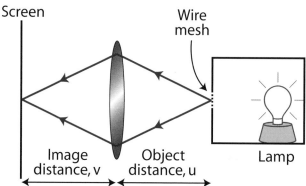

To ensure that the image is real, allowing it to be obtained on a screen, the object must be a distance from the lens greater than the focal length of the lens. Measure the distance from the mesh to the lens; this is the object distance u.

The position of the screen is adjusted until a sharp image is produced on the screen.

The distance from the lens to the screen is measured; this is the image distance v. The process is repeated for a series of different values of the object distance u, measuring the image distance v for each one. Values of u and v are tabulated and values of $\frac{1}{u}$ and $\frac{1}{v}$ calculated and tabulated. A typical set of values is shown in the table opposite.

Object distance u/m	Image distance v/m	$\frac{1}{u}$ / m^{-1}	$\frac{1}{v}$ / m^{-1}	$\frac{1}{u} + \frac{1}{v}$ / m^{-1}
0.40	0.134	2.5	7.45	9.95
0.35	0.14	2.85	7.1	9.95
0.30	0.15	3.33	6.7	10.03
0.25	0.168	4.0	5.95	9.95
0.20	0.195	5.0	5.1	10.1
0.15	0.30	6.67	3.3	10.07

Notice, allowing for experimental uncertainty, the values of $\frac{1}{u} + \frac{1}{v}$ = constant. This constant is $\frac{1}{f}$.

This is known as the lens formula and is written as;

$$\frac{1}{u} + \frac{1}{v} = \frac{1}{f}$$

Graphical analysis

The graph of object distance u against image distance v is a curve as shown. To find the focal length, a straight line is drawn. The path of the straight line is determined by points where the object distance equals the image distance, ie u = v. Where this line crosses the curve, the values of u and v represent twice the focal length.

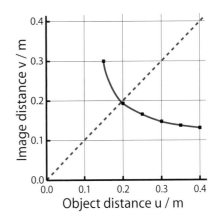

If you examine the ray diagrams for the convex lens you will see that the only situation when u = v is when the object is at a distance equal to twice the focal length. The resulting image is also at a distance of twice the focal length from the lens.

The better approach is to use your results to plot a linear graph. This is achieved by plotting $\frac{1}{u}$ against $\frac{1}{v}$. This yields a straight line as shown on the right.

The intercept on each axes provides a value for $\frac{1}{f}$.

Along the x axis ($\frac{1}{u}$) the value of $\frac{1}{v}$ is zero.

This means that v is large. In other words the image is at an infinite distance. This happens when the object is placed at the focus. The intercept on the $\frac{1}{u}$ axis gives the value of $\frac{1}{f}$.

Along the y axis ($\frac{1}{v}$) the value of $\frac{1}{u}$ is zero.

This means that u is large. In other words the object is at an infinite distance. When this is done the image is formed at the focus. The intercept on the $\frac{1}{v}$ axis also gives the value of $\frac{1}{f}$.

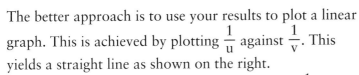

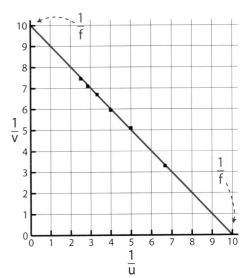

Mathematically the equation of a straight line is $y = mx + c$.

For the graph of $\dfrac{1}{u}$ against $\dfrac{1}{v}$ we can write $\dfrac{1}{v} = -\dfrac{1}{u} + \dfrac{1}{f}$.

The gradient is equal to -1 and the intercept is $\dfrac{1}{f}$.

The position, size and nature of the image formed by a lens can be determined in two ways;

1   accurate ray drawing,

2   use of the lens formula.

In the lens formula the object distance is denoted by u, the image distance by v and the focal length by f. You have already seen $\dfrac{1}{u} + \dfrac{1}{v} = \dfrac{1}{f}$

Real/virtual sign convention

When using the formula, you must apply a sign convention to each of the distances involved.

A real image is one that rays of light actually pass through. A virtual image is one that the rays of light only appear to pass through.

The distance to a real object, real image or real focal point is positive.

The distance to a virtual object, virtual image or virtual focal point is negative.

Consequently the focal length of a converging lens is positive and the focal length of a diverging lens is negative.

Magnification

The linear magnification of an image is the size of the image divided by the size of the object.

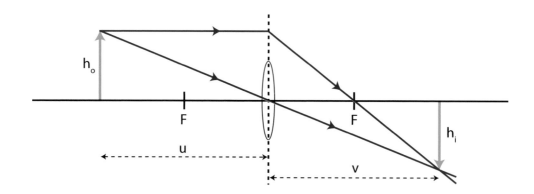

By using the properties of similar triangles we can also show that magnification is also equal to the ratio of the image distance to the object distance.

$$\text{magnification } m = \frac{h_i}{h_o} = \frac{v}{u}$$

Power of a lens

The power of lens is defined as:

$$\text{power} = \frac{1}{f}$$

The focal length is given in metres, so the power is measured in m^{-1} or **dioptres**, symbol D.

A diverging lens has a negative power, a converging lens has a positive power.

Exercise 31

1 A converging lens produces a real, inverted image at a distance from the lens greater than twice its focal length.

 (a) Draw a ray diagram to show how this image has been formed. Use arrows to show the direction of the rays of light. Show a suitable position for the eye to view such an image.

 (b) Define the linear magnification of an image produced by a lens.

 (c) A certain lens forms an upright image of an object which is placed 60 mm from the lens. The linear magnification of the image is 2.5.

   (i)   What type of lens is used and state if the image is real or virtual?

   (ii) Calculate the position of the image relative to the lens.

   (iii) Calculate the focal length of the lens.

[CCEA June 2001]

2 (a) Explain what is meant by the principal focus and focal length of a diverging lens.

 (b) The diagram shows a diverging lens with an object OB placed at its focus and perpendicular to the principal axis.

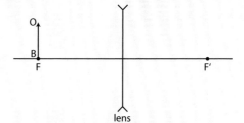

Copy the diagram and by drawing suitable construction rays, locate the image of OB. Label this image IM. On the diagram show a suitable position for the eye for viewing the image.

 (c) A converging lens has a focal length of 150 mm. An object is placed 80 mm from the lens.

   (i)   Find the position of the image relative to the lens.

   (ii) Calculate the linear magnification of the image.

   (iii) State three things that describe this image.

[CCEA June 2002]

3 (a) An object OA is placed perpendicular to the principal axis of a converging lens so that a virtual, magnified image is produced.

    (i) Draw a diagram to show the lens and mark clearly where the object should be placed to produce such an image. Label the object OA.

    (ii) Complete the ray diagram for this image. Label the image IB. Show a suitable position for an eye to view the image.

  (b) A diverging lens has a focal length of 250 mm. An object 20 mm tall is placed 375 mm from the lens.

    (i) Calculate the distance of the image from the lens. State the position of the image relative to the lens and the object.

    (ii) Calculate the height of the image.

[CCEA January 2003]

4 (a) (i) Define linear magnification produced by a lens.

    (ii) State another expression for the linear magnification. This expression should be in terms of the distance of the object from the lens and the distance of the image from the lens.

  (b) Suppose you are asked to carry out an experiment to show that the expression in (a) is equivalent to that in (a)(ii). You are supplied with a converging lens, an illuminated object, a white screen and a metre rule. State clearly the readings you would take, and how they would be used. Experimental details are not required.

  (c) An illuminated object is placed 240 mm from a converging lens. A sharp image is formed on a screen on the opposite of the lens, 360 mm from the object.

  (i) Calculate the focal length of the lens.

  (ii) Find the linear magnification produced by the lens.

[CCEA January 2004]

5 A diverging lens forms an image of an object OA. The position and height of the image can be determined by tracing two rays through the lens. A third ray may also be traced as a check.

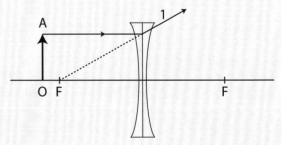

The diagram shows the diverging lens with the object OA. One of the three rays has already been drawn. This ray is numbered 1.

  (a) Copy the diagram and trace a second ray from A and use it to locate the image. Number the ray 2 and label the image IB.

  (b) On your diagram confirm the position of the image by tracing the third ray from A. Number this ray 3.

  (c) On your diagram indicate a suitable position for an eye to view the image.

  (d) How do you know that the base of the image must be on the principal axis?

Myopia and hypermetropia

The human eye has a lens which can alter its focal length. It does this by altering its shape: thick to give a short focal length (high power) for focussing on near objects and thin for a long focal length (low power) for focussing on distant objects. This ability of the eye to see objects clearly at different distances is known as **accommodation**. Most of the refraction of the light takes place at the boundary between the air and the cornea because this is where the largest change in refractive index occurs.

The farthest point which can be seen clearly by the unaided eye is called the **far point**. For the normal eye this is at infinity. Light from the far point reaches the eye as parallel rays. The rays are refracted by the eye so that they meet on the retina forming a sharp image of the distant object.

The nearest point which can be seen clearly by the unaided eye is called the **near point**. For the normal eye this is at 25 cm. The light from the near point reaches the eye as diverging rays. These are refracted by the eye so that they meet on the retina forming a sharp image of the object at the near point.

Myopia

A person who suffers from myopia (short sight) is unable to see distant objects sharply.

They cannot make the lens thin enough to view distant objects. This causes the light from distant objects to converge towards a point in front of the retina. The image seen by the person is blurred.

The person's far point is much closer to the eye than the normal infinite distance. It might be only a few metres or possibly less.

Light from this point is correctly focused by the eye so that a sharp image of an object at this point is obtained.

To correct this defect a concave (diverging) lens is used. The focal length of the lens is equal to the distance to the person's actual far point. This means that parallel rays of light from a distant object are refracted so that they appear to diverge from the person's far point.

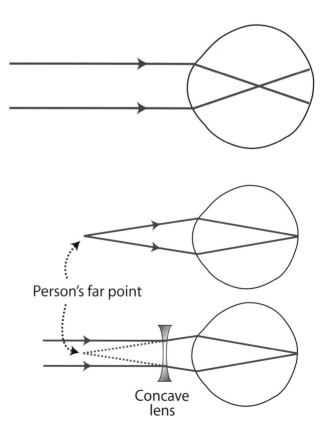

Person's far point

Concave lens

Hypermetropia

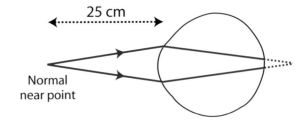

This is also known as long sight. A long sighted person sees distant objects clearly but does not see near objects clearly. This happens because the ciliary muscles are too weak to make the lens thick and so have a shorter focal length.

Normal near point

An object held at the normal near point distance of 25 cm will not be seen clearly. The rays of light from the object are not bent sufficiently to form an image on the retina.

The near point is much further than 25 cm. Rays of light from an object placed at their near point are bent so that they meet on the retina resulting in the object being seen clearly.

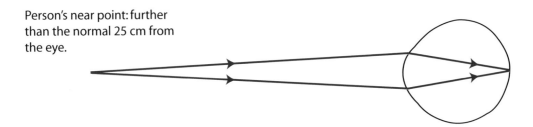

Person's near point: further than the normal 25 cm from the eye.

To correct for this defect a convex lens is used. The focal length of this lens has to be such that an object at 25 cm appears to be at the person's near point. If a person has a near point at 100 cm then for an object at 25 cm the convex lens has to create a virtual image at 100 cm of an object at 25 cm.

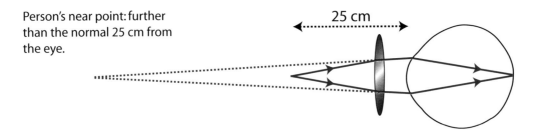

Person's near point: further than the normal 25 cm from the eye.

25 cm

The use of a converging lens means that the object that is really at 25 cm from the eye appears to be 100 cm from the eye. The converging lens forms a virtual image at the person's near point. The lens formula is used to find the focal length of the lens. If the person's near point is 100 cm from his eye then we have;

$$\frac{1}{u} + \frac{1}{v} = \frac{1}{f} \text{ substitution of values gives } \frac{1}{25} + \frac{1}{(-100)} = \frac{1}{f}$$

The negative sign is used because the image at the person's near point is virtual. The lens has a focal length value of 33.3 cm and a power of + 3.0 D.

Worked Example

A person with hypermetropia has an unaided near point of 50 cm and a far point of infinity.

(a) What is the power of lens needed to correct the hypermetropia?

(b) What is the range of her vision when she wears these lenses?

Solution

(a) The converging lenses have a focal length so that an object at the normal near point (25 cm) would give a virtual image at the unaided near point (50 cm).

$$\frac{1}{f} = \frac{1}{u} + \frac{1}{v} \text{ so,} \quad \frac{1}{f} = \frac{1}{25} + \frac{1}{(-50)} = \frac{1}{50}$$

so f = 50 cm and P = $\frac{1}{0.5}$ = **+2 D**

(b) An object placed 50 cm from this convex lens would give rise to a (virtual) image at infinity. The patient therefore has a range of vision of 25 cm to 50 cm and would therefore be expected to remove the glasses when looking at distant objects.

Exercise 32

1. A certain student requires spectacles in order to see a book clearly at normal reading distance.

(a) What defect of vision do the spectacle lenses correct?

(b) What is the normal cause of this defect?

(c) Without spectacles, the student cannot see clearly objects which are nearer than 100 cm from the eye. Calculate the power of the spectacle lens required to reduce this distance to the normal near-point distance of 25 cm.

(d) Without spectacles, the student's far-point distance has the normal value.

(i) Calculate the distance of the student's far point from the eye when the spectacles in (c) are worn.

(ii) When wearing the spectacles in (c), the student looks at a road sign which is 8 m away. Comment briefly on the appearance of the sign to the student.

2 A person viewing objects has a near point of 75 cm.

(a) What is this defect called?

(b) Suggest one possible cause of this condition.

(c) Calculate the power of the spectacle lens needed to change this person's near point to the normal near point position. Give an appropriate unit.

(d) Without spectacles the person's far point has the normal value. Find the new far point when wearing the spectacles.

[CCEA 2005]

125

2.4 Superposition and Interference

You should be able to:

2.4.1 Illustrate the concept of superposition by the graphical addition of two sine waves

2.4.2 Demonstrate knowledge and understanding of the graphical representation of standing waves in stretched string and in air in pipes closed at one end

2.4.3 Identify node and anti-node positions

2.4.4 Understand the significance of coherence as applied to wave sources

2.4.5 State the conditions for observable interference

2.4.6 Understand the significance of path difference and phase difference in explaining interference effects

2.4.7 Describe Young's slit interference experiment with monochromatic light

2.4.8 Use the formula $\lambda = \dfrac{a\,y}{d}$ applied to Young's slit experiment

Principle of Superposition

The Principle of Superposition may be applied to waves whenever two (or more) waves travelling through the same medium at the same time meet. The waves pass through each other without being disturbed.

The Principle of Superposition states that the resultant displacement of the medium at any point in space, is the sum of the displacements that each wave would cause at that point at that time.

Remember that displacement is a vector, so direction is important when we apply the Principle of Superposition.

When the two waves overlap in phase they produce a wave of greater amplitude. This is known as **constructive interference**. At a certain point in space the crests of each wave coincide exactly (as do the troughs) and so a wave with greater amplitude is produced.

However, when the crest of one wave coincides with the trough of the other wave the displacements of the two waves are in opposite directions. If the amplitudes are equal then they cancel each other. This is called **total destructive interference**.

If the amplitudes are not the same then when destructive interference takes place the resultant wave has a smaller amplitude. This time the two waves do not completely cancel.

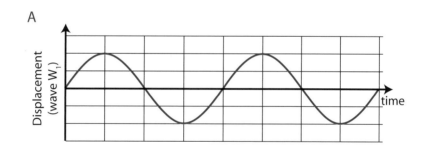

Remember the Principle of Superposition applies to all situations when two or more waves meet. To find the resultant displacement of two waves at any instant or any point represented, we apply the Principle of Superposition by adding their individual displacements at that instant or point to find the resultant displacement at that point.

Worked example

Two sinusoidal transverse waves W_1 and W_2, of the same type, are incident simultaneously on a point P. The amplitude of W_2 is the same as the amplitude of W_1. The frequency of W_2 is half the frequency of W_1. At a certain instant (time t = 0) at P both waves have zero displacement, and then both displacements increase in the same direction. Graph A shows that the displacement varies with time for wave W_1, at the point P.

A

Displacement (wave W_1) — time

(a) On a second grid B draw the displacement–time graph for wave W_2.

(b) On a second grid C draw the displacement–time graph for the resultant wave produced by the superposition at P of waves W_1 and W_2.

(c) The frequency of wave W_1 is 4.2×10^{15} Hz. What is the frequency of wave W_2 and what is the frequency of the resultant wave produced by the superposition of W_1 and W_2?

[CCEA June 2001]

Solution

The frequency of wave $W_2 = 2.1 \times 10^{15}$ Hz. Grid B shows one complete cycle.

Grid C shows one complete cycle of the resultant wave. Two complete cycles of W_1 fit into one complete cycle of W_2. This means that the frequency of the resultant wave is equal to that of the wave with the lower frequency, ie W_2. Therefore the frequency of the resultant wave is also 2.1×10^{15} Hz. The higher frequency wave W_1 simply changes the shape of the resultant wave but that shape is repeated over and over again.

B

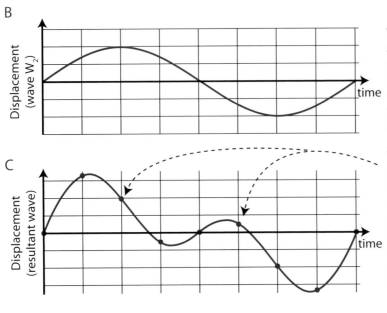

Wave W_2 has the same amplitude as wave W_1. Since its frequency is only half that of W_1, only one complete wave will fit into the time represented along the X-axis.

C

To draw the resultant wave the displacement of W_1 is added to the displacement of W_2 at each instant. The resultant is shown by the dots.

When the dots are joined the shape of the resultant wave is obtained.

The diagram below shows just over 4 complete cycles for W_2 and just over 2 complete cycles for W_2. The resultant wave W_{res} has a more complex shape, but this shape occupies the same time interval as that of W_2. So the frequency of the resultant wave is the same as that of W_2.

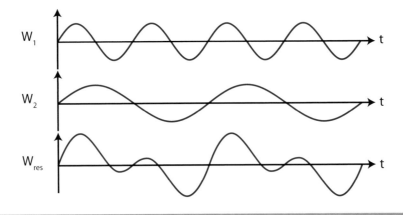

Coherence

To produce an interference pattern that is detectable, i.e. lasts long enough to seen or heard, the two sources of waves must be **coherent.** In practice coherent sources are derived from a single source.

To be coherent the sources must produce waves of the same wavelength or frequency and be in phase, i.e. each produces a wave crest at the same time, or have a constant phase difference between them.

To make the difference between constructive and destructive more obvious, it is best that the coherent sources are of equal amplitude.

Interference of sound waves

S_1 and S_2 are two speakers. To achieve coherent sources of sound, the same signal generator powers each speaker, so that they produce sound waves of the same frequency and in phase. As the sound waves from each speaker spread out they cross. This creates places where the sound is loud (constructive interference) and between these there are places where the sound is soft (destructive interference).

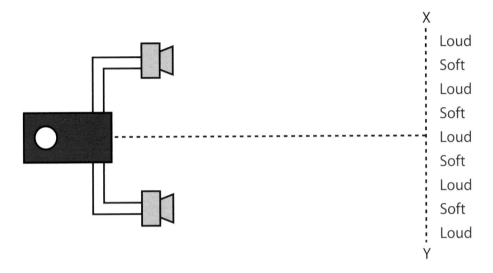

If you were to walk along the line XY you would hear these alternate loud and soft sounds.

Interference of water waves

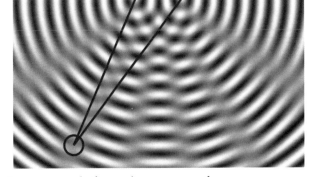

A ripple tank can be used to demonstrate interference of water waves. The shadow of the waves can be projected onto a sheet of paper below the tank as shown in the diagram or it may be projected onto a screen.

To produce coherent sources of water waves two smaller dippers vibrate in and out of the water at the same time.

Two sources of water waves are shown in the diagram below. These produce circular waves that spread out in all directions. At certain points constructive interference results and at others destructive interference is produced. The point marked is a region of destructive interference.

Notice that no waves are seen here. The two waves that reach this point have travelled different distances. They have a path difference, in this case of 1.5 wavelengths. This means that the crest of one wave reaches the marked point at the same time as a wave trough from the other source arrives. They cancel each other, so we have destructive interference and so no wave is seen.

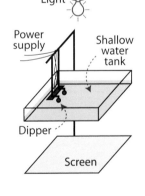

Note the regions of destructive interference radiating outwards from the sources of waves.

Interference of light waves

Light from a laser is used to illuminate two narrow slits. The light from a laser is coherent. Each slit then acts as a coherent source of light waves. The light waves spread out as they pass through the slits. This effect is known as diffraction.

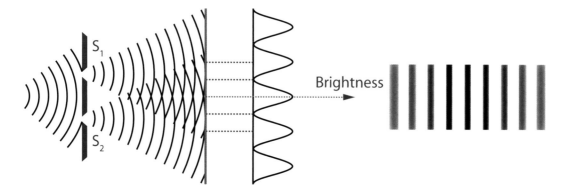

At points on the screen the light waves from each slit interfere constructively and a bright line is seen. In between the bright regions there are dark regions where destructive interference is happening. On the screen alternate bright and dark regions are seen. These are often referred to as interference fringes.

Exercise 33

1 (a) In the context of the superposition of two waves, what condition must exist for complete destructive interference?

   (b) How would you recognise that complete destructive interference has occurred?

2 Two waves A and B of equal amplitude, speed and wavelength are travelling in the same part of a medium and interfere. The diagram shows how the displacement y of each of the waves depends on time t at the point at which they interfere.

A crest of wave A arrives at the point exactly one-sixth of a period before the closest crest of wave B. In other words, there is a phase difference between the two waves.

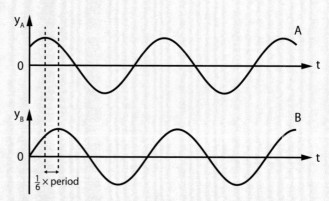

(a) State the magnitude of this phase difference.

(b) The waves can be brought into a situation where complete destructive interference occurs by increasing or decreasing the phase difference between them. What change of phase difference is required?

[CCEA January 2005]

Young's Double Slit Experiment

In Young's double slit experiment the white light first passes through a filter to produce monochromatic light (single wavelength). It then passes through a narrow single slit and as it does it diffracts (the waves spread out). Finally the waves pass through the double slit, the crest of one wave passing through each one of the double slits at the same time. This ensures that the waves are in phase. These two actions ensure that the two slits S_1 and S_2 act as coherent sources of light waves.

Young carried out his original double-slit experiment with light some time in the first decade of the 1800s, showing that the waves of light from the two slits interfered to produce a characteristic fringe pattern on a screen. This was the first piece of direct evidence for the wave nature of light.

S_1 and S_2 are two coherent sources of light, of wavelength λ, separated by a distance **a**. An interference pattern of alternate bright and dark fringes is seen on the screen. The separation of bright fringes is y. The distance from the double slit to the screen is d.

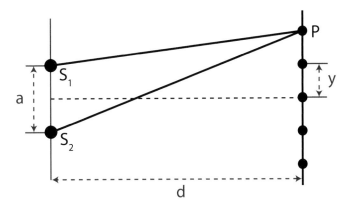

The point P is the location of a bright fringe. The waves reaching P from S_1 and S_2 have travelled different distances. If a whole number of wavelengths can fit into this path difference then constructive interference results since a crest from S_1 will arrive at the same time as a crest from S_2.

For constructive interference path difference $S_2P - S_1P = n\lambda$

If a whole number plus half a wavelength fits into the path difference destructive interference results. A crest from S_2 will arrive at the same time as trough from S_1, the waves then cancel.

For destructive interference path difference $S_2P - S_1P = (n + \frac{1}{2})\lambda$

In each of these conditions n has the value 0, 1, 2, 3, … i.e. whole numbers. The wavelength can be calculated using the formula:

$$\lambda = \frac{a\,y}{d}$$

where λ = wavelength of the light in m
    a = separation of the double slits in m
    y = fringe separation on the screen in m
    d = distance from the double slit to the screen in m

The distance from the double slit to the screen d can be measured using a metre rule. This distance is typically 1 m to 2 m. The fringe separation y is best found by measuring the separation of a number of fringes and taking an average.

The separation of the two slits in the double slit arrangement can be found by projecting a magnified image on to a screen, and measuring their separation on this magnified image. The actual magnification can be found by projecting a transparent millimetre scale on to the same screen. The actual separation of the two slits is then found by dividing their separation on the magnified image by the magnification.

The separation of the slits is a (typically 0.2 mm).

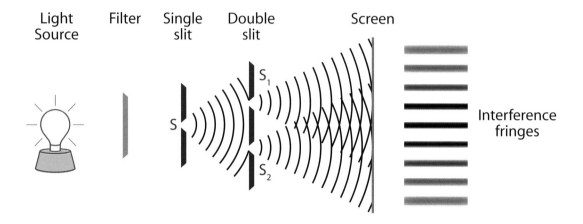

Exercise 34

1 Radio waves of wavelength 320 m travel directly to a receiver R 120 km away from the transmitter T. They are also reflected from the base of the ionosphere, which is at an effective height of 80 km above the Earth's surface. The situation is shown in the diagram.

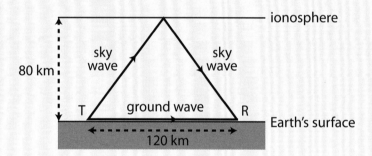

(a) Calculate the difference in the lengths of the paths travelled by the sky and ground waves when they arrive at the transmitter.

(b) When the sky waves are reflected at the ionosphere, phase change of 180° occurs between the incident and reflected waves. Use this fact, and your answer to (a), to suggest whether constructive or destructive interference occurs at the receiver. Explain your reasoning.

(c) Over a period of a few seconds, the height of the base of the ionosphere may vary. State and explain an effect this might have on the reception of the radio signals.

[CCEA January 2003]

2 A condition for observable interference fringes to be obtained with a double-slit apparatus is that two light sources should be coherent.

(a) State what is meant by coherent sources.

(b) Write down an expression for the separation of the fringes in a double-slit experiment. State the meaning of any other symbols used in your expression.

(c) Red light of wavelength 680 nm is used to illuminate two parallel, narrow slits which are 0.75 mm apart. Fringes are formed on a screen 1.60 m away from the slits.

   (i) Determine the distance on the screen between the central bright fringe and the point X where the third bright fringe is obtained.

   (ii) The red light is now replaced by light of a different wavelength. It is found that the fifth dark fringe now appears at the point X. Find the wavelength of the light from this new source.

[CCEA June 1997]

3 (a) Draw a labeled sketch to show the arrangement of apparatus in a Young's double-slit experiment.

 (b) A Young's double slit experiment was carried out with a suitable light source. At a distance of 0.850 m from the slits, 5 fringe separations per centimetre were observed. The separation of the slits was 0.250 mm. Calculate the wavelength of the light used in the experiment.

[CCEA January 2004]

Standing waves in stretched strings

These are produced by the interference of two waves, of the same type and having the same wavelength moving in opposite directions. The most common occurrence of this is a wave travelling in one direction meeting its reflection which is moving in the opposite direction.

The Principle of Superposition can be used to explain and describe what is seen when the outgoing wave and its reflection meet.

The vibration generator shown below vibrates up and down driven by a signal generator (a source of alternating voltage whose frequency can be altered). The vibration generator moves up and down with a small amplitude and this causes waves to travel along the string.

When the waves meet the pulley end of the string they are reflected back along the string. So we have two waves of the same wavelength moving in opposite directions. The result is that **standing waves**.

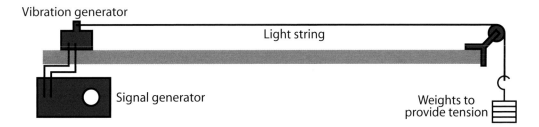

The simplest pattern and the lowest frequency at which the string vibrates is called the fundamental frequency f_o. The diagram below shows the standing wave pattern obtained as the frequency of vibration is increased. The relationship between these modes of vibration can be deduced using the wave equation. The length of the string is L.

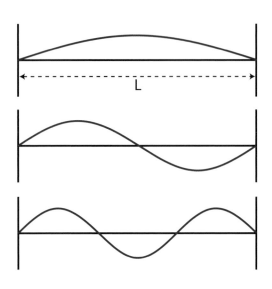

Fundamental frequency = f_0 and $\lambda_0 = 2L$
The velocity of the wave in the string = v

$$v = f_0\lambda_0 \qquad f_0 = \frac{v}{\lambda_0} = \frac{v}{2L}$$

1st Overtone frequency = f_1 and $\lambda_1 = L$
The velocity of the wave in the string = v

$$v = f_1\lambda_1 \qquad f_1 = \frac{v}{\lambda_1} = \frac{v}{L} = 2f_0$$

2nd Overtone frequency = f_2 and $\lambda_2 = 2/3L$
The velocity of the wave in the string = v

$$v = f_2\lambda_2 \qquad f_2 = \frac{v}{\lambda_2} = \frac{3v}{2L} = 3f_0$$

To explain the formation of a standing wave we have to apply the Principle of Superposition to the wave travelling out from the source and its reflected wave. The outgoing wave is shown as the dotted line (········) and is moving to the right. The reflected wave is the dashed line (⌒ ⌒) and is moving to the left. The standing wave is the resultant of these two waves and is shown by the solid line (⌒). In each of the diagrams below the incident wave is shown in steps of $\frac{\lambda}{8}$ as its moves to the right and the reflected waves in steps of $\frac{\lambda}{8}$ as it moves to the left. T is the period of the waves, i.e. the time it takes for one complete wave to pass a point.

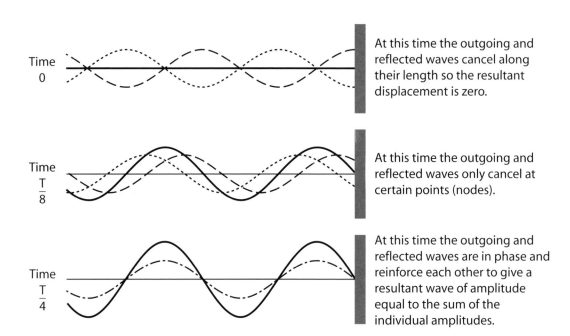

Time 0 — At this time the outgoing and reflected waves cancel along their length so the resultant displacement is zero.

Time $\frac{T}{8}$ — At this time the outgoing and reflected waves only cancel at certain points (nodes).

Time $\frac{T}{4}$ — At this time the outgoing and reflected waves are in phase and reinforce each other to give a resultant wave of amplitude equal to the sum of the individual amplitudes.

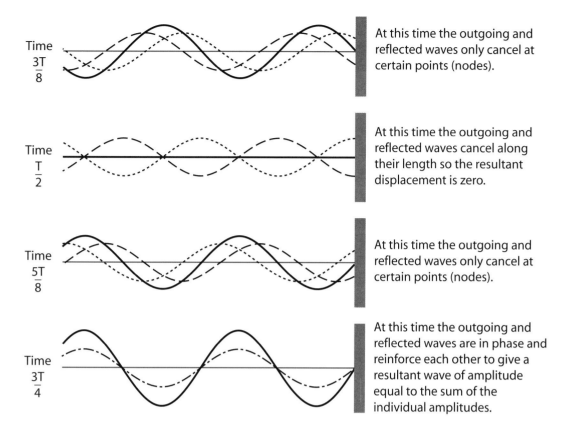

Time $\frac{3T}{8}$ — At this time the outgoing and reflected waves only cancel at certain points (nodes).

Time $\frac{T}{2}$ — At this time the outgoing and reflected waves cancel along their length so the resultant displacement is zero.

Time $\frac{5T}{8}$ — At this time the outgoing and reflected waves only cancel at certain points (nodes).

Time $\frac{3T}{4}$ — At this time the outgoing and reflected waves are in phase and reinforce each other to give a resultant wave of amplitude equal to the sum of the individual amplitudes.

Note: The wavelength of the standing wave is equal to the wavelength of the progressive waves from which it is formed.

Nodes and anti-nodes

When a standing or stationary wave is created, some points along the wave are always at rest, i.e. their resultant displacement is always zero. These points are known as **nodes**.

Between the nodes all the points are vibrating, i.e. the amplitude of vibration varies. Midway between two nodal points the amplitude of vibration is a maximum. This point is called an **anti-node**.

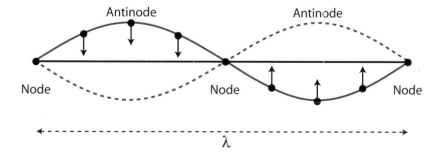

The points between neighbouring nodes are vibrating in phase with each other. However, the points between the next pair of nodes are vibrating ½ λ out of phase with these points as shown in the diagram.

The distance between neighbouring nodes is ½ λ.

The distance between a node and the nearest anti-node is ¼ λ.

135

Exercise 35

1 A string is stretched between two fixed supports 3.5 m apart. Stationary waves may be generated by vibrating the string. One mode of vibration of the string is shown in the diagram. The nodes are labelled N and the antinodes A.

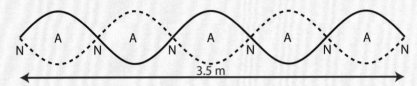

(a) Distinguish between a node and an anti-node on a stationary wave.

(b) State the phase difference between the vibrations of the particles at any two consecutive anti-nodes.

(c) What is the ratio of the frequency for the mode of vibration shown compared with the frequency of the fundamental mode of vibration.

(d) The frequency of the mode of vibration shown is 160 Hz. Find the fundamental frequency of vibration of the string.

(e) Calculate the speed of the transverse waves which produce the stationary waves on this stretched string.

[CCEA February 1998]

2 (a) A stationary wave is generated by the superposition of two travelling waves of the same type.

   (i) State two requirements for these travelling waves.

   (ii) State, in terms of energy transfer, why the name stationary wave is appropriate, in spite of the connection with travelling waves.

(b) Stationary waves may be set up on a stretched string. The wavelength λ of the fundamental mode of vibration depends on the frequency f of the waves according to the equation:

$$f = \frac{A}{\lambda}$$

   where A is a constant which depends on the tension in the string and the diameter of the string. In an experiment, frequencies f are measured in hertz, and wavelengths λ in metres. State the corresponding unit of the constant A, expressed in SI base units.

(c) The highest key on a piano strikes a string 5.0 cm long. This produces a note with a frequency 150 times that sounded by the lowest key.

   (i) Find the wavelength of the fundamental mode of stationary waves on the 5.0 cm string of the piano.

   (ii) Assume that all the strings on the piano are under the same tension and of the same diameter and that all vibrate in their fundamental. Use the equation above to calculate the length of the string for the lowest note.

   (iii) Comment on your answer to (ii) in relation to the assumptions made.

[CCEA June 2004]

Standing waves in air columns

Standing waves can be demonstrated with sound using a long glass tube closed at one end. This is commonly known as a resonance tube. Sound waves are generated at the top of the air column using a loudspeaker or tuning fork.

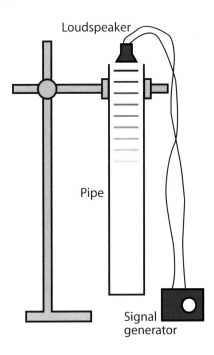

Sound waves from the speaker or tuning fork meet the reflected waves from the bottom of the air column and a standing wave is created. When a standing wave is produced the sound becomes much louder. This is easily checked by removing the glass tube. If a standing wave was present there should be a very noticeable decrease in the loudness of the sound.

The different frequencies at which this happens are called overtones. The lowest frequency of sound which creates a standing wave for a particular length of air column is called the fundamental.

The diagram shows three air molecules at three different positions along the air column in the glass tube. Sound is a longitudinal wave so the vibrations are along the length of the air column, parallel to the direction of propagation of the sound wave.

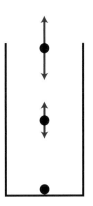

The air molecule at the closed end is not vibrating: this is a **node**.

The air molecule at the open end is vibrating with maximum amplitude: this is an **anti-node**. The air molecule further down the pipe is vibrating with an amplitude less than that of the molecule at the open end. As we move from the node to the anti-node the amplitude of vibration of the air molecules increases.

One way to represent a wave is a graph showing how the displacement of the particles varies with distance along the tube. When this is done for the fundamental mode of vibration of the air in the column we have the graph shown on the right.

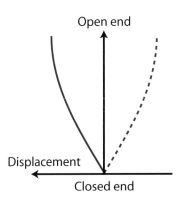

The displacement of the particles gradually increases from the closed end to the open end.

The dotted line represents the displacement of the particles half a period later.

Fixed length of air column – varying frequency

As shown on the previous page a small loudspeaker connected to a signal generator can be used to create standing waves in an air column of fixed length. As the frequency is gradually increased the loudness of the sound noticeably increases (resonates) at certain frequencies. At each of these frequencies a standing wave is created and these are known as modes of vibration. The lowest frequency is called the fundamental; the next frequency at which a standing wave is created is known as the 1st overtone; the next frequency is known as the 2nd overtone.

The diagram below shows the standing wave patterns for the four lowest frequencies for which a standing wave is created in an air column of fixed length.

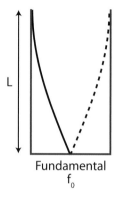
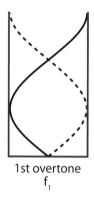
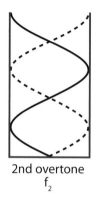
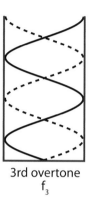

| Fundamental f_0 | 1st overtone f_1 | 2nd overtone f_2 | 3rd overtone f_3 |

Fundamental

In the fundamental mode of vibration the length of the air column L is one quarter the wavelength of the sound. Remember that the wavelength of the standing wave equals the wavelength of the progressive wave. The frequency of the sound wave is obtained from the wave equation:

$$L = \frac{\lambda}{4} \quad \text{so } \lambda = 4L \quad \text{the wave equation } v = f\lambda$$

Therefore the fundamental frequency is given by:

$$f_0 = \frac{v}{4L}$$

1st Overtone

The next mode of vibration, known as the 1st overtone, has a wavelength is λ_1 and a frequency f_1. In this case the length of the air column is three quarters of the wavelength.

$$L = \frac{3}{4}\lambda_1 \qquad \text{so } \lambda_1 = \frac{4}{3}L \qquad v = f_1\lambda_1$$

The 1st overtone frequency is given by;

$$f_1 = \frac{3v}{4L}$$

Comparing this frequency with the fundamental tells us that $f_1 = 3f_0$.

2nd and 3rd Overtones

When we examine the standing wave patterns for the second and third overtones using the approach outlined above we see that the frequencies of these modes of vibration are $5f_0$ and $7f_0$.

Mode of vibration	Fundamental	1st overtone	2nd overtone	3rd overtone
Frequency	f_0	$3f_0$	$5f_0$	$7f_0$

Fixed frequency – varying length of air column

In this case a tuning fork or a small loudspeaker connected to a signal generator can be used to produce sound waves of a constant frequency. To create standing waves the length of the air column is gradually increased.

One method of doing this is shown. A long glass tube is placed in a cylinder of water. Moving the glass tube up and down changes the length of the air column. The long glass tube is often referred to as a resonance tube.

As the length of the air column is gradually increased, loudness of the sound noticeably increases (resonates) at certain lengths. At each of these lengths a standing wave is created. The shortest length is known as the 1st position of resonance and corresponds to the fundamental frequency. The next two lengths at which a standing wave is created are known as the 2nd and 3rd positions of resonance.

The diagram below shows the standing wave patterns for the three shortest lengths for which a standing wave is created in the air column.

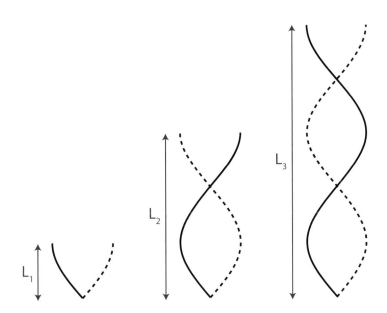

1st position of resonance

The length L_1, of the air column, is one quarter of the wavelength. $L_1 = \dfrac{\lambda}{4}$

2ⁿᵈ position of resonance

The length L_2, of the air column, is three quarters of the wavelength. $L_2 = \dfrac{3}{4}\lambda$

3ʳᵈ position of resonance

The length L_3, of the air column is one and a quarters times the wavelength. $L_3 = \dfrac{5}{4}\lambda$

2.5 Diffraction

You should be able to:

2.5.1 Describe and explain simple diffraction phenomena

2.5.2 State qualitatively, and draw diagrams to illustrate, the effect of aperture size on diffraction

As waves go through a gap they spread out. This is called **diffraction**. Diffraction also takes place when waves meet any type of obstacle. A suitable definition of diffraction is the changing of direction of waves to bend around corners and spread out as they encounter obstacles.

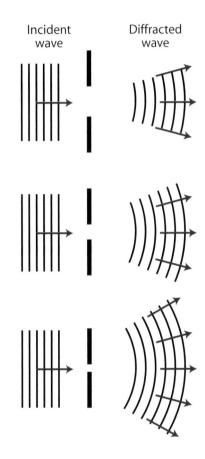

The diagrams show how the diffraction increases as the size of the gap is gradually decreased until is about the same size as the wavelength of the incident wave. The greatest diffraction happens when the size of the gap is about the same as the wavelength of the wave.

The wavelength of the wave does **not** change as a result of diffraction.

The wavelength of everyday sounds is about the same width as a door. As a result diffraction of sound at an open door results in sound waves spreading into the room, allowing us to hear sounds coming along a corridor. Light has a much smaller wavelength so very narrow openings or slits are required to observe diffraction of light.

A laser and an adjustable slit can be used to investigate the diffraction of light. The laser beam is directed through the slit and onto a screen as shown in the diagram.

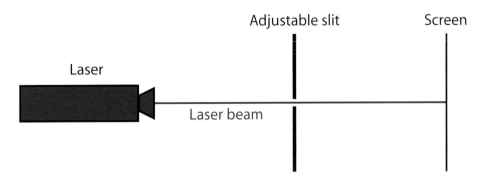

Diffraction of the light waves at a single slit produces a diffraction pattern like that shown below. As the light waves spread out in some directions destructive interference occurs, producing the dark bands. In other directions constructive interference occurs, producing the bright bands.

Most of the energy of the light waves passes through in a narrow region giving rise to the bright central maximum. The width of the central maximum depends on the width of the slit and on the wavelength of the light used. For the same slit width, red light has a wider diffraction pattern than blue light because the wavelength of red is greater than the wavelength of blue. As the width of the slit decreases, the width of the diffraction pattern increases.

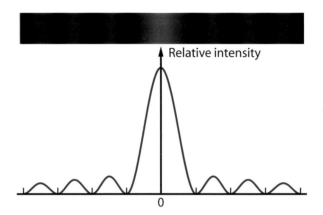

2.6 Sound

2.6.1   Determine the frequency of a pure note using a cathode ray oscilloscope

2.6.2   Measure the speed of sound in air using a resonance tube (end correction is not required)

2.6.3   Use the formula, Intensity level/dB $= 10\lg_{10}\left(\dfrac{I}{I_0}\right)$

2.6.4   Interpret, qualitatively, graphs of frequency and intensity response for the ear

Sound is a longitudinal wave. As sound travels through the air, the air molecules are made to vibrate parallel to the direction of propagation of the sound.

This means that the molecules are, in places, closer together than they would normally be, and in other places they are further apart than normal. Sound travels through the air as a series of compressions and rarefactions – it is in effect a pressure wave. A sound wave is normally represented as a displacement versus distance graph as below.

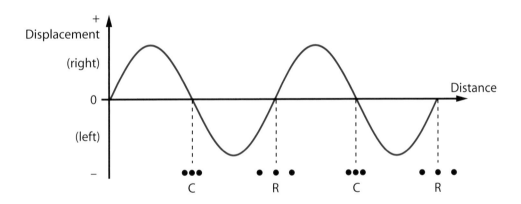

Compression (High pressure)

The air molecules to the right of the molecule with zero displacement all experience a negative displacement as the sound wave passes. This means they are displaced to the left of their normal rest position and so are closer to the molecule with zero displacement.

The air molecules to the left of the air molecule with zero displacement all experience a positive displacement as the sound wave passes. As a result they are displaced to the right of their rest positions and so are closer to the molecule with zero displacement.

Consequently the molecules in this position are forced closer than normal, the air pressure is greater and a compression is created.

Rarefaction (Low pressure)

The air molecules to the right of the molecule with zero displacement all experience a positive displacement as the sound wave passes. This means they are displaced to the right of their normal rest position and so are moved further away from the molecule with zero displacement.

The air molecules to the left of the air molecule with zero displacement all experience a negative displacement as the sound wave passes. As a result they are displaced to the left of their rest positions and so are moved away from the molecule with zero displacement.

Consequently the molecules in this position are forced further apart than normal, the air pressure is less and a rarefaction is created.

Measuring the frequency of sound

A tuning fork or a loudspeaker connected to a signal generator emits sound of a single frequency. The sound wave, when it reaches the microphone, produces an electrical signal which can be displayed on the cathode ray oscilloscope (c.r.o.). The frequency of this electrical signal is the same as that of the sound wave.

The c.r.o. display is a graph of voltage (y axis) against time (x axis). The time base setting can be used to set the scale on the x axis. A setting of 10 ms/cm means that each centimetre represents a time of 10 milliseconds.

The diagram below shows the trace obtained on the c.r.o. when a particular sound is detected by the microphone. The time base setting in this case was 2 ms/cm.

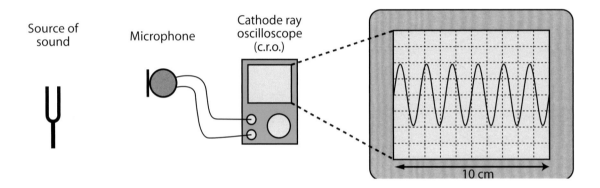

The screen displays 6 complete waves.

The x axis is 10 cm long so the total time displayed is 10 × 2 = 20 ms.

The period T of 1 wave = 20 ÷ 6

$\qquad\qquad\qquad\qquad$ = 3.33 ms = 0.0033 s

Frequency = $\dfrac{1}{T}$ = 1 ÷ 0.0033 = 333 Hz

Exercise 36

Determine the frequency of the sound waves displayed in the diagrams below. The time base setting on the c.r.o. is shown for each one.

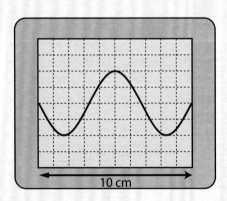

Time base setting = 1 ms/cm

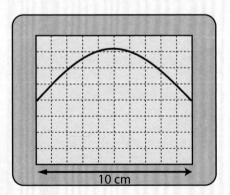

Timebase setting = 0.5 µs/cm

Measuring the speed of sound in air

Standing waves of sound in air provides a method of measuring the speed of sound in air.

Method 1 Using the fundamental mode

In this approach tuning forks of known frequencies are used to create standing waves. The tuning fork is made to vibrate and then held over the open end of a glass tube.

The glass tube is raised or lowered until the fundamental mode of vibration is produced. This is the shortest length of the air column at which the sound becomes noticeably louder. The length of the air column is measured.

This procedure is repeated for a number of tuning forks of different frequencies.

If you refer back to the previous chapter you will recall that in the fundamental mode of vibration the length of the air column L is ¼ of the wavelength of the sound.

Using this fact in the wave equation gives

$v = f\lambda$ and $\lambda = 4L$ so $v = 4Lf$

The variables are L and f

$$L = \frac{v}{4f}$$

The equation of a straight line passing through the origin is $y = mx$

A graph of L (y axis) against $\frac{1}{f}$ (x axis) yields a straight line.

The gradient of this line equals $\frac{v}{4}$. The measurements and graph from such an experiment are shown below.

Frequency of the tuning fork f/Hz	Length of the Air column L/m	$\frac{1}{f}$ /Hz⁻¹
512	0.165	1.95×10^{-3}
480	0.180	2.08×10^{-3}
362	0.235	2.76×10^{-3}
304	0.280	3.29×10^{-3}
256	0.335	3.91×10^{-3}

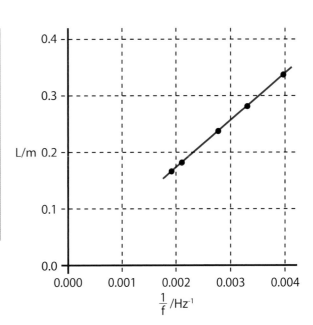

These measurements give a gradient of 86 ms⁻¹ so the speed of sound obtained is 344 ms⁻¹

Method 2 Using the 1ˢᵗ and 2ⁿᵈ positions of resonance

In this method one frequency is used. The fundamental mode of vibration is first found. This is the shortest length of the air column at which a loud sound is heard. The length L_1 of the air column is measured. This is also known as the 1ˢᵗ position of resonance. Using the same frequency the next shortest length at which a loud sound is heard is found. This is the 2ⁿᵈ position of resonance. The new length L_2 of the air column is measured.

$$L_1 = \tfrac{1}{4}\lambda \text{ and } L_2 = \tfrac{3}{4}\lambda \quad L_2 - L_1 = \tfrac{1}{2}\lambda$$

Using the wave equation $v = f\lambda$, the velocity v can be found since the frequency f is known. This method should be repeated for a number of frequencies and an average value for the velocity of sound calculated.

Exercise 37

1. A student holds a vibrating tuning fork of frequency 487 Hz above the open end of a resonance tube. She varies the length of the air column and finds the second position of resonance. The length of the air column for this position is 517 mm. Calculate the velocity of sound.

   [CCEA January 2003]

2. A student carries out an experiment to measure the speed of sound in air.

   (a) First he finds the frequency of a note emitted by a vibrating tuning fork.
   He holds the fork near a microphone connected to a cathode ray oscilloscope (c.r.o.). The trace on the screen of the c.r.o. is shown below.

   The time base control of the c.r.o. for this trace is 0.50 ms cm⁻¹. The total width of the pattern is 140 mm.

   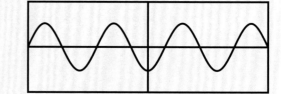

   Calculate the frequency of the note emitted by the fork.

   (b) The student then holds the vibrating tuning fork at the mouth of a resonance tube. He finds that the shortest length of air column which gives resonance is 169 mm.

   (i) Calculate the speed of sound in air in the resonance tube.

   (ii) The student then adjusts the resonance tube to find the next position of resonance. Sketch the pattern of standing waves in the resonance tube for this position of resonance.
   Mark the positions of any anti-nodes with the letter A and the positions of any nodes with the letter N.

   [CCEA June 2001]

Sound intensity level – decibel scale

Your ears pick up all the sounds around you and then translate this information into a form your brain can understand. The process is almost completely mechanical, the last part being a conversion of mechanical oscillations into electrical signals.

The auditory canal brings sound waves from outside the ear to the middle ear. At the end of the auditory canal, there is a thin layer of skin called the tympanic membrane (ear drum). The sound waves make the ear drum vibrate.

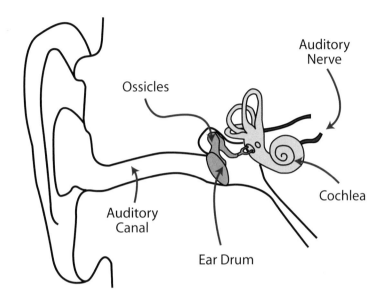

These vibrations are then transferred to the three small bones in the middle ear collectively known as the auditory ossicles: incus (anvil), stapes (stirrup), and malleus (hammer).

These structures act as a link bringing the vibrations to the fluid filled inner ear (cochlea). Finally the vibrations reach a bundle of 30,000 nerve fibres (cilia), each one responding to a different frequency. These vibrations are then converted to electrical signals allowing the brain to distinguish between sounds of different frequencies and different levels of loudness.

Sound loudness is a subjective quantity, i.e. it varies from person to person. Loudness describes the strength of the ear's perception of a sound. It is related to sound intensity but is not identical to intensity.

The intensity of sound is measured in joules per second per square metre, i.e. $Js^{-1}m^{-2}$. The unit of sound intensity is more usually stated as Wm^{-2}. Remember $1W = 1Js^{-1}$.

The lowest intensity of sound that the human ear can detect is called the threshold of hearing. This is 10^{-12} Wm^{-2}. The highest intensity, beyond which the ear may be damaged is around 100 Wm^{-2}.

Loudness is proportional to the logarithm of the intensity I.

Intensity level is defined in order to take into account this logarithmic response of the ear.

$$\text{Intensity level in dB} = 10 \, lg_{10}\left(\frac{I}{I_0}\right) \qquad \text{where } lg_{10} \text{ means logarithm to the base 10.}$$

Intensity levels are measured in decibels (dB).

Worked Example

Normal conversation has an intensity of 1×10^{-6} Wm^{-2}. Its intensity level is:

$$10 \log (10^{-6} \div 10^{-12}) = 10 \log (10^{6}) = 10 \times 6 = \textbf{60 dB}$$

Example 1

At a certain point, the intensity of a sound produced by a loudspeaker is 5.0×10^{-2} Wm^{-2}. The output from the speaker is reduced so that the intensity level at the same point falls by 6.0 dB. What is the new sound intensity at this point?

Solution

At 5×10^{-2} Wm^{-2} intensity level $= 10 \log (5 \times 10^{-2} \div 1 \times 10^{-12}) = 107$ dB
A reduction of 6 dB gives
$101 = 10 \log (I \div 1 \times 10^{-12})$
$\quad I = 1.26 \times 10^{-2}$ Wm^{-2}

Example 2

The intensity level in a classroom can range from 30 dB (rustle of paper) to 80 dB (all talking). What is this range as a ratio of intensities?

Solution

30 dB is equivelant to 1×10^{-9} Wm^{-2} 80 dB is equivelant to 1×10^{-4} Wm^{-2}

The ratio of all talking to rustle of paper is 1×10^{5}.

Frequency and intensity response of the human ear

The range of human hearing is from **20 Hz to 20 kHz.** Sound frequencies above 20 kHz are known as **ultrasound** sound. Infra sound applies to frequencies below 20 Hz.

The range of sound intensities that the human ear can cope with is very large and it varies with the frequency of the sound. The lowest intensity is the threshold of hearing and the highest (at which the sound becomes painful) is the threshold of pain.

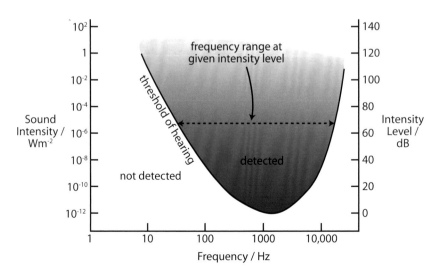

On the right hand side of the graph the intensity level is marked in dB.

The graph shows the intensity of the threshold of hearing at different frequencies. The threshold of hearing has its lowest intensity value at around 2000 Hz. The value is $1.0 \times 10^{-12} \, \text{Wm}^{-2}$.

The intensity level corresponding to this threshold of hearing is 0 dB.

At low frequencies the ear is very insensitive. The intensity of the threshold of hearing at 20 Hz is about 1 Wm^{-2}, a very loud sound. As the frequency increases, the **threshold of hearing** decreases, reaching a minimum at around 2 kHz. It then rises again.

Any sound with a frequency and an intensity or intensity level value that lies inside the shaded area will be heard. Any sound with a frequency and intensity or intensity level value falling in the white area will not be heard.

The width of the curve will give the range of frequencies that can be heard for a particular intensity or intensity level value.

Exercise 38

1 (a) (i) State the range of frequency of sound to which the normal human ear responds.

   (ii) Sketch a graph to show the variation with frequency (x axis) of the minimum audible intensity I_{min} (y axis)for the normal human ear. Indicate by shading the region corresponding to sound which can be heard.
   Your graph should indicate appropriate values on both axes.

[CCEA June 2001]

2 The graph below shows the intensity level response with frequency of the average ear. Note that the frequency scale is logarithmic.

   (a) What is the physical meaning of the fact that the graph shows a minimum?

   (b) Use the graph to obtain approximate values of the intensity level of the threshold of hearing and the frequency at the minimum.

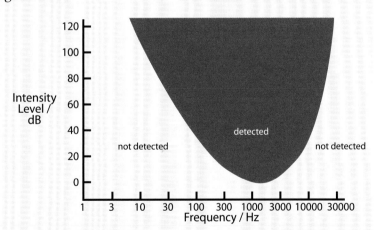

   (c) Music is being played on a CD player, producing sounds at an intensity level of 20 dB. Use the graph to deduce the approximate limits of the frequency range of the music that is heard.

   (d) An electronic circuit in the CD player is switched on, boosting the intensity level by 20 dB. State the difference this makes to the music heard.

[CCEA June 2004]

2.7 Imaging Techniques

You should be able to:

2.7.1   Describe the flexible endoscope in terms of structure, technique and applications

2.7.2   Describe ultrasonic A scans and B scans in terms of physical principles, basic equipment, technique and applications

2.7.3   Describe CT scans in terms of physical principles, basic equipment, technique and applications

2.7.4   Describe MRI scans in terms of physical principles, basic equipment, technique and applications

Medical imaging is the use of a range of techniques to examine structures within the human body without having to resort to surgery to carry out the examination. In some instances the use of imaging technique may provide information that visual inspection cannot.

Endoscopy

An endoscope is a flexible tube that allows us to look into the body. In many cases there is no need to perform surgery to do this. In other cases, a small incision is required to perform what has become known as key-hole surgery. The development of optical fibre in the 1960s allowed the construction of endoscopes that were both flexible and of small diameter.

When light travels from glass into air it is refracted away from the normal. However if the angle of incidence in the glass exceeds the critical angle c, then total internal reflection takes place. This allows light to travel along a glass tube as shown. If the glass tube is flexible, and the angles through which the glass fibre is bent are not too great, the light can be directed into body cavities.

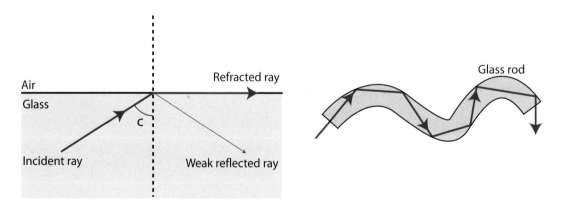

The endoscope has two bundles of optical fibres. One is called the illumination bundle and carries light to the object being viewed. The other bundle, the image bundle, carries back the reflected light. The optical fibres inside the image bundle are carefully arranged parallel to each other to create what is termed a coherent bundle.

The image is viewed or photographed through a magnifying eyepiece. In some instances a TV camera is attached and the image displayed on a monitor.

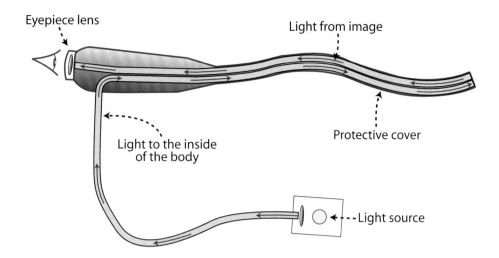

When inserted through the mouth, the endoscope can be used to view the gastrointestinal tract (oesophagus, stomach and duodenum). Alternatively, in the technique called laparoscopy, the endoscope is inserted through the wall of the abdomen to study the liver, spleen and other organs. The information obtained in this way provides direct and often very clear evidence of bleeding ulcers, constrictions, benign and malignant tumours and cirrhosis of the liver.

The endoscope also allows a range of minor surgical treatments. Forceps attached at the viewing end allows a surgeon to remove a sample of tissue (biopsy) for detailed analysis. Electrodes can be used to apply heat to stop bleeding. A range of extractors can be fitted and used to remove foreign objects from the throat or possibly drugs hidden in the lower bowel of smugglers.

Exercise 39

Optical imaging by means of a flexible fibre-optic endoscope is an important diagnostic tool in medicine. The endoscope may also be used for minor surgical procedures.

   (a) Draw a labelled diagram to show the important parts of a flexible fibre-optic endoscope.

   (b) The terms coherent and non-coherent (or incoherent) are applied to parts of the endoscope.

      (i) To which parts of the instrument do the terms apply?

      (ii) Explain the terms and their significance.

   (c) State one example of the use of the endoscope for a diagnostic purpose.

[CCEA June 2004]

Ultrasound

The range of human hearing is approximately 20 Hz to 20 kHz. Sound waves with a frequency greater than 20 kHz are called ultrasound. Ultrasound waves are longitudinal pressure waves. Typical diagnostic ultrasound frequencies used in medicine are in the range 1 MHz to 15 MHz.

Low intensity ultrasonic waves pass through tissue without causing harm, unlike X-rays which cause ionisation and damage cells. Ultrasonic waves are reflected at the boundaries between biological structures. These reflections allow images of internal organs to be created by an ultrasound scanner.

The ultrasound transducer probe generates and receives sound waves using a principle called the piezoelectric effect, which was discovered by Pierre and Jacques Curie in 1880. When a high frequency alternating voltage is applied to certain crystals, the crystals expand and contract when the voltage is applied. In other words the crystals vibrate at the same frequency as the applied alternating voltage. These changes of shape of the crystal, or vibrations, produce sound waves that travel outward. Crystals such as lead zirconate-lead titanate, or PZT for short, are commonly used.

The structure of a typical ultrasound transducer is shown below. The backing material is used to prevent the crystal oscillations continuing when the alternating voltage is removed. This ensures the pulse ends abruptly. A silver electrode attached to the piezoelectric crystal provides the electrical connection to the high frequency voltage supply.

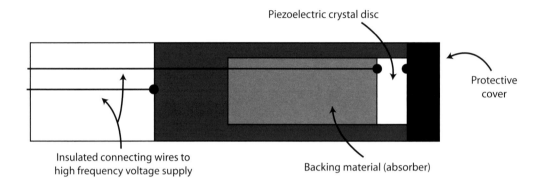

The ultrasound transducer also acts as a receiver of reflected ultrasound waves. The incoming waves distort the crystal's structure which generates a small electrical signal. To do this the ultrasound waves are emitted in short pulses that may last for only 5μs. There is then gap of perhaps 100 μs.

During the 100 μs the transducer is in receive mode – it receives reflected waves. These reflected waves are associated with pressure changes that cause changes in the shape of the piezoelectric crystal which produces an electrical voltage which is detected and processed by a computer system.

The diagram shows the timing for the ultrasound pulses.

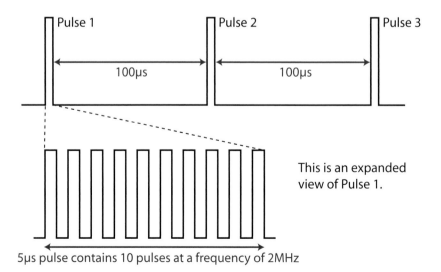

A Scan

The A in 'A scan' means amplitude. When used in this way a pulse of ultrasound is sent into the body and its reflection displayed in the manner shown below. The horizontal axis on the display represents time and the vertical axis represents the amplitude of the reflected wave.

In the diagram, an ultrasound scanner is being used to scan a foetus. The ultrasound waves are reflected from various structures within the womb and this method is commonly used to measure the diameter of the foetal head. The display shows a typical A-scan of a foetal head.

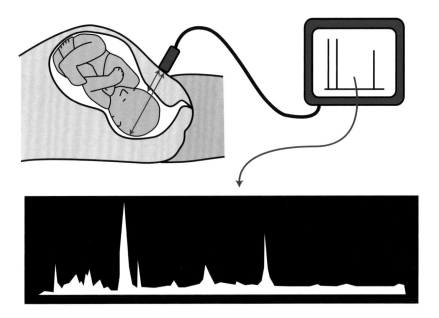

A measure of the diameter of the baby's head is an indicator of the age and the development of the foetus. The measure is based on the time interval between the peaks.

The diagram on the right shows a simplified version of an actual display. The vertical lines represent the echoes from two structures within the body. Speed of ultrasound in the body is around 1500 ms^{-1}.

This trace indicates that the separation of the two structures is:

$$\left(\frac{60\times10^{-6}}{2}\right) \times 1500 = 4.5\times10^{-3}\text{m (45mm)}$$

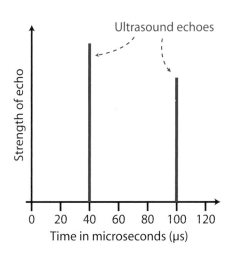

B Scan

The B in 'B scan' means brightness. The B scan produces an image that is easier to interpret. The ultrasound probe is scanned across the body in a series of lines. The strength and position of the reflected ultrasound is stored electronically. The data stored is then used to produce an image on a TV screen. The strength of the signal is used to determine the brightness of the spot on the screen.

B scans can identify tumours in the liver and other organs, but the most common use is to monitor foetal development.

Below is a B scan of a section of a foetus.

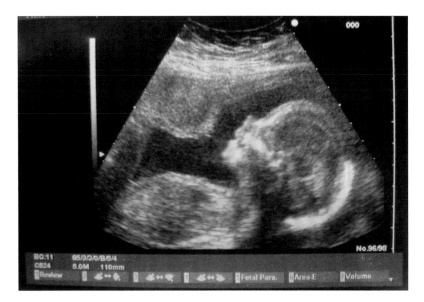

Ultrasound waves are strongly reflected at the air–skin boundary. To overcome this problem a water based cellulose jelly is smeared on the skin. This jelly acts as a coupling agent to ensure that most of the ultrasound enters the body.

Resolution

The image of an object in the body is made up of reflections from small pieces of tissue. Diffraction takes place when waves are scattered or reflected by small objects. If the object is small, a lot of diffraction will take place and the image will lack clarity, i.e. small details will be lost in the final image. As a general rule, ultrasound will resolve details of the same size as the wavelength of the ultrasound.

This means that if we need to resolve details of around 1 mm, then the ultrasound must have a wavelength equal to or smaller than 1 mm. Diagnostic ultrasound uses frequencies in the range 1 to 15 MHz and can resolve details as small as 0.1 mm.

Dangers of Ultrasound

Ultrasound waves carry energy. Some of it is absorbed in tissue and this causes heating. Bones are particularly energy absorbent. At some frequencies, small objects in the body could resonate and literally be shaken to pieces. This is actually used in the treatment of kidney stones when ultrasound is used to break up the stones into small pieces that are passed out of the body in the urine.

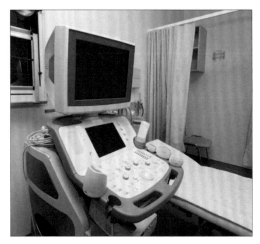

Ultrasound can also cause cavitation. This is the production of small gas bubbles which absorb energy, expand and may damage surrounding tissue. However, the effect can also be used to promote wound healing and the repair of broken bones.

A typical ultrasound machine.

Computed Tomography or CT Scanning

Computed tomography (CT) imaging, also known as 'CAT scanning' (Computed axial tomography), was developed in the early to mid 1970s. CT has the unique ability to image a combination of soft tissue, bone, and blood vessels. Today CT enables the diagnosis of a wide range of illness and combines the use of a digital computer with a rotating X-ray device to create detailed cross sectional images or 'slices' of the different organs and body parts such as the lungs, liver, kidneys, brain, spine, and blood vessels.

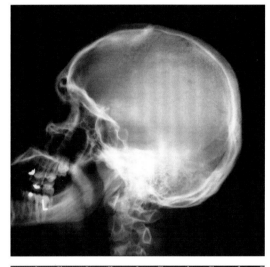

A conventional X-ray image of the head (on the right) can show only the dense bone structures of the skull. CT images (overleaf) allow us to see soft-tissue structures like the valves of the heart or grey and white matter in the brain.

CT is an invaluable tool in the cancer diagnosis process and is often the preferred method for diagnosing lung, liver and pancreas cancer.

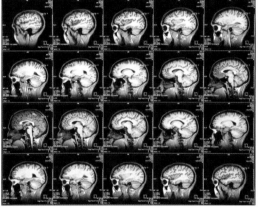

CT imaging has a role in the detection, diagnosis and treatment of heart disease, acute stroke and vascular diseases which can lead to stroke. Additionally, CT can be used to measure bone mineral density for the detection of osteoporosis.

CT has excellent application in trauma cases and other emergencies. All dedicated trauma departments have a CT scanner so patients can be scanned immediately to look for major internal injuries such as internal bleeding.

CT is used extensively for diagnosing problems of the inner ears and sinuses because of its ability to generate very high resolution images. The anatomy of the inner ear and sinuses is made up of delicate soft tissue structures and very fine bones. CT is excellent for imaging tumors or polyps in the sinuses and diseases that cause degeneration of the small bones in the inner ear.

Unlike other medical imaging techniques, such as conventional X-ray imaging (radiography), CT enables direct imaging and shows the differences within soft tissue structures, such as liver, lung tissue, and fat. CT imaging of the head and brain can detect tumors, show blood clots and blood vessel defects. Due to the short scan times (500 milliseconds to a few seconds), CT can be used for all regions of the body, including where the body is in motion, such as breathing.

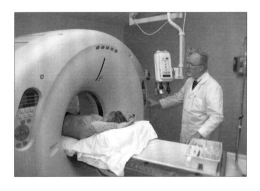

How is CT scanning carried out?

During the scan the patient lies on a bed, with the body part under examination placed in the round tunnel or opening of the scanner. The bed then moves slowly backwards and forwards to allow the scanner to take pictures of the body, although it does not touch the patient. The length of the test depends on the number of pictures and the different angles taken.

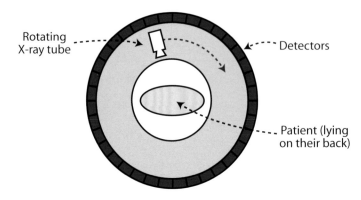

The X-ray tube is rotated around the patient. There is a large number of detectors on a complete circle around the patient. This means that a complete scan can be completed in less than 5 seconds. This is much safer for the patient and it is less likely that the image will be affected by the patient moving. The computer is able to reconstruct the structures within the body from the detector signal using sophisticated software.

Disadvantages of CT scanning

Computed tomography is considerably more expensive than conventional radiography. As a rough guide, a chest X-ray might cost £10-£25 whereas a computed tomogram of the chest could cost £50 to £150.

Secondly, the X-ray dose from computed tomography is much larger than for conventional radiography. During computed tomography of the chest the patient receives the equivalent dose to that from 100 chest radiographs.

Another factor to consider is patient preparation. For scans of the abdomen patients often have to drink several large cupfuls of contrast agent about an hour before scanning. The contrast agent has a high density so in the scan the entire bowel is highlighted in white and readily distinguished from possible intra-abdominal masses. Because of the large X-ray dose from computed tomography other methods are always considered before computed tomography is carried out on children as they are particularly sensitive to radiation.

Exercise 40

1 (a) Write a brief account of the use of the CT X-ray scanner in medical imaging.
     In your answer you should refer to:
    (i) the principle of the CT scanner;
    (ii) the major difference between the way in which the information is handled in a CT scanner and in a conventional X-ray photograph;
    (iii) a principal advantage of the CT scan.   [CCEA June 2001]

2 (a) Outline the difference in procedure employed using conventional X-ray technique and that employed in a CT scan.
   (b) State the difference between the images obtained by the two methods above.
                                                                                  [CCEA June 2002]

How are X-rays Produced?

X-rays are produced by high speed electrons striking metal targets. The electrons are emitted by a **cathode** which is heated to a very high temperature (white heat). This heating is produced by an electric current passing through the cathode. The electrons are then accelerated toward a metal **anode** using a very high voltage (typically 100 kV).

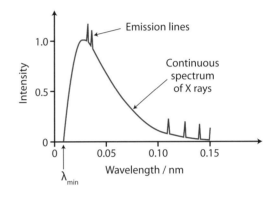

At the centre of the anode is a metal target. This target is made of metal of a high melting point and high atomic number. Around **0.5%** of the electrons produce **X-rays,** the other 99.5% simply heat the anode. The anode therefore needs to be constantly cooled. In the case of the rotating anode tube shown above this is achieved by conduction, convection and radiation.

The diagram opposite shows a typical X-ray spectrum. There are three characteristics that must be understood.

1. The Continuous Spectrum

When the high speed electrons encounter the atoms of the target material they are slowed by the attraction of the positively charged nucleus. The energy lost by the electron appears as an X-ray photon. The electrons lose varying amounts of energy so X-rays photons of different energy (wavelength, frequency) are produced. This type of X-ray production is known as **braking radiation** as shown in the diagram.

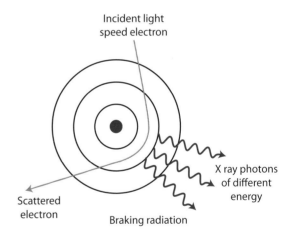

2. The Minimum Wavelength λ_{min}

Some high speed electrons lose all of their kinetic energy in a single encounter with the atoms of the target material. This produces an X-ray photon with maximum energy (minimum wavelength or maximum frequency). The value of λ_{min} can be calculated.

The kinetic energy of the electron = loss of electric potential energy = eV
where e is charge of the electron
         V is the tube voltage

The energy of this X-ray photon = $\dfrac{hc}{\lambda_{min}}$ = eV.

3. The Sharp Emission Lines

These are characteristic of the element used as the target. These elements have high atomic numbers and consequently the electron shells are generally filled with the total complement of electrons. An incoming electron will knock an electron out of these filled electrons shells, as shown in the diagram. The vacancy left is immediately filled by a electron from a higher energy shell dropping down to a lower energy shell. It loses its energy as an X-ray of very specific energy or wavelength.

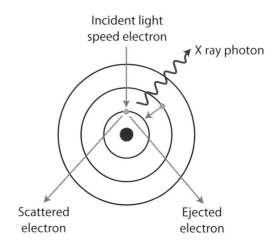

Magnetic Resonance Imaging (MRI)

The basis for this technique is Nuclear Magnetic Resonance or NMR. Although it involves the nuclei of atoms the only radiation involved is that of radio signals.

The nucleus of some atoms spin. This spinning positive electric charge creates a magnetic field. You can think of the spinning nuclei as subatomic bar magnets. When no magnetic field is present the nuclei are randomly orientated but when placed in a magnetic field they line up with the magnetic field.

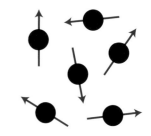

Some of the nuclei become aligned in the same direction as the magnetic field and some become aligned in the opposite direction to the magnetic field. This means there are two spin states for the nuclei, those nuclei that become lined up with the magnetic field are in the lower energy state. Those nuclei that have become aligned in direction opposite to the magnetic field are in the higher of the two energy states.

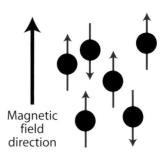

However, the picture is a little more complicated. The spinning nuclei, because of thermal motion, wobble about the axis of rotation. This effect is called precession. The frequency at which they wobble is known as the Larmour frequency. If an electromagnetic radio frequency pulse is applied at this frequency, then the nuclei can absorb that energy. This results in the nuclei in the lower energy state jumping to the higher energy state and they are now aligned in a direction opposite to that of the magnetic field direction.

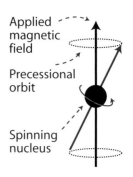

When the pulse of radio waves is stopped, the nuclei return to the lower energy state and as they do they re-emit the radio wave they absorbed. It is this re-emitted radio wave that is detected and processed to provide information on tissues in the body.

For example, in the case of hydrogen atoms in a magnetic field of strength 1.41 T the frequency of the electromagnetic radiation required is around 60 MHz. This lies in the radio frequency region of the electromagnetic spectrum. For example, BBC Radio 1 uses a frequency, in Northern Ireland, of 97.7 MHz.

Hydrogen ($_1^1$H) nuclei are not the only nuclei that spin, deuterium ($_1^2$H), carbon ($_6^{13}$H), nitrogen ($_7^{14}$N) and oxygen ($_8^{17}$O) are also nuclei that spin. Each of these nuclei requires a different radio frequency to make them flip from the lower energy state to the higher. Hydrogen, because of its abundance in human tissues, is the nucleus used in MRI imaging.

Similar atoms in different environments, such as a hydrogen attached to an oxygen and a hydrogen attached to a carbon, flip at different frequencies. This provides us with a means of discriminating between different soft tissues in the body. X-rays are of limited use in this respect.

How MRI is carried out on a patient

The photograph shows a typical MRI imaging system. The patient is placed inside the coil as shown. Surrounding the patient is the magnetic field produced by a super conducting magnet. The patient is placed on the table which is then slid inside the large cavity which contains the magnetic field and radio coils.

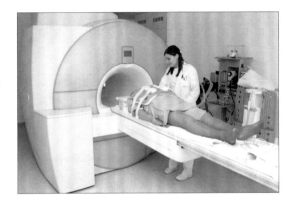

A pulse of radio waves is emitted by the coils surrounding the patient. This causes the hydrogen nuclei to flip to the higher energy state. The radio waves are then switched off and as the hydrogen nuclei return to the lower energy state they emit radio signals. These radio signals are detected and with use of computers are processed to provide a display of the tissues in the body.

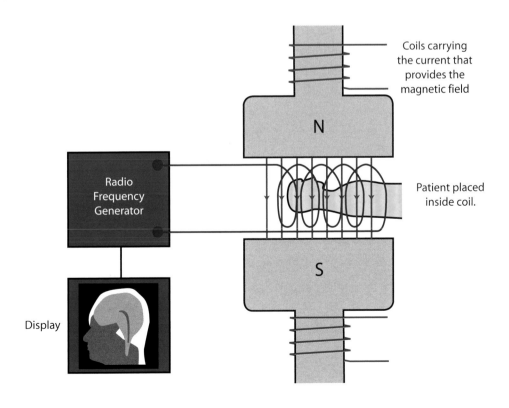

Some examples of the images of the body obtained using MRI are shown below.

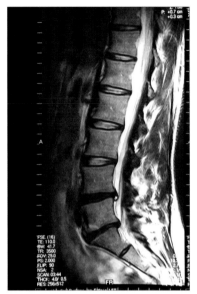
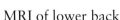

MRI of lower back

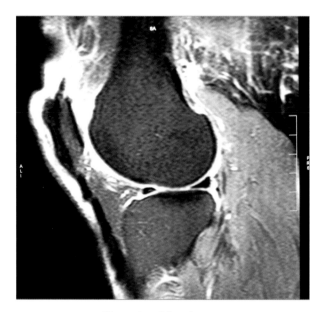

Knee in side view

The magnetic field is very strong, typically between 0.1 and 4 T and some concern has been expressed about the potential effects such strong magnetic fields have on tissues. Many studies have been carried on the subject and presently the evidence indicates there are no adverse effects from such magnetic fields.

More serious is the effect such a magnetic field has on objects made of iron or steel. Such objects are turned into projectiles by such a strong magnetic field and any tools kept in the vicinity of the MRI laboratory must be made of non magnetic materials. Everyday objects such as keys, pens, belts and metals studs or buttons on clothing are not permitted in the MRI facility.

The strong magnetic field is produced by currents flowing in superconducting alloys. However these alloys have to be cooled to -269 °C by immersing them in liquid helium. This is expensive and is a major running cost in the use of MRI.

Exercise 41

Magnetic Resonance Imaging (MRI) is a recent development in medical imaging.

Briefly compare the MRI technique with that of CT scanning.

In your answer you should refer to

    (i)   the major advantage of MRI over the CT scan;

    (ii) two disadvantages of MRI scanning as an imaging technique;

    (iii) one precaution which must be taken when a patient is given an MRI scan.

Summary of imaging techniques

Technique	Advantages	Disadvantages	Most suited to
Endoscopy	Removes the need for major surgery. Does not expose the patient to ionising radiation.	Can be an uncomfortable experience for the patient.	It is mostly used to diagnose problems in the oesophagus, stomach and intestines. Can be used to take a small sample of tissue for analysis (biopsy). Laparascopy is an extension of the technique where the endoscope is used to look inside the abdomen and pelvis through a small incision. Endoscopic (keyhole) surgery can be used to treat hernias and remove tumours.
Ultrasound	It is thought to be safe as it doesn't use an ionising radiation.	Limited in its ability to see very fine detail.	Detecting cysts, which are pockets of fluid in the liver, ovaries and breasts. Used to identify gallstones and kidney stones. Commonly used during pregnancy to check on the development of the foetus. Useful in diagnosing blockages in blood vessels.
CT scanning	Takes a relatively short time to complete.	The radiation dose is about 100 times that of standard chest X-ray.	Useful for diagnosing internal injuries in trauma victims such as those involved in a car crash. CT scans are used to show a range of very different tissues clearly such as lung, bone, soft tissue and blood vessels.
M R I	Is based on the detection of radio waves and not ionising radiation. Requires strong magnetic field which is though to be safe. Can produce images that allow very fine detail to be seen.	The strong magnetic field requires special safety measures with regards to metal objects. A scan can takes up to 20 minutes. The changing magnetic field can be noisy and frightening to patients.	Can be used to identify tumours. Can identify multiple sclerosis. Often used on athletes to identify ligament damage and problems in the knee and other joints. Used to examine the anatomy of the brain and how it works. MRI can reveal the small differences between tissues that are very similar.

2.8 Photon Model

You should be able to:

2.8.1   Recall and use the formula E = hf

2.8.2   Use the photon model to explain the photoelectric effect qualitatively using the terms 'photon energy' and work function.

In photoelectric emission, electrons are ejected from the surface of a metal when electromagnetic radiation of sufficiently high frequency falls on it. The electrons emitted by this process are called photoelectrons. The effect was first discovered by Hertz in 1887. However, a full explanation was not given until Einstein published his famous paper in 1905. It was for his explanation of the photoelectric effect that Einstein was later to receive his Nobel Prize.

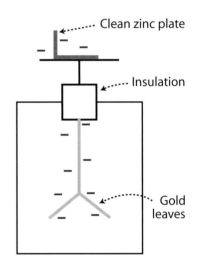

The effect can be readily demonstrated with a gold leaf electroscope. The experiment uses the fact that zinc metal emits electrons when exposed to ultraviolet light.

When the electroscope is negatively charged, by momentarily connecting the metal cap of the electroscope to the negative terminal of a high voltage supply (eg 300 V), the leaves diverge due to the electrostatic repulsion between them.

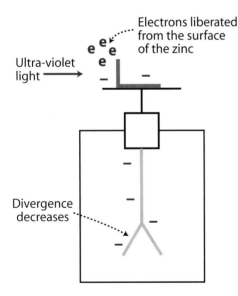

The clean zinc strip is then illuminated with ultraviolet light, and it is observed that the divergence of the leaves becomes less. The zinc is losing electrons due to the ultra-violet light, so the excess of electrons that we started of with is decreasing.

A sheet of glass inserted between the source of the ultra-violet light and the zinc will stop this collapse of the leaves. Glass absorbs ultra-violet light. When the glass is removed the collapse of the leaves continues.

To explain interference of light we used the wave theory. Wave theory considered radiation to be emitted continuously in waves. To explain the photoelectric effect we need to use the **photon** model of light. In this model we regard light as packets or **quanta** (singular: **quantum**) of energy. The energy of a quantum or photon of light depends on the frequency of the radiation.

According to Max Planck, the energy E of the quantum of radiation (photon) of frequency f is given by:

$$E = hf$$

where E = energy of the photon in J
h = Planck's constant 6.63×10^{-34} Js
f = frequency of the radiation in Hz

Einstein assumed that not only were light and other forms of electromagnetic radiation emitted in whole numbers of photons, but that they were also absorbed as photons. But first, we need to define what physicists call the work function of a metal.

Work function Φ is defined as the minimum quantity of energy needed to liberate electrons from the surface of a metal and to just allow it to escape to an infinite distance from the metal. Einstein proposed that a photon of energy will cause the emission of an electron from the metal if the energy of the photon is equal to or greater than the work function of the metal.

If the photon's energy is greater than the work function of the metal then the difference appears as kinetic energy of the ejected electron. Since the work function is the minimum energy needed to eject an electron from the metal this means that the electrons that are ejected have a range of kinetic energy from zero to a maximum.

$$hf - \Phi = \frac{1}{2}mv^2_{max}$$

The above is known as **Einstein's Photoelectric Equation.**

The frequency of electromagnetic radiation that just liberates electrons from a metal is known as the threshold frequency f_0. The photons of this frequency have energy equal to the work function of the metal.

$$hf_0 = \Phi$$

The Electron-Volt (eV)

The kinetic energy of a photo electron, the work function and the energy of a photon can all be measured in joules (J). However the electron-volt (eV) is often used as an alternative unit for energy when dealing with these quantities.

The work function is measured in joules or electron-volts. An electron-volt (eV) is defined as the energy an electron gains or loses when it moves through a potential difference of 1 volt.

$$1 \text{ eV} = 1.6 \times 10^{-19} \text{ J}$$

Worked example

A strip of magnesium ribbon in an evacuated chamber is illuminated with monochromatic light of wavelength 300 nm. The work function of magnesium is 2.8 eV. Calculate the following:

    (a) the photoelectric threshold frequency for magnesium;

    (b) the frequency and energy of a photon in the incident beam;

    (c) in what part of the electromagnetic spectrum radiation of wavelength 300 nm is found.

Solution

    (a) $\Phi = 2.8$ eV $= 2.8 \times 1.6 \times 10^{-19}$ J $= 4.48 \times 10^{-19}$ J
        $f_o = \Phi \div h = (4.48 \times 10^{-19}) \div 6.63 \times 10^{-34} = \mathbf{6.76 \times 10^{14}}$ **Hz**

    (b) $f = c \div \lambda = 3 \times 10^8 \div 300 \times 10^{-9} = \mathbf{1 \times 10^{15}}$ **Hz**
        $E = hf = 6.63 \times 10^{-34} \times 1 \times 10^{15} = \mathbf{6.63 \times 10^{-19}}$ **J**

    (c) Radiation of wavelength 300 nm is found in the **ultraviolet** region of the spectrum

Exercise 42

1 (a) What is a photon?

  (b) (i) The output power in a beam of a certain helium-neon laser, which emits light of photon energy 3.1×10^{-19} J, is measured as 0.70 mW. The laser beam is pointed at a nearby wall. How many photons arrive at the wall in one second?

    (ii) Calculate the range of photon energies corresponding to the spectrum of visible light, which extends from a wavelength of 400 nm (violet light) to one of 700 nm (red light). Give your answers in electron volts (eV).

  (c) Caesium has a work function of 1.90 eV.

    (i) Explain what is meant by work function. Suggest why different metals have different work functions.

    (ii) Calculate the maximum kinetic energy of the electrons emitted when a caesium surface is illuminated by violet light of wavelength 400 nm. (Make use of your answer to (b)(ii)). Find also the speed of these electrons.

    (iii) Explain whether or not photoelectric emission would occur if the caesium surface were illuminated by red light of wavelength 700 nm.

[CCEA February 1998]

2 (a) When describing the photoelectric effect a student writes the following:

    "In order to emit photons from a metal surface, incident electromagnetic radiation of wavelength greater than a certain threshold value must be used."

    Identify two important errors in this statement.

  (b) Calculate the energy of a photon of ultraviolet radiation of wavelength 250 nm.

3 (a) Define the work function of a metal surface.

(b) When photons with a frequency greater than the threshold are incident on a metal surface, electrons are emitted with a range of kinetic energies.

(i) Explain the requirement of a threshold frequency for emission.

(ii) Explain why the photoelectrons emitted have a range of kinetic energies.

(c) A metal surface has a work function of 2.1 eV. Photoelectrons are emitted when light of wavelength 420 nm is incident on the surface. Calculate the maximum speed of the electrons emitted.

[CCEA June 2005]

2.9 Quantum Physics

You should be able to:

2.9.1   Understand that electrons exist in energy levels in atoms.

2.9.2   Recall and use the formula $hf = E_1 - E_2$.

2.9.3   Provide a simple explanation of laser action.

When sunlight is made to pass through a triangular glass prism, a spectrum is obtained. We observe a range of colours which gradually changes from deep red through orange to yellow and so on to violet. There are no sudden changes of colour and no gaps. Between the limits of red light and violet light all possible colours and hence all possible wavelengths are present. We call such a spectrum **continuous**. We can also obtain a continuous spectrum from hot filament lamps.

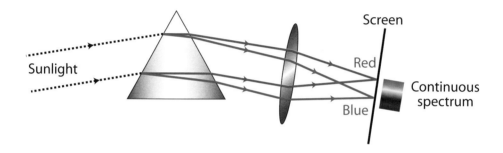

However, when we look at the light from a gas discharge lamp containing a gaseous element such as sodium vapour or neon, we obtain a very limited range of wavelengths indeed, for example:

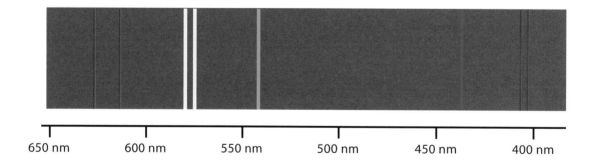

Why do elements like sodium give an emission spectrum consisting of a series of discrete wavelengths? In the early years of the twentieth century physicists simply had no answer as to why this should be so.

Niels Bohr, a Danish physicist and friend of Albert Einstein, made a remarkable suggestion to explain atomic line spectra. Bohr's idea was that electrons in atoms could orbit the nucleus only in certain allowed circular paths.

An electron has a fixed amount of energy in each orbit, those being closest to the nucleus having the least energy and those most distant from the nucleus having the most energy. Each orbit therefore had an energy level associated with it. Electrons orbiting a nucleus are in bound states and must acquire a minimum quantity of energy to break free from the attraction of the nucleus.

An electron at an infinite separation from the nucleus was considered to have zero energy. The energy of the electrons in the bound states was therefore considered to be negative. When all the electrons in an atom have the lowest possible energy, then that atom is said to be in its ground state.

Bohr argued that an electron could move from one energy level to a higher energy level by absorbing a photon of energy equal to the energy difference between the two states. This process is called **excitation**. As a result, the electron moves to an unstable, higher energy state and the exciting photon ceases to exist.

Similarly, if an electron in an excited state moved from a high energy level to a vacant lower energy level, a photon of light of energy exactly equal to the energy difference between the two states would be emitted. This process is called **relaxation**.

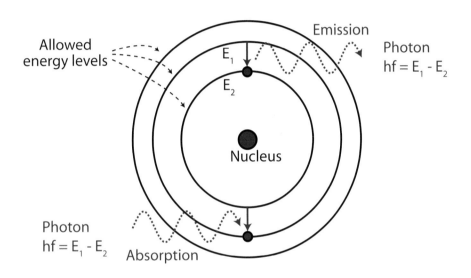

For both excitation and relaxation the same equation is true:

$$\Delta E = hf$$

where ΔE = energy difference between the two levels (J)

h = Planck's constant = 6.63×10^{-34} Js

f = the frequency of the photon emitted or absorbed (Hz)

You should appreciate that the equation above is an example of the principle of conservation of energy in a form that applies to electron transitions between orbits.

The diagram overleaf is called an energy level diagram and it shows the main electron transitions in hydrogen. The lowest energy level or ground state has value of –13.6 eV. Higher energy levels are less negative, –3.4 eV, –1.5 eV and so on. The difference between the energy levels gradually becomes smaller as the energy of each level increases. There are an infinite number of energy levels.

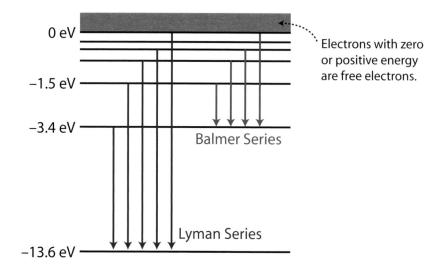

0 eV

Electrons with zero
or positive energy
are free electrons.

−1.5 eV

−3.4 eV

Balmer Series

Lyman Series

−13.6 eV

Lyman series

The longest wavelength in this series corresponds to a photon with minimum energy.

This photon is emitted when the electron moves from level with energy −3.4 eV to the ground state level with energy −13.6 eV.

The energy of the emitted photon = 13.6 − 3.4 = 10.2 eV = 1.63 × 10⁻¹⁸ J = hf or $\frac{hc}{\lambda}$.

This gives a frequency of 2.46 × 10¹⁵ Hz and a wavelength of 121.9 nm.

The shortest wavelength in this series corresponds to a photon with maximum energy.

This photon is emitted when the electron moves from an energy of 0 to the ground state level of energy −13.6 eV.

The energy of the emitted photon = 13.6 − 0 = 13.6 eV = 2.18 × 10⁻¹⁸ J = hf or $\frac{hc}{\lambda}$.

This gives a frequency of 3.29 × 10¹⁵ Hz and a wavelength of 91.2 nm.

Balmer series

Performing an analysis similar to that used for the Lyman series gives the following:

The longest wavelength photon has an energy of 1.9 eV, frequency = 4.59 × 10¹⁴ Hz and wavelength = 654 nm (red).

The shortest wavelength photon has an energy of 3.4 eV, frequency = 8.21 × 10¹⁴ Hz and wavelength = 365 nm (UV).

Exercise 43

1 (a) The hydrogen atom possesses discrete energy levels. Explain the meaning of this statement. Describe the experimental evidence that supports it, making clear the link to energy levels.

(b) High intensity, monochromatic, electromagnetic radiation is incident on atoms of hydrogen in a container. However, the electrons in the atoms do not become excited. Suggest how this may be possible.

(c) The diagram below shows some of the energy levels of an isolated hydrogen atom. The diagram is not to scale.

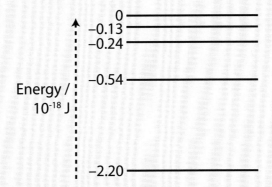

Identify the electron transition which would result in the emission of a photon with the longest possible wavelength for this set of levels. State clearly the direction of such a transition.

(d) Calculate the wavelength of the photon in (c).

[CCEA January 2004]

2 The diagram below shows a simplified energy level diagram for the hydrogen atom. The diagram includes the ground state.

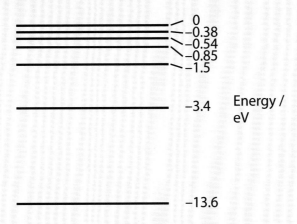

(a) Identify the ground state of the hydrogen atom. Explain what the term ground state means.

(b) The longest wavelength in the visible emission spectrum of hydrogen was measured as 654 nm.

Make a calculation to indicate the energy levels between which an electron transition would result in the emission of a photon of this wavelength.

[CCEA June 2005]

Laser action

Lasers were first invented in the late 1950s and today we see lasers being used almost everywhere. You will find a laser in every CD player and DVD player. But they are also used by surgeons to arrest bleeding, by metal workers to cut through metal, by tradesmen to obtain a 'level' during construction and by teachers and lectures in optical pointers.

The photons emitted by a laser are coherent, they have the same wavelength and they are in exactly the same phase (or more accurately, they maintain exactly the same phase difference all the time).

Stimulated emission is extremely unlikely to occur in nature. This is because there are normally many more electrons in the ground state than in any excited state. The length of time an electron spends in an excited state is typically 10^{-8} s. It then makes a transition to a lower energy level and a photon of light is emitted. This is a random process and is called spontaneous emission.

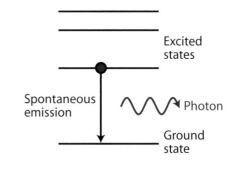

We need to arrange things so that there are more electrons in the excited state than in the ground state. This is called a **population inversion**. Some excited energy levels allow the electrons to spend a longer time in them. These are called metastable levels and the time spent can be around 10^{-3} s. This is 100 000 times longer than normal. This gives us time to have more electrons in this excited state than in the ground state.

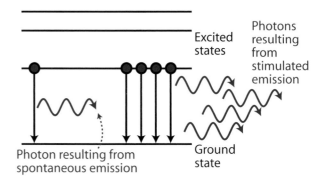

However electrons in a metastable excited state can be induced to make a transition by the presence of a photon of energy equal to the difference between the levels. This is known as stimulated emission. This 'inducing' photon results from spontaneous emission.

The helium-neon laser is commonly found in schools but can still be dangerous and looking into the laser beam is to be avoided. A 1mW He-Ne laser has a brightness equal to sunshine on a clear day and is just as dangerous to stare at directly.

2.10 Wave – Particle Duality

One of the amazing success stories of 19th century physics was the development of the wave theory of light. It was used to deepen our understanding of the transmission of light, of reflection and refraction, of dispersion and, most spectacularly, of interference and diffraction. Moreover, the realisation that light could be polarised seemed to prove beyond doubt that light was not only a wave, but that it was a transverse wave.

It came as a shock when Einstein demonstrated conclusively that an explanation of the photoelectric effect required us to consider light as a stream of particles or photons. Einstein explained the observations associated with the photoelectric effect using the idea that light and other forms of electromagnetic radiation were both emitted in whole numbers of quanta and absorbed as quanta. A quantum is a discrete amount of energy. The energy of a quantum (photon) of electromagnetic radiation is given by $E = hf$ or $E = \dfrac{hc}{\lambda}$

This implied that electromagnetic radiation could exhibit particle-like behaviour when being emitted or absorbed and led to the idea that light has a dual nature. In some circumstances it appears to behave as waves (reflection, refraction, diffraction, interference and polarisation) and in others as particles (photoelectric effect, line emission).

Therefore to explain some aspects of light behavior, such as interference and diffraction, it is treated as a wave. To explain other aspects it is treated as being made up of particles. Light exhibits wave-particle duality, because it exhibits properties of both waves and particles.

Phenomenon	Can be explained in terms of waves	Can be explained in terms of photons
Interference of light	Yes	No
Diffraction of light	Yes	No
Polarisation of light	Yes	No
Photoelectric effect	No	Yes

Electron diffraction

The wave-particle nature of light caused some physicists to consider if matter (beams of particles) could exhibit wave-like properties. In 1924, Louis de Broglie (pronounced de Broy), having considered the particle-wave duality of light, presented a thesis suggesting that matter might also have a dual nature. The proposal was that a particle, having a momentum p, has an associated wavelength λ, given by:

$$\lambda = \frac{h}{p}$$

where λ = de Broglie wavelength (m)
    h = Planck's constant (6.63×10^{-34} Js)
    p = momentum of the particle (kg ms^{-1})

De Broglie's suggestion that electrons with momentum possessed an associated wavelength was followed up by two enterprising physicists called Davisson and Germer. In 1926 they succeeded in obtaining a circular diffraction pattern using electrons and a nickel crystal.

Calculations show that if electrons were accelerated through 100 V then their momentum would indicate a wavelength of around 10^{-10} m. This is the distance between atoms and so it might be possible to use the layers of atoms in a crystal to produce diffraction and interference effects.

This can be demonstrated using the apparatus shown below. This shows how a crystal of graphite can be used to produce interference of electrons in a beam. Where lots of electrons reach the fluorescent screen a bright ring is seen. This is a region of constructive interference. The absence of light from the screen indicates a region of destructive interference: few electrons reach the screen.

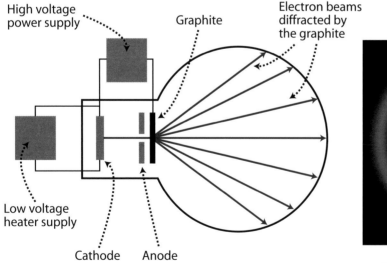

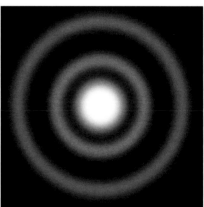

Electron diffraction rings
seen on the fluorescent screen

It appears that wave-particle duality is not confined to light. Everything exhibits wave-particle duality, from electrons to golf balls. The behavior of relatively large objects, like a golf ball, is dominated by their particle nature, but to explain the behavior of very small things like electrons, both the wave properties and particle properties have to be considered. The experiment discussed above shows that electrons exhibit the same kind of interference pattern as light does when it passes through a double slit (Young's experiment).

If the accelerating voltage is increased, the speed of the diffracting electrons (and hence their momentum) also increases. The rings then become narrower and have a smaller radius, showing that the wavelengths of the electron waves decrease with increasing momentum.

Why then do we not observe other moving objects such as cars, trains and buses displaying wave-like properties? The answer is that their mass (and hence their momentum) is so large and Planck's constant is so small, that the wavelength of these objects is much too small to produce observable interference and diffraction effects.

Exercise 44

1 Describe an experiment to demonstrate the wave aspect of an electron beam.
  Your answer should include:

  (a) a labelled diagram of the apparatus;

  (b) a description of what is observed;

  (c) a full explanation of how the observations demonstrate the wave-like behaviour of the electron beam.

  [CCEA January 2003]

2 (a) State what is meant by wave-particle duality as applied to electromagnetic radiation.

  (b) The fact that light can be polarised is regarded as conclusive evidence for the wave aspect of wave-particle duality.

   (i) Describe what is meant by polarised light.

   (ii) Describe how you would test whether a beam of light was polarised.

  (c) Wave-particle duality applies to situations other than electromagnetic radiation.

   Make an appropriate calculation to decide whether the wave aspect of duality is relevant in describing the behaviour of a minibus of mass 5100 kg travelling at a speed of 13 ms^{-1} (29 mph).

  [CCEA June 2004]

Unit AS 3: Practical Techniques

3.1 Measuring

The correct use of common school laboratory apparatus is described in the pages that follow. Physics relies on accurate measurements of physical quantities such as mass, length, time and temperature. To improve the accuracy and precision of such measurements instruments such as metre rules, vernier callipers, stop clocks and thermometers are used.

It is important that you know how to use these devices properly. In measuring any quantity there is always some degree of uncertainty. Appreciation of the uncertainty associated with each measuring instrument is equally important.

Measuring length

Using a metre rule

Although this may be one of the simplest length measuring instruments to be found in a school laboratory, care must be taken with its use to avoid errors.

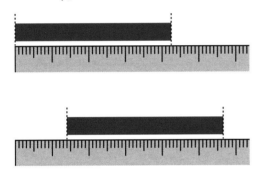

This is bad practice. The end of the metre rule may be worn giving rise to a zero error and an inaccurate measurement of the length.

It is good practice to place the metre rule against the object so that you have two readings to take and subtracting them will give you the length of the object. It avoids a zero error in the measurement. Of course the measurement of length still has an uncertainty associated with it.

The smallest division on the metre is usually 1 mm. If we say that each reading of the metre rule has an uncertainty of ± 0.5 mm then subtracting the two readings to obtain the length has an associated uncertainty of ± 1 mm.

For example, if the two readings are 14.0 cm and 56.5 cm the length is 42.5 cm and if we quote the length with the associated uncertainty then we would write this as (42.5 ± 0.1) cm i.e. an uncertainty in the length of about 0.25%.

For lengths greater than 1 m it is better to use a tape measure, with 1 mm divisions. Tape measures can be used to measure distances up to several hundred metres with good accuracy.

Parallax error

Parallax error occurs when any scale is not viewed at right angles as shown. Failure to view the scale at right angles will give a reading which is either too high or too low.

Having the scale of the metre rule as close as possible to the object will reduce the possibility of a parallax error.

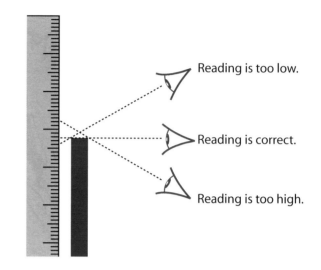

Reading is too low.

Reading is correct.

Reading is too high.

The object to be measured is too far from the scale increasing the possibility of parallax error.

Moving the object closer to the scale as shown is good practice since it reduces the possibility of parallax error.

Vernier Calliper

The Vernier Calliper is a precision instrument that can be used to measure internal and external distances extremely accurately. The example shown below is a manual calliper. Measurements are interpreted from the scale by the user.

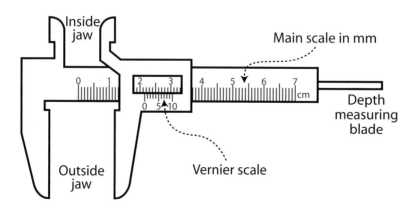

The internal jaws can be used measure the internal diameter of a tube, the external jaws can be used to measure the external diameter of the tube or the width of a block. The depth measuring blade can be used to measure the depth of, say, a hole drilled in a metal bar.

The calliper in the diagram below can read to ± **0.1 mm**. To take the reading you should follow the two steps shown.

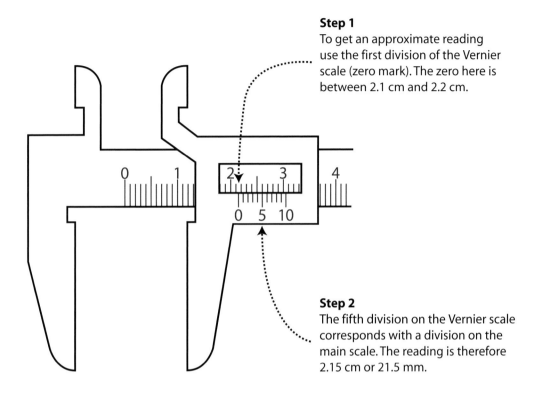

Step 1
To get an approximate reading use the first division of the Vernier scale (zero mark). The zero here is between 2.1 cm and 2.2 cm.

Step 2
The fifth division on the Vernier scale corresponds with a division on the main scale. The reading is therefore 2.15 cm or 21.5 mm.

Exercise 45

Work out these readings.

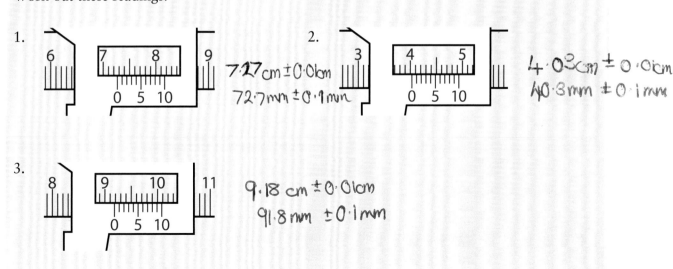

1. 7.27 cm ± 0.01 cm
   72.7 mm ± 0.1 mm

2. 4.03 cm ± 0.01 cm
   40.3 mm ± 0.1 mm

3. 9.18 cm ± 0.01 cm
   91.8 mm ± 0.1 mm

Using a micrometer gauge

A micrometer gauge can measure distance to an accuracy of ± 0.01 mm. It is particularly useful for measuring the diameter of a wire or the thickness of a glass microscope slide. The area of cross section of a wire can be calculated when the diameter of the wire is measured using a micrometer gauge.

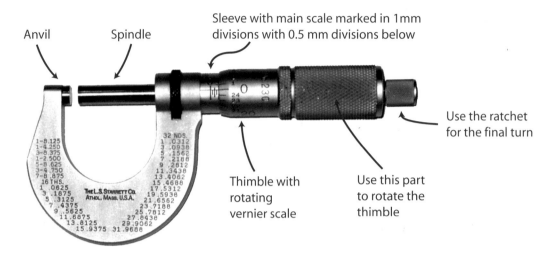

Anvil   Spindle   Sleeve with main scale marked in 1mm divisions with 0.5 mm divisions below

Use the ratchet for the final turn

Thimble with rotating vernier scale   Use this part to rotate the thimble

The divisions along the micrometer are 1 mm.

There are (in the micrometer normally used in school) 50 divisions around the barrel.

To move the thimble 1 mm along the barrel requires the thimble to moved through 2 complete turns. There are 50 divisions around the thimble, so to move 1 mm the barrel is turned 100 divisions. This means that 1 division around the barrel = 0.01 mm

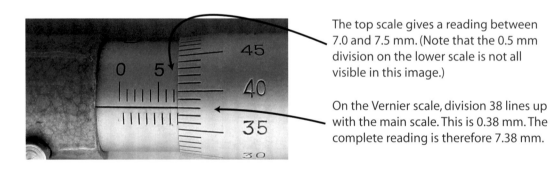

The top scale gives a reading between 7.0 and 7.5 mm. (Note that the 0.5 mm division on the lower scale is not all visible in this image.)

On the Vernier scale, division 38 lines up with the main scale. This is 0.38 mm. The complete reading is therefore 7.38 mm.

Exercise 46

Work out these readings.

1.

3·56mm ±
0·01mm

2.

5·80mm ±
0·01mm

3.

7·72mm ±
0·01mm

Measuring volume

Using a graduated cylinder

Graduated cylinders are used to measure the volume of a liquid. They come in a range of sizes from 10 cm^3 to 1000 cm^3. Liquids in glass containers curve at the edges; this curvature is called the **meniscus**. With water in glass, the meniscus will curve up at the edges and down in the centre so we say you read the bottom of the meniscus. When reading the volume you should have your eye level with the curved surface (meniscus) of the liquid to avoid parallax error. In some plastic cylinders water has a flat surface. However it still best to take the reading at the centre rather than at the edge.

The visibility of the meniscus can be improved by using a card with a dark stripe on it, placed behind the cylinder. Adjusting the position of the card you will either see a white meniscus against a black background or a black meniscus against a white background. There are some liquids where the curve goes the other way. In this case you would take the reading at the top of the meniscus.

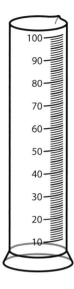

Like most measuring instruments it is important to work out the volume represented by each of the marked divisions.

The volume of an irregular object such as a stone can be found using the displacement method. In this technique a graduated cylinder is partly filled with water and the volume measured. The stone is carefully lowered into the water and when completely covered with water the new volume is measured. The difference between the two readings gives the volume of the stone.

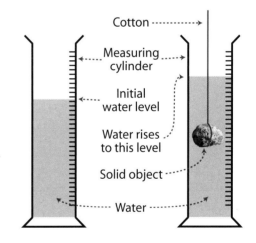

The method can be adapted to find the volume of an object that floats, like a cork. The stone is tied to the cork and, provided both are completely covered, the volume of the cork can be found.

Measuring angles – using a protractor

Notice that numbers marked on the protractor run in both directions so be careful which you use when taking measurements.

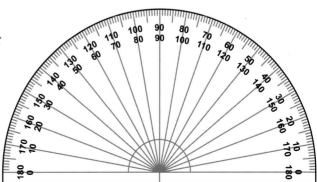

To measure the angle between two lines follow the steps below.

Find the centre of the straight edge of the protractor. This is the cross as shown below.

Place the cross over the point of the angle you wish to measure or draw.

Line up the zero on the straight edge of the protractor with one of the sides of the angle or the line already drawn.

Find the point where the second side of the angle intersects the curved edge of the protractor (you may need to extend the lines). The value at the intersection is the measure of the angle in degrees.

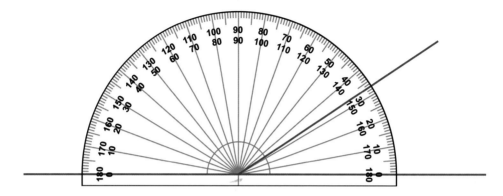

There is of course uncertainty associated with the measurement of this angle. The reading on the scale can be read to ± ½ of one division. This corresponds to ± 0.5°. The positioning of the line along the zero of the protractor also involves an uncertainty of ± ½ of one division, again this is ± 0.5°.

The overall uncertainty in the measurement of the angle is ± 1°.

The angle shown above should be quoted as (33 ± 1)°.

Measuring weight – using a spring balance or Newton meter

This is used to measure force. It consists of a spring which extends when a force is applied to one end. The spring obeys Hooke's law, so the extension produced is proportional to the force. This allows a scale calibrated in newtons to be placed alongside the spring.

The maximum force that can be measured depends on the strength of the spring. Spring balances with ranges of 0 – 10 N, 0 – 20 N and 0 – 50 N are common.

Measuring mass – using an electronic top pan balance

This is used to measure the mass of an object. The object is placed on the pan and the force it exerts is detected by a sensor which converts this to an electrical signal. A conversion factor is applied and the display will show the mass of the object in grammes or kilogrammes.

Most electronic balances have a 'tare' facility which when pressed sets the reading to zero. This is useful when measuring a required mass of a solid or liquid in a beaker or other container.

The container is placed on the pan, the tare button is pressed and the reading goes to zero. The reading then shown is the mass of material added to the container.

The final decimal place indicates the uncertainty. For the electronic balance shown above this is ± 0.1 g.

Measuring temperature

In Physics we use the Kelvin and the Celsius temperature scale. On the Celsius scale water freezes at 0 °C, on the Kelvin scale this is 273 K. Water boils at 100 °C or 373 K.

The thermometers found in school laboratories are normally calibrated from -10 °C to 110 °C. It is possible to get thermometers capable of measuring higher temperatures than 110 °C.

It is important to determine the temperature difference indicated by the smallest division shown on the thermometer. This is normally 1 °C, so it is possible to read the scale to ± 0.5 °C. Therefore a temperature change would measured to ± 1 °C.

Thermometers are made of glass and therefore fragile. Most are round and they can easily roll off a bench. However some are triangular in cross section or have a small plastic triangle around them to reduce the likelihood of rolling.

When recording the temperature of a liquid it is important to stir the liquid to ensure thorough mixing. When heating a liquid do not use the thermometer to stir the liquid unless it is a robust type clearly intended for the purpose. When recording the temperature of a liquid ensure than the bulb of the thermometer is completely covered by the liquid or is as close as possible to the position at which the temperature is to be measured.

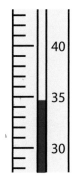

The example on the left shows how to measure temperature accurately using a thermometer.

Smallest division: 1.0 °C

Uncertainty: ±0.5 °C

Reading: 34.5 °C

Measuring current – using an ammeter

An ammeter measures electric current. An ammeter is connected in **series** with the other components in a circuit. The positive terminal of the ammeter is connected to the positive side of the cell. If there are other components in the circuit you should trace the connections from the positive terminal of the ammeter to the positive terminal of the cell. The circuit below shows an ammeter in series with a bulb.

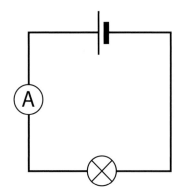 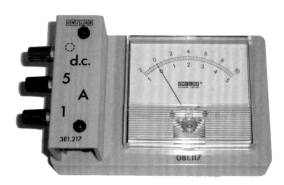

The scale of an ammeter can measure amperes (A), milliamps (1 mA = 1 × 10⁻³A) or possibly microamps (1 μA = 1 × 10⁻⁶A). You should also determine what the smallest division of the scale represents. This is important when it comes to considering the uncertainty associated with a measurement of current. The uncertainty is normally taken as ± ½ the smallest division on the scale.

The ammeter shown above is of a type found in many school laboratories. The top scale can measure currents up to a maximum of 1.0 A, the lower scale to a maximum of 5.0 A. The scale to be used is determined by which of the terminals 1A or 5A is used to connect the meter into the circuit.

Using the ammeter shown above, the top scale has the following features:
Maximum current is 1.0 A
Smallest division is 0.02 A
Uncertainty is ± 0.01 A (± ½ division)

Using the ammeter shown above, the bottom scale has the following features:
Maximum current is 5.0 A
Smallest division is 0.1 A
Uncertainty is ± 0.05 A (± ½ division)

The type of meter shown can easily be converted to a milliameter by changing the shunt. The procedure outlined above can be used to determine which scale to use and the uncertainty associated with that scale.

Digital ammeters are also found in school laboratories. The one shown below can measure current as large as 10 amperes. The final decimal place indicates that the uncertainty associated with the use of this ammeter is ± 0.01 A.

Measuring potential difference - using a voltmeter

A voltmeter measures potential difference. It is connected in **parallel** with the component across which the potential difference is to be measured. The positive terminal of the voltmeter is connected to the end of the component which is nearest to the positive terminal of the cell, battery or power supply and the negative terminal to the other end of the component.

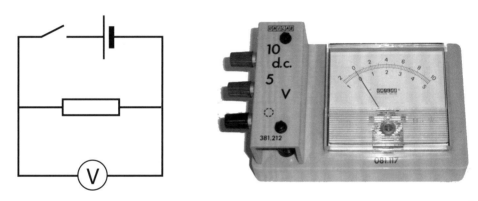

When building a circuit the voltmeter can be the last item attached.

The voltmeter shown has a multiplier which allows the top scale to have a maximum reading of 10V and the lower scale a maximum of 5.0V.

Using the voltmeter shown above the top scale has the following features:
Maximum current is 10.0 V
Smallest division is 0.02 V
Uncertainty is ± 0.01 V (± ½ division)

Using the voltmeter shown above the bottom scale has the following features:
Maximum current is 5.0 V
Smallest division is 0.1 V
Uncertainty is ± 0.05 V (± ½ division)

Digital voltmeters are also found in school laboratories. The one shown below can measure a potential difference as large as 20 v.

The final decimal place indicates that the uncertainty associated with the use of this voltmeter is ± 0.01 V.

Zero error

Before you use a meter it is important that it reads zero before any current passes through it or a potential difference is applied to it. The one shown below has a zero error. It may be possible to set the pointer to read zero. If this cannot be done then the zero error value must be subtracted from all your readings.

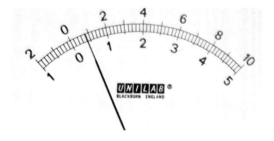

3.2 Precision, Accuracy and Errors

It requires skill to carry out an experiment well. Skill involves being able to manipulate equipment, identifying variables that can be measured, varied and controlled, and being able to take readings from a range of measuring instruments. To become a skilful experimenter requires practice but what follows is a number of simple techniques that can improve your experimental technique and lead to more precise measurements.

What is the difference between an accurate measurement and a precise measurement?

An accurate measurement is one that is close to the true value of a physical quantity. A precise measurement is one taken with a measuring device that can give an exact value when used with skill. For example using a vernier scale that reads to 0.1 mm will give a more precise value than a metre rule that reads to 1 mm. Of course it requires more skill to take a reading with a vernier scale than with a metre rule.

Precise and **accurate**
The measurements that are close to the true value and the measurements are very similar ie random and systematic uncertainties are small.

Precise but **inaccurate**
The measurements show very small differences but their average value is far from the true value.

Imprecise but **accurate**
The measurements show large variation but an average value that is close to the true value.

Imprecise and **inaccurate**
The measurements show large variations and an average value far from the true value.

	True 2.45 Readings taken 2.42, 2.46, 2.44, 2.45 Average 2.44
	True 2.45 Readings taken 2.82, 2.84, 2.85, 2.87 Average 2.85
	True 2.45 Readings taken 2.82, 2.26, 2.72, 2.15 Average 2.49
	True 2.45 Readings taken 2.62, 2.76, 2.14, 2.95 Average 2.62

What are systematic errors?

A systematic uncertainty will result in all readings being either above or below the accepted value. In other words it leads to inaccuracy of the measurement although the measurements taken may well be precise (very small differences between them). This uncertainty **cannot** be eliminated by repeating readings and then averaging.

Examples of systematic uncertainty are:

Zero error

Zero error on an instrument (the scale reading is not zero before measurements are taken).

Where appropriate, instruments should be checked for any zero error. Where there is a zero error, the meter should be adjusted to zero or, if this not possible, the zero error should

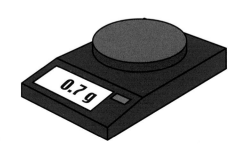

be noted and all recorded readings should then be adjusted.

Note: Remember to record all readings as they are taken. Do not allow for zero error 'in your head' and then write down the adjusted value.

Parallax error

Parallax error occurs when the scale is not viewed normally when taking a reading. To reduce parallax errors, always:

• have the scale as close as possible to the pointer;

• view the scale normally.

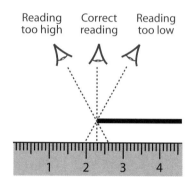

Over-tightening a micrometer

Over-tightening a micrometer gauge when taking a measurement will lead to a systematic error that will always give a smaller value than the true value.

Always use the ratchet, because this will slip when the jaws meet any resistance. This is particularly important if you are measuring the diameter of a wire.

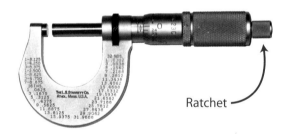

Ratchet

Techniques designed to improve the accuracy of your measurements

Timing oscillations

Start your timing when the oscillation is at one extreme, ie when the vibrating object is momentarily at rest. In the case of the simple pendulum, one oscillation would be from C to A to B and back to C again. Start the object oscillating before you start timing and watch the object until the vibrations are no longer noticeable. This will determine how many oscillations are noticeable.

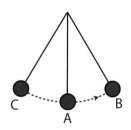

It is poor practice to measure the period of oscillation by timing just one. The error in human timing is likely to be around 0.2 s. It is better to time 20 such oscillations. However in some circumstances the oscillations may die out quickly and only 3 or 5 complete oscillations may be noticeable.

When you decide to start timing, begin by saying zero as you start. Timing 20 oscillations will reduce the uncertainty in determining the time for 1 oscillation, the period. A simple pendulum with a period of just 1 second would have an error of 0.2 s, i.e. 20% . However, if you time 20 such oscillations the error is only 0.2 s in 20 seconds, ie 1%.

When you take measurements, vary the quantity in a logical manner, e.g. increase the length of the pendulum in equal sized steps. This will allow trends to be more noticeable.

Measuring current and potential difference

Always draw the circuit diagram before you start building the circuit.

Start at the positive terminal and insert components as you follow the circuit from positive to negative.

Voltmeters should be left until all the series components have been connected. Remember voltmeters are connected in parallel.

Ammeters and voltmeters are always connected as positive to positive or red to red.

When using analogue meters establish what each division on the scale represents.

When taking a reading look vertically down on the scale. This reduces the possibility of parallax error in your reading.

If you are using a digital meter do not change the scale in the middle of the experiment.

In many cases try to change the potential difference in equal steps. However when dealing with light emitting diodes (LEDs) it may be necessary to change the potential difference in very small steps when the current is beginning to increase.

$$\frac{1}{2} m v^2 = m g h$$

$$\frac{1}{2} \times v^2 = g h$$

3.3 Analysis and Interpretation of Results

The first step in the analysis of your data is the recording of measurements in a suitable table. The table should have sufficient columns for all the measurements and possible calculations you need to make.

Columns need headings. These should be the quantity in the appropriate units for that quantity.

As an example, consider the table that could be used for the investigation of the period of a simple pendulum and the length of the pendulum.

Measurement repeated 3 times to give an average

Units shown on all column headings

Systematic and a good range

Length of the pendulum/m	Time for 20 oscillations/s			Average time for 20 oscillations/s	Period/s
	1st	2nd	3rd		
1.2					
1.0					
0.8					
0.6					
0.4					
0.2					

The length is varied in a systematic manner: it is gradually increased in length using steps of 0.2 m.

Increasing the length from 0.2 to 1.2 m covers a good range of values. For each length the time for 20 oscillations is measured. To improve the accuracy and ensure reliability, this is done 3 times and the average taken. The final step is to calculate the period of the pendulum by dividing the average time by 20.

To reduce the uncertainty in the measurement of the periodic time of any vibrating system, it is advisable to time sufficient oscillations so that a total time of around 20 seconds or better is to be measured. In the case above, a pendulum with length of 0.2 m would yield around 18 seconds and the length of 1.2 m would yield a total time of around 40 seconds.

However it is not always possible to obtain sufficient oscillations to achieve a total time of at least 20 seconds. In this case you need to determine the maximum number of oscillations that you can detect before they cease to be noticed.

AS Practical 2002

In this a bifilar pendulum was set up for you. The pendulum was made to vibrate about its centre. The length of the vertical cords was to be varied and the effect this had on the periodic time of oscillation was to be investigated.

The timing was to be carried out using a stopwatch or stopclock. The length of the supporting cords was to be decreased from 400 mm to about 200 mm and 5 sets of readings were to be taken.

The results were to be recorded in a table that was partly completed with the first value of L and the period T column shown with the appropriate unit.

When the bifilar pendulum was set swinging it was found that 5 oscillations were easily observable. More than this and they became very difficult to see. As you can see from the table, it was decided that 5 oscillations should be timed.

L/mm	Time for 5 oscillations/s				T/s
	1st	2nd	3rd	Average	
400	9.55	9.40	9.51	9.48	1.90
350	8.90	8.85	8.82	8.85	1.77
300	8.21	8.30	8.25	8.25	1.65
250	7.35	7.51	7.53	7.46	1.49
200	6.52	6.75	6.62	6.63	1.33

The relationship between T and L is given by one of the following equations. Which one?

$$T^2 = A^2 L \qquad T^2 = \frac{A^2}{L}$$

$$1.\ T = A\sqrt{L} \qquad 2.\ T = \frac{A}{\sqrt{L}} \qquad 3.\ T = \frac{A}{L^2}$$

From the trend shown by the results it is clear that 1 is the correct relationship. As the length L increases the period T also increases. Equations 2 and 3 indicate that as L increases T would decrease.

To draw a suitable straight line graph from the results to find the constant A then $\sqrt{L}$ should be plotted on the x-axis and T on the y-axis. A new table containing the appropriate values is then produced.

$\sqrt{L}$ / mm$^{1/2}$	14.14	15.81	17.32	18.71	20.0
T/s	1.33	1.49	1.65	1.77	1.90

The graph obtained using these values is shown below.

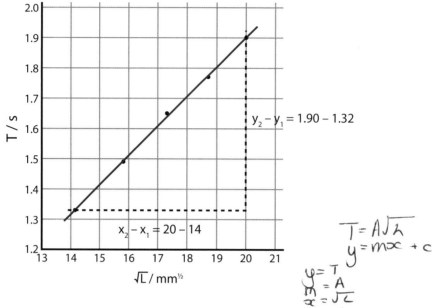

To find the value of A we need to take the gradient of this line. Why?

The relationship between L and T is given by $T = A\sqrt{L}$. This corresponds to $y = mx$, the equation for a straight line that passes through the origin (0,0). Note that in this case there is no requirement to find the intercept so there is no need to plot the graph from the origin.

By comparing the two equations we see that $y \equiv T$ $x \equiv \sqrt{L}$ and the gradient $m \equiv A$.

The gradient $= \dfrac{y_2 - y_1}{x_2 - x_1} = \dfrac{1.90 - 1.32}{20.0 - 14.0} = \dfrac{0.58}{6.0} = 0.097$

The gradient may have units and in this case it has the units of $s\ mm^{-\frac{1}{2}}$.

Graphs

Graphs are commonly used to show the results of experiments. Graphs allow you to deduce relationships much more quickly than using a table. They provide a visual picture of how two quantities depend on each other: they show up anomalous readings and, if straight lines, the gradient can be used to find an average value of the ratio of the two quantities.

Dependent and independent variables

Plot the independent variable (the one you have been changing) along the horizontal axis and the dependent variable along the vertical axis. The exception to this rule occurs where you need to plot a particular graph to find a required quantity. For example, in the case of stretching a spring, the equation $F = kx$ applies. F is the force, x is the extension and k is the spring constant. In this instance F is the independent variable but to find the spring constant, the force F is plotted along the y-axis and the extension along the x-axis, because the gradient is then the spring constant.

Labels and units

Label both axes to show the quantity that is being plotted.

Indicate on the axes the unit of measurement used for the quantity. Sometimes the quantity may just be a number so a unit is not required.

In (V/V) would be noted as this as logs have no units

Scales

Choose scales on the axes to make the plotting of values simple. Generally this means letting 10 small divisions on the graph paper equal 1, 2, 5, 10 or some multiple of these numbers. Do not make life difficult for yourself by letting small divisions equal 3 or 7. This will take you longer to plot the graph, increase your chances of mis-plotting points and makes it difficult for others to read the data.

Choose the range of the scales on the axes so that the points are spread out. As a general rule the graph you draw should fill at least three quarters of the graph paper grid in both the x and y directions.

Plotting points

Plot the results clearly, and use a sharp pencil rather than a pen. Pencil is much easier to erase should you make a mistake in plotting. Use crosses or dots with circles around them.

Lines and curves

The graphs that you will encounter during an A level course will generally represent a smooth variation of one quantity with another so a smooth curve or straight line will be appropriate. Draw a best fit line, which may be a smooth curve or a straight line that passes through or close to all your points as shown below. In general you should **not** join the points with short straight lines.

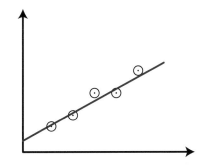
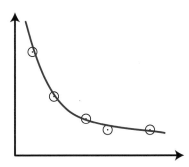

Worked Examples

1 A ball rolls from rest down a sloped plane. Measurements are made of the distance travelled along the slope, d, and the time taken, t.

   The relationship between d and t is: $d = \frac{1}{2}at^2$ where 'a' is the acceleration of the ball.

   (a) What **straight line** graph would you plot to display your results?

   (b) How could you find the acceleration from the graph?

Solution

The equation of a straight line that passes through the origin (0,0) is $y = mx$.

By comparing this with the relationship above we see that d should be plotted on the y-axis and t^2 on the x-axis.

In the equation for the straight line m represents the gradient. The gradient of the graph of d against t^2 is equal to $\frac{1}{2}a$.

2 The unknown e.m.f. of a cell, E, is linked to the terminal voltage, V, and the current I by the equation $E = V + Ir$ where r is the unknown internal resistance of the cell.

   In an experiment, corresponding values of V and I are recorded as the resistance in an external circuit is changed. The e.m.f. and the internal resistance are both constant.

   (a) What **straight line** graph would you plot? Which variable would be on the vertical axis?

   (b) Draw a sketch of the graph you would expect to obtain.

   (c) How would you find the e.m.f. of the cell and the internal resistance from this graph?

Solution

First the equation has to be arranged so that V becomes the subject of the equation.

This gives $V = E - Ir$. The equation of a straight lines is $y = mx + c$. By comparing these two equation we see that V should be plotted on the y-axis and I on the x-axis. The intercept on the y-axis is c and in this case it will give us a value for E. The gradient of the graph is negative and will give a value for r.

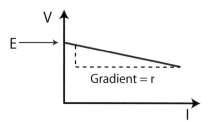

3 The focal length f, of an inaccessible lens (inside a cylinder) can be found by a technique called 'the displacement method'. The distance between an illuminated object and a screen is measured, this is s, as shown in the diagram. The cylinder containing the lens is moved until a sharp image is obtained on the screen. The position of the cylinder is noted. The cylinder

is moved again until a new image on the screen is obtained. The distance between the two positions of the cylinder containing the lens is found, this is d, as shown in the diagram.

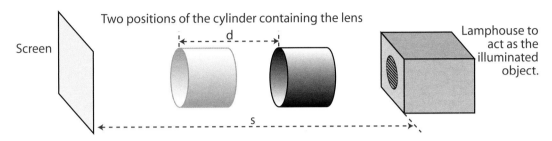

Two positions of the cylinder containing the lens

The mathematical relationship between the quantities is $f = \dfrac{s^2 - d^2}{4s}$

Below is a table of results of s and d.

s in cm	50.0	54.0	58.0	62.0	66.0	70.0
d in cm	22.4	27.5	32.3	36.9	41.4	45.8

(a) What **straight line** graph should you plot so that the gradient can be used to calculate the focal length of the lens?

(b) Copy the table above and calculate the values required to plot the graph. Insert the values in the appropriate spaces in your table and add appropriate labels.

(c) Plot the graph, labelling carefully the units on each axis and use it to find the focal length of the lens.

Solution

Rearrange the equation to give

$s^2 = d^2 + 4sf$

Divide both sides by s

$s = \dfrac{d^2}{s} + 4f$

Plot s on the y-axis and $\dfrac{d^2}{s}$ on the x-axis. The intercept is equal to 4f.

Alternatively, rearrange the equation to give

$4fs = s^2 - d^2$

$(s^2 - d^2) = 4fs$

Plot $(s^2 - d^2)$ on the y-axis and s on the x-axis. The slope is 4f.

Combining uncertainties

Often the aim of an experiment is to find the value of a quantity that depends on the measurement of several quantities, each with its own associated uncertainty.

In an experiment to determine the resistivity of a material the diameter of a wire is measured. Then that value is used to calculate the area of cross section of the wire. What is the uncertainty in the calculation of the area of cross section? There are two methods of dealing with this.

Method 1: Maximum, minimum and range

In this method the first thing to do is to calculate the area using the best value of the diameter and using the maximum and minimum values as determined by the measuring instrument. The average diameter of the wire was measured as 0.32 mm using a micrometer gauge giving an uncertainty of $\pm$ 0.01 mm.

$$A_{Best} = \frac{3.142 \times (0.32 \times 10^{-3})^2}{4} = 8.0 \times 10^{-8} \, m^2$$

$$A_{Min} = \frac{3.142 \times (0.31 \times 10^{-3})^2}{4} = 7.55 \times 10^{-8} \, m^2$$

$$A_{Max} = \frac{3.142 \times (0.33 \times 10^{-3})^2}{4} = 8.55 \times 10^{-8} \, m^2$$

This gives a range of 1.0×10^{-8} in the values for the area. The calculated value for the area can be written as: $(8.0 \pm 0.5) \times 10^{-8} \, m^2$

Method 2: Combining percentage uncertainties

Consider a measured quantity A and its associated uncertainty ΔA, and another measured quantity B with its associated uncertainty ΔB. X is the quantity we wish to measure and its uncertainty is ΔX. The value of X may be found by combining the values of A and B in various ways. For each way that A and B could be combined the final uncertainty ΔX is simply the sum of the uncertainties in A and B. This is a simplified version of a statistical method that is applicable to AS and A2 Physics.

How X is found from A and B	Final uncertainty in X
$X = A \times B$	$\Delta X = \Delta A + \Delta B$
$X = A \div B$	$\Delta X = \Delta A + \Delta B$
$X = A \times B^n$	$\Delta X = \Delta A + n \, \Delta B$
$X = A \div B^n$	$\Delta X = \Delta A + n \, \Delta B$
$X = kA^n$ where k is a constant	$\Delta X = n \, \Delta A$

The uncertainties, ΔA and ΔB, are best quoted as percentages of the measured values A and B. The uncertainty ΔX is then a percentage of the final measured value.

For example, if the period of an oscillating pendulum is 1.1 s with an uncertainty of $\pm$ 0.1 s, the percentage uncertainty in this measurement is $(0.1 \times 100) \div 1.1 = \pm 9\%$

The numerical examples below show how the rules shown in the table are applied.

Example 1 Measurement of resistance

The resistance of a length of wire is found by measuring the current passing through it and the potential difference across it. In such an experiment the values of these quantities and their uncertainties were found to be V = 5.2 ± 0.2 and I = 1.2 ± 0.1.

$$\Delta V = \frac{0.2 \times 100}{5.2} = 3.8\% \quad \Delta I = \frac{0.1 \times 100}{1.2} = 8.3\%$$

$$R = \frac{V}{I} \quad \Delta R = \Delta V + \Delta I = 3.8\% + 8.3\% = 12.1\%$$

$$R = \frac{5.2}{1.2} = 4.3 \ \Omega \pm 12.1\% = (4.3 \pm 0.5) \ \Omega$$

Example 2 Measurement of density

The diameter of a steel ball was measured using a micrometer gauge and found to be 8.65 mm and the uncertainty was ± 0.01 mm. The mass of the steel ball was found using an electronic balance, the measured value being 2.82 g with an uncertainty of ± 0.01 g. What is the density of the steel?

The volume of the sphere is given by $\frac{\pi d^3}{6}$, d being the diameter of the sphere.

The uncertainty in the measurement of the diameter is $\Delta d = \frac{0.01 \times 100}{8.65} = \pm 0.12\%$

However, the uncertainty in the volume ΔV is three times this since diameter has to be cubed to find the volume.

The uncertainty $\Delta V = \pm 0.36\%$

$$\text{Density} = \frac{\text{Mass}}{\text{Volume}} = \frac{2.82 \times 10^{-3}}{3.39 \times 10^{-7}} = 8318 \text{ kg m}^{-3}$$

$\Delta m = 0.01 \times 100\% \div 2.82 = 0.35\%$

The uncertainty in the density $\Delta D = \Delta m + \Delta V = 0.35\% + 0.36\% = \pm 0.71\% = \pm 59 \text{ kg m}^{-3}$

The final value for the density can be quoted as $(8318 \pm 59) \text{ kg m}^{-3}$

Exercise 47

In an experiment to measure the resistance of a piece of wire a voltmeter capable of measuring a maximum potential difference of 10 V was used. The smallest division on the scale was 0.2 V. The ammeter used was capable of measuring current as large as 1.0 A and the smallest division on its scale was 0.1 A. The experiment yielded readings of 4.9 V and 0.3 A.

Calculate the resistance of the wire along with the uncertainty in its value. Use the percentage method to determine the uncertainty in the resistance.

Uncertainties from graphs

The slope or gradient of a graph provides a means of determining an average value for a physical quantity. The intercept on either the x- or y-axis is dependent on the slope. A small change in the slope can produce a large change in the value of the intercept.

The points plotted may not all lie on a straight line. It may be necessary to judge the best fit line.

The slope of the best fit line will give you the best value for a physical quantity and the intercept on the appropriate will give you the best value for this quantity. The placing of this line of best fit can be aided by calculating the average x value and average y value and plotting this point. This is known as the **centroid** and the line of best fit is drawn so that it passes through this point.

To estimate the uncertainty in the slope and the intercept, follow the procedure outlined below:

Draw the line of best fit as outlined above.

Now draw two more lines, one of maximum slope and one of minimum slope through the plotted points. The gradients of these two lines will give you a maximum and minimum value for the slope. The difference between these two values gives you a range and the uncertainty can be taken as half the value of the range.

Similarly the line of best fit will give best value for the intercept. The range of the intercept values can be found from where the lines of maximum and minimum slope cut the appropriate axis. The uncertainty in the intercept value is again half the range.

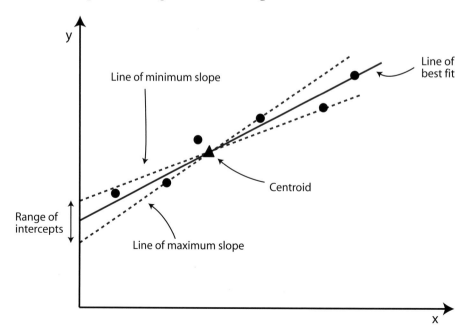

Answers

Answers – Exercise 1

1 (a) joule: $kg\ m^2s^{-2}$ (b) watt: $kg\ m^2s^{-3}$ (c) $kg\ ms^{-1}$ (d) ms^{-2}
   (e) newton: $kg\ ms^{-2}$ (f) hertz: s^{-1}

2 FAT^2

3 The 2π term has no unit.
   The unit of $(L \div g)^{\frac{1}{2}} = (m \div ms^{-2})^{\frac{1}{2}} = (s^2)^{\frac{1}{2}} = s$, which is the unit of time on the LHS of the equation.

4 The 2π term has no unit.
   The unit of $(m \div k)^{\frac{1}{2}} = (kg \div Nm^{-1})^{\frac{1}{2}}$
   Substituting the derived units for the newton gives:
   $(kg \div kg\ ms^{-2}m^{-1})^{\frac{1}{2}} = (s^2)^{\frac{1}{2}} = s$, which is the unit of time on the LHS of the equation.
   Since both side have the same base units the equation is homogeneous.

Answers – Exercise 3

1 (a) 35 m (b) 25 m 36.9° to the north of east

2 (a) 3.13 ms^{-1} (c) 17.73 ms^{-1}

Answers – Exercise 4

1 **26.93 N, 58.7°** (or 121.3°)

2 (a) Horizontal component of S_{BL} = 500 cos 40° = **383.0 km** = 380 km to 2 sig fig

   Vertical component of S_{BL} = 500 sin 40° = **321.4 km** = 320 km to 2 sig fig

   (b) S_{WL} = vector sum of vertical component of S_{BL} and horizontal component of $(S_{BL} - 160\ km)$
   Using the figures given in part (a):
   $S_{WL}^2 = 320^2 + (380 - 160)^2 = 150800$ giving S_{WL} = 390 km
   tan ϕ = (vertical component of S_{BL} ÷ Horizontal component of S_{WL}) = 320 ÷ 220 = 1.4545
   and ϕ = **55.5°**

Answers – Exercise 5

3 (a) 5 ms^{-2} (b) 178 m (c) 17.8 ms^{-1}

4 (b) 7.7 ms^{-1} (c) 12 m to the left of P

5 (a) From t = 0 to t = 3 s, the ball is rising vertically. After t = 3 s, the ball is falling. The change in sign is due to the change in the ball's direction of motion.

   (b) 1.6 ms^{-2} (c)(i) 7.2 m above the surface (ii) 0 m   (d)(i) 7.2 m (ii) 14.4 m

Answers – Exercise 6

1 (a) 20.26 ms^{-1} (b) A takes 3.333 s to reach finish. B takes 3.136 + 0.100 = 3.236 s so B wins by 0.097 s

2 10.8 s

3 (a) (i)

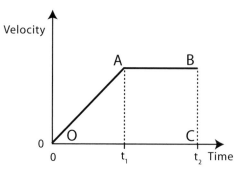

(a) (ii) Displacement = area between v–t graph and time axis from t = 0 up to t = t_2 = area of trapezium OABC

(b) (i) 120 km h^{-1} = 120 ÷ 60 km min^{-1}
$$= 2000 \text{ m min}^{-1} = 2000 \div 60 \text{ ms}^{-1}$$
$$= 33.3 \text{ ms}^{-1} \approx \textbf{33 ms}^{-1}$$

(ii) S = $(v^2 - u^2) \div 2a = (0^2 - 33.3^2) \div (2 \times -8.7)$
$$= \textbf{63.7 m}$$

(iii) t = (v–u) ÷ a = (0–33.3) ÷ (–8.7) = **3.8s**

Answers – Exercise 7

1 (a) speed = 0, acceleration = –9.81 ms^{-2} (b) 78.48 m (c) 4 s

2 (a) 49.1 ms^{-1} (b) 24.6 ms^{-1} (c) 123 m

3 (a) 37.3 m (b) 1.22 s (c) 2.76 s (d) 27.1 ms^{-1}

4 (a) velocity = +4.00 ms^{-1}, acceleration = –9.81 ms^{-2} (b) 22.8 m (c) –21.2 ms^{-1} (d) 2.57 s

5 8.75 m

1st bounce: mgh_1 = 0.9 × initial energy

2nd bounce: mgh_2 = 0.9 × 0.9 × initial energy

3rd bounce: mgh_3 = 0.9 × 0.9 × 0.9 × initial energy = 0.9^3 × initial energy

h_3 = (0.9^3 × initial energy) ÷ mg = (0.9^3 × mg × 12) ÷ mg = 0.9^3 × 12 = 8.748 m

n^{th} bounce mgh_n = $(0.9)^n$ × initial energy = 0.9^n × mg × 12

h_n = $(0.9)^n$ × mg × 12 ÷ mg = $(0.9)^n$ × 12 – which goes not depend on g

So height does **not** depend on g.

The height, h_n, after the nth bounce is given by: h_n = 0.9^n × 12 (metres)

Answers – Exercise 8

(a) 0.202 s

(b) 14.9 ms^{-1}

(c) 15.0 ms^{-1} at an angle of 7.6° below the horizontal

Answers – Exercise 9

1 **15.8° and 74.2°**

Comment: The artilleryman is more likely to have elevated the gun to the smaller angle of 15.8°. At this angle the shot is in the air for a shorter period of time, reaches a smaller maximum height and is less affected by weather conditions

2 (a) Horizontal velocity component = v cos θ, Vertical velocity component = v sin θ

(b)

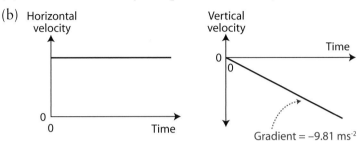

(c) The stone is travelling at its smallest speed at instant of horizontal projection.

Answers – Exercise 10

1 (a) 24.5 N (b) 4.1 ms^{-2} (c) 8.2 m

2 (a) 12 m (b) 8 ms^{-2} (c) 37 m (d) No. The child was 40 m away and the motorist stopped in 37 m.

(e) Alcohol increases reaction time, so it increases stopping distance. Wet roads reduce friction and hence reduce the resultant force causing the car to stop. This reduces the deceleration and hence increases the stopping distance.

3 709 N (b) 589 N (c) 469 N

4 (a) 3 ms^{-2} (b) 600 N

5 (a) 1.96 ms^{-2} (b) 23.5 N

6 (b) 5 ms^{-2} which occurs at the start of the motion (c) 5 ms^{-1}

Answers – Exercise 11

1 (a) 1.03 N, 1.27 N (b) Sum of upward reactions at C and D = Sum of downward forces.

2 (a) 425 N (b) No (c) equal to

3 (a) Reaction at C = 760 N, Reaction at D = 320 N (b) 2.2 m (c) 0.4 m

Answers – Exercise 12

1 (a) 150 mm (b) 75 mm

Answers – Exercise 13

1 (a) Reaction at each front wheel = 348g or 3414 N
Reaction at each rear wheel = 252g = 2472 N
(b) Car is front–engined (greater reaction at front wheels than rear wheels)

2 (a) 0.7g or 6.9 N (b) 0.7g or 6.9 N

Answers – Exercise 14

(c) (i) 1201.2J (ii) 5.7ms^{-1}

Answers – Exercise 15

1 (a) 1.5 MJ (b) 3.6 MW
2 (a) 120 kJ (b) 2940 Js^{-1}
3 (a) 5.10 ms^{-1} (b) 4.49 ms^{-1}
4 (a) Acceleration is not constant.
   (b) From trigonometry, at the start the bob is 1 – cos 60 or 0.5 m vertically above lowest point.
   ½ mv^2 = mgh gives
   v = $\sqrt{9.81}$ = 3.13 ms^{-1}
5 (a) Student is correct,
   Total energy (PE + KE) is constant throughout and is ½mu^2
   At height h, PE = mgh, so KE = ½mv^2 = ½mu^2 – mgh
   Giving v = $\sqrt{(u^2 - 2gh)}$ which is independent of projection angle α.
   (b) Initial KE = ½m 15^2 = 112.5 m (J)
   PE at 2.00 m = mgh = m × 9.81 × 2 = 19.62 m (J)
   KE at 2.00 m = 112.5m – 19.62 m = 92.88 m
   Using KE = ½mv^2 gives
   v = $\sqrt{2 \times 92.88}$ = 13.6 ms^{-1}

Answers – Exercise 16

2 (a) 10.4 J (b) 206 J

Answers – Exercise 17

1 (i) 5 cm (ii) 7.2 N cm^{-1} (iii) 36 N
2 spring with constant of 15 Ncm^{-1} has a tension of 37.5 N and extends 2.5 cm; spring with constant of 25 N cm^{-1} has a tension of 62.5 N and extends 2.5 cm.
3 (a) 0.08 Nmm^{-1} (b) 1250 mm
4 (a) 0.125 mm (b) 4.8 MNmm^{-1}

Answers – Exercise 18

1 (a) 2.58 × 10^{-4} m^2 (b) 18.1 mm
2 (a) 34.3 MPa (b) 4.91 × 10^{-4} (c) 0.981 mm
3 (a) copper: 0.9 m, 9 × 10^{-7} m^2, iron: 1.4 m, 1.3 × 10^{-6} m^2
   (c) (i) 1.5 (copper wire stretches 1.5 times as much as the iron wire) (ii) copper stretches 6 mm, iron stretches 4 mm (iii) 780 N
4 (a) 2.50 × 10^{-3} (b) 7.50 MPa (c) 589 N (d) 589 N (e) tension unchanged, extension reduced (f) 1.50 ms^{-2}

Answer – Exercise 19

0.06A or 60 mA

Answers – Exercise 20

1 (a) 1.25 A (b) 1.25 A (sections are in series)

2 (a) electrons (b) 9.375×10^{15}

3 44 000 s

Answers – Exercise 21

1 e.m.f. is the energy converted to electrical form when 1 C of charge passes through the battery (or e.m.f. is the pd across the battery terminals when it delivers zero current)

2 (a) Work = QV = 2.5 × 15 = **37.5 J** (b) Power = Work ÷ time = 37.5 ÷ 5 = **7.5 W**

Answers – Exercise 22

1 (c) $d_{silver} = d \div \sqrt{(6.7)} = 0.39d$

3 (b) Iron (highest resistivity);
   $l = RA \div \rho = \pi(0.25 \times 10^{-3})^2 \times 6.80 \div (9.71 \times 10^{-8}) = 13.75$ m

Answers – Exercise 23

2 (b)(i) E = I(R + r) = 0.25(5.0 + 0.6) = 1.4 V (ii) $P = I^2r = 0.25^2 \times 0.6 = \textbf{0.0375 W}$

3 (b)(i) E = V + Ir (ii) r = E ÷ I − R = 1.5 ÷ 0.5 − 2.94 = 0.060 Ω
      (iii) $P = I^2r = 0.5^2 \times 0.06 = 0.015$ W

Answers – Exercise 24

AB: 5 A from B to A, BC: 3 A from C to B

Answers – Exercise 25

1 (a) 0.50 A
   (b) Across single 12 Ω resistor p.d. = 5.33 V, across parallel combination p.d. = 2.67 V
   (c) 0.67 A

2 (b) 4 A away from P to the left (c)(i) 0.02 A (ii)

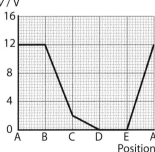

Answers – Exercise 26

1 9.0 V

2 (a) Resistance of parallel combination of 5.0 kΩ and illuminated LDR (0.20 kΩ)

$$= \frac{5 \times 0.2}{5 + 0.2} = 0.192 \text{ k}\Omega$$

V_{out} across parallel combination $= \dfrac{12 \times 0.192}{0.192 + 5} = \textbf{0.444 V} \approx 0.4 \text{ V}$

(b) When the rheostat's resistance is reduced to zero, voltage across the LDR is 12 V. The current in the LDR under conditions of maximum illumination is $12 \div (0.2 \times 10^3)$ A = **60 mA** and the power dissipated in the LDR is $60 \times 12 = $ **720 mW**

In dark conditions the same LDR takes a current of $12 \div (5 \times 10^3)$A = **2.4 mA** and the power dissipated in the LDR is $2.4 \times 12 = $ **28.8 mW**

Reducing the resistance of the rheostat to zero would therefore not be a good idea as the excessive current and dissipated power in bright conditions might destroy the LDR.

3 (i) Since 6 V is across 10 kΩ, 3 V must appear across unknown resistor. So, by proportion, unknown resistance = 3 × 10 ÷ 6 = **5 kΩ**.

(ii) When a voltmeter is connected and slider is at the mid-point value of rheostat, the output voltage is across a combined resistance of 5 kΩ and 20 kΩ in parallel. This has a total resistance of

(5 × 20) ÷ (5 + 20) = 4 kΩ.

The voltmeter reading is therefore:

$V_{out} = R_1 V_{in} \div (R_1 + R_2) = (4 \times 9) \div (5 + 4)$

$V_{out} = 36 \div 14 = $ **2.57 V**

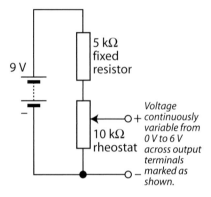

4 (a) Total resistance = V ÷ I = $3 \div 10 \times 10^{-6} = 300\ 000 \ \Omega$

Output resistance = V ÷ I = $1.2 \div 10 \times 10^{-6} = 120 \text{ k}\Omega$

Other resistance = 300 kΩ – 120 kΩ = 180 kΩ

(b) Combined resistance of new 1.0 kΩ and 120 kΩ in parallel is 0.992 kΩ. So, output voltage is now across 0.992 kΩ, rather than 120 kΩ as before. This reduces output voltage from 1.2 V to 0.016 V and increases current drawn from battery from 10 μA to 16.6 μA.

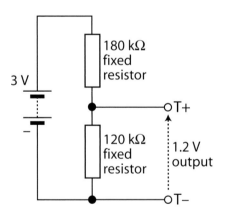

Answers – Exercise 28

1 (a) approx 4 cm (b) Period of wave B = 2 ms (2×10^{-3}) f = 1 ÷ T = 500 Hz (c) Wave has maximum when B is zero, the phase difference is equivalent to ¼ wavelength = 90°.

2 Amplitude is the magnitude of the maximum displacement.

Frequency is correct.

The time to complete one oscillation is the periodic time.

The final one is correct.

Answers – Exercise 29

1 (a) Red ray bent less towards the normal in the glass than the blue ray. (b) 0.4°

2 (a) Draw the normal to the prism at X. Angles are measured from the normal.
(b) 32.6° (c) 27.4° (d) 44.4° (e) 1.97×10^8 ms^{-1}

3 (b) 26.8° (c) 1.95×10^8 ms^{-1}

Answers – Exercise 30

1 (a) 41.8° (b) Total internal reflection will occur.

2 (a) 1.52

Answers – Exercise 31

1 (c) (i) Upright and magnified can only be a virtual image and a convex lens. (ii) 150 mm (iii) 100 mm

2 (c) (i) 171.4 mm (ii) 2.14 (iii) virtual, magnified, upright

3 (b) (i) 150 mm situated between the lens and the object (ii) 8 mm

4 (c) (i) 80 mm (ii) 0.5

Answers – Exercise 32

1 (c) + 3.0 D (d) (i) 33.3 cm

2 (c) + 2.67 D (d) 37.5 cm

Answers – Exercise 33

2 (a) $\frac{1}{6}$ of period = 60° or $\frac{\lambda}{6}$ (b) Increase the phase difference of B by 120° or $\frac{\lambda}{3}$

Answers – Exercise 34

1 (a) 80 km (b) destructive

2 (c) (i) 4.35×10^{-3} m (ii) 453 nm

3 (b) 588 nm

Answers – Exercise 35

1 (b) ½λ or 180° (c) 5 to 1 (d) 32 Hz (e) 224 ms^{-1}

2 (c) (i) 0.1 m (ii) 7.5 m

Answers – Exercise 36

1 150 Hz

2 1×10^5Hz

Answers – Exercise 37

1   335.7 ms^{-1}

2   (a) 500 Hz (b)(i) 338 ms^{-1}

Answers – Exercise 42

1   (b)(i) 2.26×10^{15} (b)(ii) 3.11 eV and 1.78 eV (c)(ii) 1.21 eV or 1.94×10^{-19}J
(iii) 6.53×10^5 ms^{-1}

2   (b) 2.96 eV or 4.74×10^{-19} J

3   (c) 5.5×10^5 ms^{-1}

Answers – Exercise 43

1   (c)(i) Transition –0.13 to –0.24 eV (d) 1.13×10^{-5} m

2   (b) Transition –1.5 to –3.4 eV

Answers – Exercise 45

1   7.27 cm

2   4.03 cm

3   9.18 cm

Answers – Exercise 46

1   3.56 mm

2   5.80 mm

3   7.72 mm

Answer – Exercise 47

1   $16.3 \pm 6 \ \Omega$